ISLAM vs. ISLAMISM

ISLAM vs. ISLAMISM

The Dilemma of the Muslim World

Peter R. Demant

Foreword by Asghar Ali Engineer

Westport, Connecticut
London

Library of Congress Cataloging-in-Publication Data

Demant, Peter R., 1951–
 Islam vs. Islamism: the dilemma of the Muslim world / Peter R.
Demant ; foreword by Asghar Ali Engineer.
  p. cm.
 Includes bibliographical references and index.
 ISBN 0–275–99078–8 (alk. paper)
 1. Islam—21st century. 2. Islamic renewal—Islamic countries. 3. Islamic
fundamentalism—Islamic countries. 4. Islam and politics—Islamic countries.
5. Islamic countries—Politics and government. 6. Religious awakening—Islam.
I. Title. II. Title: Islam versus Islamism.
BP161.3.D46 2006
297.2'7209—dc22 2006019253

British Library Cataloguing in Publication Data is available.

Library of Congress Catalog Card Number: 2006019253
ISBN: 0–275–99078–8

First published in 2006

Praeger Publishers, 88 Post Road West, Westport, CT 06881
An imprint of Greenwood Publishing Group, Inc.
www.praeger.com

Printed in the United States of America

The paper used in this book complies with the
Permanent Paper Standard issued by the National
Information Standards Organization (Z39.48–1984).

10 9 8 7 6 5 4 3 2 1

For Arnold Demant

In loving memory of Katja Komkommer

CONTENTS

Part II Today

FIGURES

FOREWORD

Peter Demant has written a very perceptive book on Islam and the problems faced by Islamic countries, particularly those of West Asia. Newspapers and journals today are full of hastily written articles displaying their writers' prejudices, and plenty of books are published with an agenda. The concept of an inevitable clash of civilizations has been widely discussed in many Western forums, and has been lapped up as a new gospel in the Western press. Meanwhile, many well-researched books that cast doubt on such impending doom, written with objectivity by scholars of repute and integrity, go without mention in newspapers of wide readership.

In such circumstances, any book written with objectivity and perceptiveness is received with great relief. Peter Demant is firmly grounded in his subject and has done justice to it. He has analyzed events with honesty and sensitivity, without being swept off his feet by the events of 9/11 and post-9/11, as most Western scholars have been.

As Demant rightly points out, Islam can be shown to be peaceful or to be violent, just like any other religion. Scriptural pronouncements must be situated in historical context. All scripture, if it is revealed in this world, is revealed in history, but also transcends any given historical era. It is this transcendence that makes it relevant for the present as well as the future. Often, however, the followers themselves confuse history and transcendence.

It is also true that many Muslims find great relief in demonizing the West—everything Western is evil in their eyes. By thus seeing the world, they transfer their own responsibility to the West and absolve themselves—as if, if the West ceased to exist, the Muslim world would be transformed into paradise. Such a self-congratulatory approach, besides being misleading, would prove self-destructive.

What is needed is honest reflection and critical analysis of the situation. Muslim intellectuals confront an onerous task. Some of the questions before them are quite fundamental: Why is there a lack of pluralist democracy in the Islamic world today? What props up corrupt monarchies and dictators? Even conceding that America has, in some cases, shored up these monarchs and dictators to serve its own purposes—all framed in the rhetoric of freedom and democracy—are Muslims absolved of all responsibility?

Muslim intellectuals should also critically reflect on the role played by the Iranian masses in peacefully overthrowing their powerful monarch. Although the Iranian Revolution deposed a powerful and corrupt shah supported to the hilt by the U.S. government, it failed to usher in a truly pluralist and secular democracy. As Demant rightly points out, the Islamic world occupies perhaps the lowest rung of the human development index—but why? Why the dismal position despite the Islamic rhetoric? Can mere Islamic rhetoric answer the West's rhetoric of democracy and freedom? Today both sound utterly hollow.

The dismal economic situation of the Muslim world contributes to the proliferation of violence in it. Yet poverty alone does not explain this violence—it can also flare up in an oil-rich country like Saudi Arabia, due to its long-standing traditions of intolerance and lack of intellectual freedom. Although change is occurring in Saudi Arabia, it is far from adequate to meet the challenges of modern times. Genuine intellectual freedom, indeed, is a *sine qua non* precondition for ushering in a pluralist democracy, but the Islamic world is far behind in this area, and no amount of Islamic rhetoric can ever substitute for authentic freedom of thought.

The events of 9/11 may prove to be a blessing in disguise. They have set Muslims thinking seriously and may have initiated a degree of critical awareness among them. 9/11 has, for instance, been an eye-opener for the ruling elite as well as for the common people of Saudi Arabia, who have woken up to the implications of utter religious intolerance and have begun to seriously reconsider their school and college syllabi. This may be the beginning of a long road, but a lot remains to be done. Thus, although the position of women in Islam fails to measure up to Qur'anic standards, and patriarchal values continue to reign supreme in the name of Qur'an and Shari'a, women are now demanding changes in their status. They insist on a more active role in public life. Kuwaiti women have won the right to vote and run for public office. Their Saudi sisters have not progressed this far yet, but it is just a matter of time.

On the other hand, Western scholars should not blame Islam and Islamic teachings alone for the current social and cultural crisis of the Muslim world, and for all the ills besetting Western-Muslim relations. Thinkers of the West must develop deeper insight into the societal roots of the Muslim world's current problems—specifically, insight into the economic and political malaise of West Asia today. For this to occur, though, they must let go of the prejudices imbibed through political propaganda, and realize that the mere rhetoric of freedom and democracy is inadequate to engender democratic change. The Western public should ponder this question: is the U.S. government truly interested in promoting democratic changes in West Asia, or just in perpetuating American interests? We need more unbiased and objective studies to genuinely understand the problems of the Islamic world. This book can prove to be an important link in these efforts.

—Asghar Ali Engineer

Asghar Ali Engineer's motto might be "It is not civilizations, but barbarians, who clash." Born in Salumbar, Rajasthan, in 1939, Engineer is a Muslim scholar and engineer active in interfaith dialogue and issues of communal harmony in South and Southeast Asia. He holds liberal, rational views on Islam and promotes a culture of peace. The author of numerous books on liberation theology and human rights in Islam, he is a founding member of the Asian Muslim Action Network, director of the Indian Institute of Islamic Studies, and head of the Center for the Study of Society and Secularism in Mumbai, India.

ACKNOWLEDGMENTS

Writing a book as wide-ranging and ambitious in scope as this demands not only extensive research, but even more requires the intellectual and practical input of friends, colleagues, and tutors. The History Department of the University of São Paulo provided the material conditions and the stimulating environment for this text to take shape. Conversations with fellow historians and social scientists, as well as with my students, have found their way into the discussions in this book. I thank all of them. The bibliography lists those earlier authors to whom I am most indebted, but for their especially insightful ideas, I would like to mention in particular the fruitful influence of books by Fred Halliday, Shireen Hunter, Gilles Kepel, Bernard Lewis, Olivier Roy, and Bassam Tibi. Any mistakes are, of course, my own responsibility. This book is a thorough reworking of my earlier *O mundo muçulmano* (São Paulo: Contexto, 2004); the encouragement of my publisher, Jaime Pinsky, is gratefully acknowledged. Thanks are also due to Hilary Claggett, Senior Editor at Praeger Publishers, for helping to reshape the original and for shepherding it to its final form, and to Jena M. Gaines for improving the English and the coherence of the text. Diagrams by Gilberto Rosenberg Colorni and maps by Giorgio Zoffoli provide visual aids for understanding complex phenomena. Of the many people who have helped in the gestation of this work, I wish in particular to thank my wife, Eliane. If the text is now better and more readable, it is due in no small measure to her efforts.

I dedicate this book to the memory of my mother, Katja Komkommer, and to my father, Arnold Demant. My parents' values and their unceasing support have been the most formative influence that brought me to develop the ideas expounded in this book.

NOTE ON SPELLING

Islamic terms and proper nouns are often based on Arabic proto-types, because Arabic is the language of the Qur'an and has, for believing Muslims around the world, a status much like Latin once had in European Christendom. I have generally used a simplified transliteration of the Arabic original, maintaining ' for *hamza* (glottal stop) except at the beginning of the word, ` for the guttural sound `*ayn,* and q for the deep throat sound *qaf*, but otherwise omitting the diacritical signs, "broken plurals," and other conventions found in the scholarly literature. However, complete consistency is not possible. Where other renderings have gained wide acceptance, I have followed them: thus Nasser (not Nasir), Hussein, Osama, al-Qaeda, and so on.

INTRODUCTION

Over the last fifteen years, many books have been published about the world of Islam and its complex relationship with the West. After the terrorist attacks of September 11, 2001, this information river has turned into a waterfall. However, few of these books combine a concise introduction to Islam as a religion and civilization with an in-depth discussion of Islamic fundamentalism and its threat to the modern world. This book, written by a Westerner for a non-Muslim readership, offers a general analysis of Islamic civilization, and it explains how and why significant portions of the Islamic world have been radicalizing, politicizing their religion, and attacking the West.

Humankind's future will depend on our collective success or failure in answering the hard question of coexistence. And few differences between the West and the rest of the world confront us with a more urgent challenge than Islamism. We can avoid Samuel Huntington's announced "clash of civilizations" between Islam and the West—a war in which all will be victims—*if* both make the required efforts and concessions. The first, and indispensable, task is to understand. The West must understand how Islam's historical riches are linked to its current anger—and how the Western world is in a way complicit in Islam's contemporary crisis. Understanding the Islamic world's internal dynamics and its interaction with non-Islamic peoples and cultures is a first step on the road to more compassionate and effective policies.

The Islamic world encompasses about 1.3 billion people—one-fifth of all humanity—living along a wide arc stretching from West Africa, over the Middle East and India, to Indonesia. In most countries of this vast region, Muslims constitute the majority; in others, they are important minorities. Histories, nations, tongues, ways of living together, ecology, and relations with neighbors vary immensely. Yet all components of this Islamic world share a single distinctive factor: Islam itself. Contrasts abound, not only in the visible, ritual, and social forms but even in the core beliefs. It could not have been otherwise. Islam emerged nearly 1400 years ago and spread over three continents and countless societies, meeting vastly differing conditions.

Let us remove the terminological confusion first. *Islam* and *Islamic* refer first of all to the religion, and the culture it created; *Muslim* refers to the sociological phenomenon: the believer or the person who identifies with the culture. The word *Islam* also defines the geographical and civilizational areas where Islam has become the predominant religion. Thus, although Pakistan has a Muslim majority, it is not necessarily an Islamic state. *Islamism* and *Islamist* denote the radical religious movement of "political Islam"; its popular synonym *Islamic fundamentalism* has also gained acceptance. As distinct from Islam, *Arab* and *Arabic* refer to a people and a language; the *Arab world* is located within the wider *Middle East*, a region encompassing roughly West Asia and North Africa.

The confusion surrounding these terms is historically grounded and has as its origin the totalistic character of Islam itself: more than a body of beliefs, Islam permeates social life, even economics, politics, and international relations. Initially, the terms *Arab* and *Muslim* did coincide, as most Arabs living on the Arabian Peninsula at the time of Islam's arrival converted to Islam. In a second stage, however, the expansion of this population created a new cultural sphere, presently known as "the Middle East." The Middle East adopted Arabic as its *lingua franca*, and its majority embraced Islam as religion. At this point, "Islamic world" and "Middle East" coincided, but "Islam" and "Arab" no longer did, because non–Arabic-speaking Middle Eastern peoples such as the Persians were converting to Islam as well.

Next, Islam gained followers in other parts of the earth, reducing the Middle East to one region of the Islamic world—although it remains ideologically its most important center, locus of the revelation, and action radius of Muhammad, the prophet of Islam. It was from here that Islam radiated, and it was in its language, Arabic, that the Qur'an (Koran) was written. Even today, the overlap between the definitions is understandable: after all, Arabs live in the Middle East and most Arabs are Muslims. However, the Middle East is also home to non-Muslim Arabs (Lebanese Maronites and Egyptian Copts among others), non-Arab Muslims (Turks, Kurds, Iranians, etc.), and even to non-Arab, non-Islamic nations such as Israel.

The use of "Middle East" as shorthand for a geographic area harboring 400 million Muslims is a questionable one. It originated with the colonial administrators of the British Empire, and it reflects their Eurocentric worldview. Since the term has entered popular parlance, however, this book will use it. The Middle East, then, located at the crossroads of multiple historical influences and transected by caravan routes and sea lanes, was for centuries the contact point between civilizations to the east—India, China, Southeast Asia—and what was for a long time an insignificant promontory of Asia: Europe. Eventually the European backwater and its offshoots in America and on other continents ("the West") came to dominate the others. Geopolitics made the Middle East the most complex region of the Islamic world, in terms of collective identities, political problems, and ethnic-religious conflicts. Western intervention has also turned it into a flashpoint of anti-Western sentiment. In the last decades, the (especially Arab) Middle East has become the field of action for most Islamist thinkers and militants. It continues to be a lightning rod for international tensions.

This book therefore pays particular attention to the Middle East as part of the Islamic world, even though less than one-quarter of the world's Muslims live there. Religious assimilation with other civilizations runs counter to Islam, which prescribes the unity of all believers within one single *umma* (community) and (in theory at least) under a single state. Diversity of experiences has created a very divided Islamic world, split into four large and geographically and culturally distinct blocks: Middle Eastern, Indian, Malay, and African. (In addition, there is Central Asia, vast, overwhelmingly Muslim, but sparsely populated.) Together these encompass over 95 percent of all Muslims. These four blocks are discussed in Part I ("Yesterday") of this text. So are, in a separate section, smaller Muslim minorities, present nowadays in all continents.

This book is more about Muslims than about Islam—more about specific populations, their histories, and the challenges confronting them than about theology. However, both the current difficulties and possible solutions are at least partly rooted in religion. Think, for instance, of the impassioned debate on the role of religious law (the *shari`a*) in public and private life in countries such as Egypt, Iran, or Turkey, or of terrorist movements trying to destabilize regimes, states, and recently even international society itself because they see these institutions as hostile or corrupt. Their political positions are based on particular interpretations of Islam. Yet other groups and individuals, less well known than media-savvy extremists, find in the same religion their inspiration to struggle for democracy and peaceful

dialogue with other civilizations. So religion is both the point of departure and the end of the road, although the myriad ways of getting
there differ vastly. Understanding the religion, therefore, is essential
to understanding today's Islamic world—the aim of the book's second
part.

Islam, like Christianity, is a proselytizing faith and a monopolist of
truth. Consecutive Muslim empires spread the faith, the Arabic language, and a distinctive culture. Today 95 percent of the Middle East
is Muslim. Yet before Islam arrived, 1400 years ago, perhaps as much
as 90 percent of it was Christian. The diminution of Christianity in
the region of its birth engendered an enduring conflict between the
two rival religions. Over the past 200 years, Christianity has lost
much of its influence over Europeans themselves, but meanwhile
Europe's antagonistic relationship with the Middle East has been
exacerbated by economics and geopolitics. Indeed, while the Muslim
states of the Middle East were weakening, the strategic importance of
the region was growing. A major portion of the world's oil is found
there, and it has become a privileged space for rivalries with and
among outside powers.

The overlapping of religious, strategic, economic, and other factors
explains why the Middle East commands so much of the world's attention. As Muslim populations try to recapture their former geopolitical
might, their demands challenge the vital interests of Western powers
and, by extension, of all developed capitalist countries. The resulting
struggle constitutes *the* central drama of today's international relations. Since this struggle has assumed more noticeably religious color-
ings, conflicts of interest threaten to mutate into a "clash of
civilizations."

Islam's confrontation with modernity is the lodestar of Part II
("Today"). The Islamic world, and especially the Middle East, was
poorly prepared for the political, economic, and cultural penetration of
Western powers imposed by military force in the nineteenth and
twentieth centuries. However, that supremacy was in itself an effect
of the West's own modernization, through the political and industrial
revolutions that began in the late eighteenth century.

Confronted with Western military superiority, Muslims may well
have felt more humiliated than other "overrun" civilizations, for
Allah, or God,[1] had promised the Muslims not only spiritual but also
worldly supremacy. For Islam, equality with (let alone inferiority to)
the West is thus a theological absurdity. There are in principle two
ways of reacting to such an absurdity: the Islamic world can cut its
losses, accept the West's "recipe" for modernization, and limit the public role of Islam as a "God that failed"; or it can retreat into religious

traditionalism. The choices are modernization or fundamentalism, flight forward or flight backward, progress or regress, and so on. Even projects of an "Islamic Reformation" would have trouble escaping this dilemma. This book analyzes how a sequence of military, socioeconomic, and cultural defeats in the Arab world undermined the legitimacy of regimes and projects tainted with modernization, or Westernization. Thus an ideological breach opened, widened from year to year, and was progressively exploited by proponents of the alternative: Islamic fundamentalism, or Islamism.

"Return to religion" is, of course, a global phenomenon, seen periodically among Christians and Jews, not solely among Muslims. But nowhere has it had more dramatic effects than in the Islamic world. Islamism's self-referential logic is simple: "We lost not because we were too religious and not modern enough, but because we tried to imitate the West and forgot religion. God abandoned us because we abandoned Him." Islamist thinkers' wholesale rejection of the Western model includes not just criticism of the "unjust" behavior of Christian powers, but also a condemnation of the "dissolute" Western social mores that are "infecting" the Islamic world. Islamists have their own blueprint for a better society, one that will re-create the pristine community established by Islam's founder, the Prophet Muhammad. What is most surprising of this "utopia in reverse," however, is Islamism's selective adoption of Western-based technologies, from radio and television to weapons of mass destruction. This differentiates Islamism from earlier Islamic traditionalisms, and stamps it as a modern movement—however antimodern its ideology!

Although unity among all Muslims is printed on its banner, Islamism is no unified movement, and differs from country to country and from one period to the next. Nor have most Islamists been prone to violence. But, whether peaceful or armed, Islamist growth has been the *leitmotiv* of the Islamic world over the last three decades. As we analyze the expansion of Islamism and dissect its varieties, we cannot but ponder its wider implications. Islamism obtained its first, limited hearing in the 1970s, in countries such as Egypt and Syria, but gained international notoriety only with Iran's Shiite revolution in 1979 and with the first hostage takings and suicide bombings in Lebanon in the 1980s. Since the 1980s, predictions to the contrary notwithstanding, Islamism has continued to grow, and it has grown ever more extreme. The 1990s witnessed an explosion of violent incidents provoked by Islamist groups from Nigeria to Indonesia; since 9/11 at the latest, the West itself has become its target. Ironically, policies designed to cope with Islamist violence have actually helped the Islamists.

How then should—and can—the West react? Are we facing real danger—or sensationalist exaggeration? Is Islam inherently a religion of violence, or have Islamists corrupted a beautiful tradition, one that has enriched the world, and could do so again? The answers will depend first on shifts within Islam. However, interfaith and inter-civilization dialogue plays a role in stimulating answers that can be helpful for us all. Part III ("Tomorrow") explores the arguments in favor of and against coexistence and its opposite: the "clash of civiliza-tions." Our conclusions cannot be but ambiguous, yet some lessons may be learned.

The first is that Islam is potentially more flexible than either its detractors, or the Islamists, would have us believe: it admits of, and needs, dialogue with the Other. Correspondingly, and in order not to plunge into new wars of religions, the West is no less in need of such a dialogue. Second, dialogue is hardly conceivable with a violent Islam-ism that calls for war to establish God's rule on earth. Nor is the struggle to contain violent Islamism only a Western interest: Muslims are its first and the majority of victims. Finally, we need to transform the structural global inequality that keeps most of the Islamic world trapped in a cycle of impoverishment and isolation. Without hope for change, extremism will only intensify and spread. So the task at hand is formidable—and could not be more urgent.

KEY DATES

Ten Crucial Episodes of Islam

622   The *hijra,* or migration of Prophet Muhammad from Mecca to Medina; start of the Islamic calendar

661–689   Civil wars lead to the split between Sunnis and Shiites

744–750   `Abbasid revolution ends the first, Arab-dominated, Omayyad caliphate and establishes political equality among believers. Start of Islam's Golden Age

1258   Mongols sack Baghdad—end of `Abbasid caliphate and of Golden Age

1453   Ottoman Turks capture Constantinople; end of Byzantine Empire

1492   Discovery of America breaks Middle Eastern monopoly of trade with Asia; fall of Granada ends Muslim hold over Spain

1683   Ottoman Turks fail to conquer the Habsburg capital Vienna; beginning of Ottoman decline

1798   Napoleon Bonaparte's Egyptian expedition breaks Mamluk power and opens the Middle East to Western influences

1856–1857 Heyday of *tanzimat* reforms to modernize Ottoman Empire; in India, Sepoy Rebellion is crushed, end of Mughals, India becomes British Crown colony

1915–1919 During World War I, British-instigated Arab Revolt against Turks; Britain and France plan colonization of Arab East; Balfour Declaration promises Palestine to Jews; end of Ottoman Empire; joint Hindu-Muslim anti-British agitation in India; Wilson's Fourteen Points and Russian Revolution inspire hope for independence among Muslims worldwide

Ten Crucial Episodes of Islamism

1924   Republic of Turkey under Atatürk abolishes caliphate

1928   Hassan al-Banna establishes Muslim Brotherhood in Egypt

1947–1949   Partition of British Mandate of Palestine, independence of Israel, the Palestinian *nakba* (catastrophe); partition of British India, independence of India and Pakistan

1967   Six Day War or June, 1967 War, Israel defeats Arab states; conquers and occupies Sinai, West Bank and Gaza Strip, and Golan Heights; crisis of secular pan-Arabism

1977–1978   Israeli-Egypt peace accord breaks taboo on negotiating with Jewish state; Islamic Revolution establishes mixed theocratic-democratic regime in Iran, led by Khomeini

1981–1983   Islamists assassinate Egyptian president Sadat; Israeli invasion of Lebanon militarily breaks PLO; massacre of Palestinians in Sabra and Shatila; failure of U.S.-French intervention. First suicide bombs by Shiite resistance

1988–1993   Islamist resistance leads to Soviet retreat from Afghanistan; Iraq-Iran War breaks Iran's Islamist dynamism, ends in stalemate; Iraq invades Kuwait, Western-led international intervention defeats Iraq in Gulf War, fueling anti-Westernism; *intifada* (Palestinian revolt) and Israeli-PLO peace process. Ahmad Yassin Islamists establishes Hamas

1996   Hamas's terrorism interrupts peace process. Taliban establish fundamentalist regime in Afghanistan

2000–2001   Failure of Israeli-Palestinian peace process leads to second *intifada* and emergence of Hamas; 9/11 al-Qaeda of Osama bin Laden 2001 terror attack against United States, Western-led international intervention dislodges Afghan Taliban

2003   U.S.-led invasion and occupation of Iraq; attempts at democratization and international anti-Western Islamist mobilization

PART I

Yesterday

ISLAM IN TIME

Islam: Origins and Historical Trajectory _____

Sixth and Seventh Centuries: Geopolitical Panorama

Islam started at a specific time and place, about 610 CE, in Mecca, Western Arabia. The Middle East, cradle of some the world's oldest civilizations, had already had experience with two earlier monotheistic religions, and these experiences facilitated the reception of a third. To understand Islam's character and extraordinary expansion, we must look both at its geopolitical context and at the religious influences of Judaism and Christianity.

In the sixth and seventh centuries, Arabia was peripheral to two regional "superpowers": the Byzantine Empire, the long-lasting Greek-speaking offshoot of the Roman Empire, and Persia, the only neighbor the Romans had never conquered. Byzantium was emphatically Christian. Its powerful church was closely aligned with the state (Byzantine "caesaropapism" may have stood as a model for Islam), but suffered from two problems. First, with Christianity as a state religion, non-separation of state and religion meant that theological disputes automatically became political. Debates on the nature of the Christ—divine, human, or both—led to destabilizing strife. The orthodox position ("Christ has two natures") became dominant in the Balkans and

Anatolia; in the Fertile Crescent (today's Israel/Palestine, Syria, and Iraq), however, more people accepted monophysitism ("Christ has only one, divine nature"). Religious persecution of Christian Middle Easterners by Constantinople, and the ethnic proximity of its Semitic population with the Arabs, would later facilitate acceptance of Islam. In the second place, the Byzantines were externally weakened by invasions and mutually exhaustive struggles against the Persians, followers of dualist Zoroastrianism.

Byzantine-Persian wars made trade dangerous for caravans coming from East Asia over the Silk Road. Merchants developed alternative routes over the Red Sea and Arabia. That in turn, benefited Mecca, a commercial nexus and, with its Kaaba housing a black meteorite, a traditional pilgrimage site for the polytheistic Arabs. The Prophet Muhammad would later erect a mosque over it.

The Arabian Peninsula's inhabitants spoke Arabic (a southern Semitic language), were pagans (though Christian and Jewish pockets existed), and had a tribal kinship structure. The inclement climate forced most to live as nomad pastoralists or caravan traders. These Bedouin looked down upon the sedentary populations of oases and towns. Bedouin values permanently marked Arab culture: freedom of movement, honor (linked to control of female sexuality), and clan solidarity. Eventually Islam overcame tribal traditions, but only partially; subsequent Islamic conquests exported Arab customs throughout the Middle East.

Muhammad (ca. 570–632) was born in what for Islam was the pre-revelation period of ignorance and barbarism, *jahiliyya*. The future prophet belonged to a minor branch of the powerful Quraish clan; he married an older merchant widow, Khadija, and his business trips in Arabia may have brought him into contact with Jews and Christians. At the age of 40, he started to have visions of the archangel Gabriel (Jibril), who spoke in God's name. The first visitation, in which Gabriel revealed what would become the Qur'an's oldest verses, frightened him, but Muhammad eventually believed that he was elected by God to be His messenger, and he continued receiving revelations for the rest of his life. The message was one of an omnipotent and unique God Who called upon every human being to acknowledge and venerate Him: the word *Islam* means "submission." The oldest messages are exhortations to prayer and conversion; later ones, more concrete, instruct on how to organize the community of believers. The revelations received their final compilation as the **Qur'an** (Koran, "recitation") some thirty years after Muhammad's death.

Initially Muhammad's preaching had little success. The Meccan elite were irritated by his demand to destroy their deities' images. In

622 Muhammad fled with a small band of followers to Yathrib (later *al-Madina*, "the City") 300 kilometers north of Mecca. This migration, or *hijra*, marked the beginning of the Islamic calendar. Here Muhammad succeeded in imposing his rule, established the first Islamic community, and waged war against neighboring polytheistic and Jewish tribes. Muhammad's victories resulted in the destruction, expulsion, or conversion of his enemies: constant wars of expansion led more tribes to accept Muhammad's leadership and join his wars. Thus, the despised preacher grew into a political-military leader. Eventually he defeated and converted the Meccans, cleansed his native town of pagan deities, and turned it into the prime pilgrimage center of the new religion. By the time of Muhammad's death, Muslims controlled most of Arabia.

The Five Pillars

Islam presents itself as a simple religion with clear obligations and prohibitions. It has five core principles, or "pillars":

1. *Shahada* (testimony): "There is no God but God and Muhammad is His Prophet"; accepting one all-powerful God and Muhammad as His messenger is what makes one a Muslim.
2. *Salat* (prayer): Five times a day the *muezzin* calls the believers to prostrate themselves before God. *Salat* is veneration; benefits to the believer are a result of God's grace, not of a contract or covenant. Although prayer may happen anywhere, believers meet once per week, on Friday, communally in the mosque.
3. *Zakat* (alms or charity): A portion of capital and income is levied for social beneficence. This levy expresses the solidarity among all believers, who constitute the *umma*, a type of nonterritorial nation.
4. *Ramadan*: In an act of self-purification, believers fast from sunrise to sunset during the month that celebrates the "descent" of the Qur'an. Nights, however, are for visiting relatives and friends.[1]
5. *Hajj* (pilgrimage): At least once in a lifetime, each healthy believer who can afford it must visit the Holy Places. Mecca replaced Jerusalem as the focus (*qibla*) of prayers after Muhammad's breach with the Jews. Although the pilgrimage was even more arduous in the Middle Ages than it is today, untold thousands made the journey. The shared spiritual experience bound the pilgrims into a transnational community and helped standardize ritual, practice, and belief. Paradoxically, *hajj* became easier, and more massive, thanks to Europe's colonization of Asia

and Africa in the nineteenth century and the Western transportation technologies of the railway, the steamship, and the airplane. Saudi Arabia, custodian of the Holy Places, now receives two million pilgrims annually.

The Two Earlier Monotheistic Revolutions

Islam has much in common with Judaism and Christianity: primacy of one true faith, a single life that is the one opportunity to gain or lose salvation, a God "descending" to human beings too weak to ascend to Him by their own forces. (Non-revelatory religions, such as Hinduism and Buddhism, invite human beings to "ascend" and reach a higher consciousness.) Fruit of the same monotheistic tree, Islam views itself as the perfection of Judaism and Christianity; Muhammad is an exponent of the monotheistic revolution, and the last (the "seal") of a lineage of prophets starting with Adam, sent by God to humanity to call man, who repeatedly strays, back to the straight path.

Like Judaism and Christianity, Islam demands ethical behavior. It partakes of a monotheistic revolution that began in Israel, rejecting existing pantheons of immortal but often immoral gods and goddesses. Although stronger and demanding of propitiation from mortals (e.g., through sacrifice), these deities were hardly admirable role models. In the eighteenth century BCE, Abraham (Ibrahim) believed that he had been contacted by one more powerful and benevolent God, Who, according to the Biblical account, led him to Canaan. His descendants eventually denied not just the power but even the existence of other deities. In 1300 BCE God's revelation on Mount Sinai to the Hebrews, led by Moses (Musa), formalized His covenant with the Elected People in a code of legal, ritualistic, but also ethical rules.

This first monotheism was revolutionary, not only because it eliminated all of Yahweh's rivals, but also because of its contractual nature; the Covenant transformed erratic nature into a world where human beings relate to one all-powerful, all-knowing, and all-good entity. Henceforth, catastrophes were no longer the doings of blind fate or angry Olympians, but punishments meted out when humans do not keep their side of the bargain: if they did, they would live (individually and collectively) the good life. Yet it was still a particularistic revolution, committing only one priestly nation to the One God in one Promised Land. Still, Islam accepts the major part of the Old Testament narrative, with the patriarchs, Joseph (Yusuf), Moses, David (Da'ud), Solomon (Suleiman), Jesus (`Isa), and others cast as prophets. Jerusalem remains in Islam the third holiest city, *al-Quds*, after Mecca and Medina.

Political crises culminating in destruction and loss of independence stimulated expectations of an end-time, when the Messiah, originally a this-worldly savior, would restore the Jews and usher in a realm of peace on earth. Christianity later spiritualized the concept, and Messianic ideas percolated into Islam, and especially into Shiism.

The Babylonian exile and its resolution transformed Judaism, importing from Persian Zoroastrianism a dualism of Good and Evil locked in cosmic battle, and the call to each person to be a soldier in the army of the Good. Post-exilic Judaism was henceforth torn between particularism and universalism. Jewish Diasporas in the Middle East underwent the impact of Hellenistic civilization with its universalism, humanism, and rationalism. Eventually, a "fundamentalist" backlash in Israel resulted, emphasizing the Jews' specificity and erecting ritual barriers against assimilation. Zealots revolted, first against Hellenistic rulers and then against Rome. The outcome was catastrophic, but before the end, Jesus of Nazareth had introduced a second monotheistic revolution. While Jesus's first followers saw him as the Jewish Messiah, Saul of Tarsus (later the apostle St. Paul) provoked a breach with Judaism; early Christianity came to define Jesus as one expression of a Trinitarian God. Abolishing "superseded" ritualism that erected barriers against Gentiles, Paul facilitated mass conversion. Thus, Christianity universalized Jewish monotheism, which had been restricted to one people. It took the idea of humanity as God's coadjutant, of human dignity and equality, into the world. Christianity grew in the Middle East, and then infiltrated the rest of the Roman Empire. By 381, it had become the official faith. By then, the Empire had split, with Constantinople the capital of its eastern, more resistant, half.

Where Islam Differs

God is for all three monotheisms unborn, eternal, omniscient, and omnipresent; on Judgment Day, He will conduct the good to paradise and the evildoers to hell. Yet a number of differences distinguish Islam from its two predecessors. The distance between Creator and creature is greater: God must receive absolute obedience. His unicity is more emphasized: *shirk*—giving Him "partners"—is the worst sin, hence no Trinity, no spirits, no saints. There is no mediation between God and man—no Christlike figure, no Church—only immediate confrontation. That makes His word so much more important—hence the centrality of Qur'an. Somewhat like Orthodox Judaism and to a far greater extent than Christianity, Islam penetrates (and means to control) all life spheres: it is at once religion (*din*), community (*umma*), and comprehensive lifestyle (*sunna*). Islam, then, becomes for pious

Muslims *the* determinant of their collective identity. This has the following consequences:

1. A juridical-religious system determining rules of behavior, the *shari`a*, based on the interpretation of sacred sources in response to changing circumstances.
2. Nondifferentiation of religion and politics: no life sphere can *not* be under God. The unity of State and Church that prevailed in Medina under Muhammad was transplanted to the huge Muslim empire. The caliph, leader after the Prophet, combined military with juridical-religious authority; absolutism, though, was tempered by the idea that community consensus reflects God's will.
3. No Church, and hence no clergy. There is a specialist class of religious interpreters, the `ulama*, but no mediators; all believers are equal.
4. Militancy for the faith. *Jihad*, often incorrectly translated as "holy war," more properly corresponds to "struggle in the path of God." Accepting Islam has always implied total commitment to conduct one's life according to God's precepts, to infuse society with the letter and spirit of God's word, and to propagate the true religion in the world. *Jihad* means both the disciplining inner transformation (the Greater Jihad) and efforts to convert the infidels, if necessary through violence (the Lesser Jihad).
5. Like Christianity, Islam views itself as bearer of the only true faith, and it combines this exclusivity with proselytizing. While bloody religious conflicts abound in Christianity, the military aspect is even more present in Islam, whose prophet and founder was also leader in war. The expansion Muhammad started continued over the next generations with undiminished vigor. After the first decades of rapid wars of expansion, more gradual and pacific expansion and conversion became the rule. However, the geopolitical antagonism between the House of Islam and the House of War remained: armistices are possible, but no peace—until the latter absorbs the former.

Rapid Military-Political Expansion

Islamic enthusiasm proved irresistible. Within decades, Islam had conquered an unprecedentedly vast area stretching from Spain over North Africa and the Middle East. India, Indonesia, and parts of China and Sub-Saharan Africa were reached later. The history of Islam largely coincides with that of this Islamic world. Four stages may be distinguished. The first is the "classical" phase: from the seventh through the tenth century, the Arabs established the world's largest state and its most advanced civilization. In a second stage, the Islamic Middle Ages from the eleventh through the fourteenth century, Islam suffered reversals in the Middle East but continued to advance in Central Asia and India. The third epoch, from the fifteenth through the eighteenth century, witnessed renewed dynamism in a range of Muslim "gunpowder empires": the Ottoman in the Middle East, the Safavid in Persia, and the Great Mughal in India. Islam now also penetrated Southeast Asia and Africa. The nineteenth and first half of the twentieth century constitute a fourth period, when the Islamic world fell under European influence. Finally, recent decolonization—and experiments to strike a new balance between Islam and Western modernity—have opened a fifth period. Each of these epochs will now be briefly characterized, with more detail given as the discussion comes nearer to our own times.

Stage 1: "Classical" Islam

The Rightly Guided Caliphs and the First Schisms, 632–661

The period of the first four successors of Muhammad, the "Rightly Guided Caliphs" (*rashidun*) was also that of the first schisms in a still primitive Islamic community (see Figure 1.1). At the Prophet's death, Islam was in control of the larger portion of Arabia, but no successor had been designated. Two currents soon confronted each other. The first held that succession could only be legitimate within the Prophet's family; its candidate was `Ali ibn Abi Talib, Muhammad's cousin and son-in-law.

The second claimed that any Muslim was eligible to succeed the Prophet, and this opinion prevailed, turning `Ali's adherents into a party (*shi`a*, hence Shiism/Shiites) of disgruntled oppositionists. The winning party was that of the *sunna*, or "beaten track"; its followers, Sunnis, are now a 90 percent majority in Islam. Abu Bakr, an old comrade of Muhammad, was appointed caliph (*khalifa*) by consensus; after him, `Umar ibn al-Khattab, a stern legislator, completed conquests of Egypt, Palestine, Syria, Mesopotamia, and parts of the Caucasus—so many losses for the Byzantine Empire.

Arab Islamic garrisons controlled the mostly Christian populations. The third caliph, `Uthman ibn `Affan, conquered Persia. However, as the caliphate expanded, doctrinal dissensions and social disparities grew. When `Ali finally became caliph, strife among Muslims could no longer be controlled. In 661, civil war (*fitna*) broke out, and `Ali was killed by Mu`awiyya of the Umayyad clan. Mu`awiyya moved the caliphate's seat to Damascus and founded the Umayyad

Main Divisions of Islam

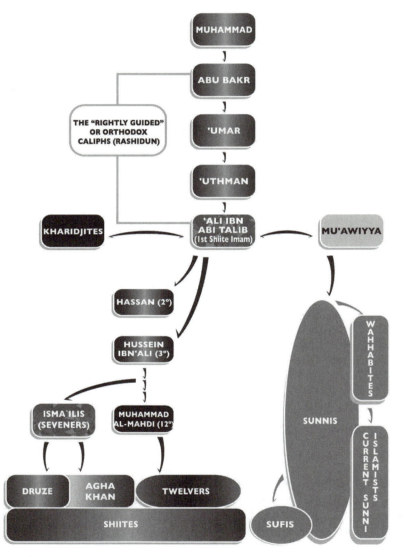

Figure 1.1
Divisions of Islam

dynasty. A stunned *umma* realized Muhammad's golden era of an ideal Islam close to God was now past. `Ali's loyalists set their hopes upon his surviving son, Hussein. With the succession of Yazid, Mu`awiyya's son, however, the dynastic principle seemed consolidated. A Shiite rebellion was easily defeated in a second civil war. In 689, on day ten (`*Ashura*) of the month of Muharram, Hussein and his followers were beheaded in a battle at Karbala. The Umayyads now reigned supreme. `Ali's defeated and persecuted party maintained an underground existence, developing traditions that glorified Hussein's sacrifice, contesting the legitimacy of the "usurpers" and insisting on the restoration of `Ali's line. Eventually, Shiism developed a millennial ideology of justice restored. Sunnism developed into a kind of establishment. But the *fitna* left a lasting trauma, and revolt against an Islamic ruler was henceforth condemned: "Better a hundred years of tyranny than one hour of anarchy."

The Umayyads (661–750)

The Umayyads ruled the first Islamic Empire—the largest state the world had ever known, stretching from Spain to India. The expansion stopped only in 732, when Frankish leader Charles Martel defeated the Muslims at Poitiers. The Umayyad structure was multi-ethnic but remained under Arab control. Arab frontier garrisons were turning into cities such as Cairo, Baghdad, and Kairouan, whose soldiers formed an exploitative ruling stratum yet increasingly mixed with non-Arab merchants. As strengthening links with the local population bred regionalism, the need to defeat it strengthened the caliphs and turned what had been an egalitarian religious community into an absolutist, centralized state.

Although there was little pressure to convert, Arabization and Islamization both proceeded apace. Islam's relationship with other religions took shape in this period: the sword for idolaters, but tolerance for monotheistic "People of the Book" (Jews, Christians, and Sabeans—the concept was later expanded to include Zoroastrians, Hindus, and some others). The Christian majority thus entered the statute of *dhimma*, or community protection: while free to continue worship (albeit discreetly) and exercise any profession, external symbols such as colored badges marked their inferiority, and disarmament showed their vulnerability. A poll tax, or *jizya*, was paid in lieu of military service.

Better treated than non-Christians in Christendom, *dhimmis* were nonetheless never secure; better periods alternated with worse. Political and military power was a Muslim monopoly, and conversion, an ongoing, one-way process, gradually made Muslims the majority. Yet non-Arabs did not achieve full equality by conversion, and many converts felt the sting of discrimination.

The Abbasids (750–1258)

In the 740s a series of revolts led by Abu al-`Abbas, a distant relative of the Prophet, exterminated all Umayyads (except one, who fled to Spain, where his descendants ruled until the eleventh century). The new "Abbasid" dynasty ended Arab racial privilege and based its legitimacy on political equality among Muslims. With religion as the only cement of the *pax islamica*, though, theological questions became paramount. Over time, this would undermine the unity of the caliphate. For now, however, expansion continued. In 755 the Abbasids defeated China, opening Central Asia for Islamization. Sicily fell in the mid-ninth century. The Middle East, with the scattered demography and proliferation of ethnic and religious groups we know today, started to emerge. While some Christian minorities held on to their own tongue as liturgical language, such as Syriac or Coptic, Arabic was now spoken from the Atlantic coast to the Persian Gulf, in addition to being the sacred language of all Muslims.

Most Middle Easterners adopted Islam as religion and Arabic as language. However, Islamization and Arabization were not always overlapping processes. Thus there were Arabic-speaking, non-Muslim minorities (e.g., Maronites, Jews); non-Arabic speaking, Muslim minorities (e.g., Berbers, Kurds); and non-Arabized, non-Muslims (e.g., Armenians). (See Figure 1.2.) To these minorities must be added Islamic schismatics, often esoteric Shiite sects such as Druze, Isma`ilites, and `Alawites, as well as Kharijites.

Pressures for cultural homogenization existed, but Muslims never had the administrative means to impose uniformity in their states. The resulting Middle Eastern ethnic-religious mosaic has survived until today—except in Turkey, which achieved a degree of homogeneity through massacres and enforced population exchanges, but only in the twentieth century.[2]

Orthodoxy and the Defeat of Rationalist Theology: Shiism

Islam's Golden Age lasted from 750 to 950. The empire and its merchants prospered through their caravan trade with Asian empires and Europe. It was also a period of cultural flowering. A detailed analysis falls outside our scope, but some relevant philosophical tendencies must be mentioned. Today's normative Islam is a result of expansion and confrontation with unfamiliar customs. The danger of fragmentation strengthened the need for a definitive code of belief and behavior. How was one to perform ablutions in the desert? How were inheritances

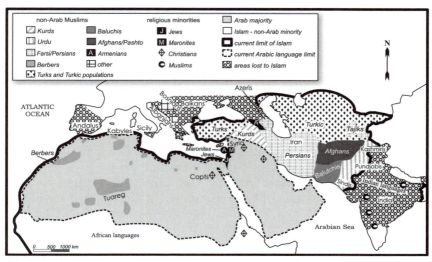

Figure 1.2
The Middle East: Arabization, Islamization, and minorities

to be apportioned? When was the death penalty the fitting punishment? The answers were based on *fiqh*, a system for interpreting religious law. Its sources were the Qur'an, whose often contradictory or unclear lessons were checked against the *hadith*, or sayings and actions of the Prophet. When there was a question, either logical reasoning by analogy or community consensus (*ijma`*) would help.[3] Through discussion and education in *madrasas* (religious academies), the process gradually institutionalized a corpus of rules: the *shari`a*. Eventually, four orthodox schools gained a monopoly on interpretation; the youngest and also the strictest, the Hanbalites (after Ahmad ibn Hanbal, 780–855), laid the basis for later medieval puritans such as Ibn Taymiyya and is today the law in Saudi Arabia.

The first two Abbasid centuries became Islam's Golden Age. It witnessed the development of new forms of economic organization (such as credit mechanisms, maritime companies) as well as significant advances in medicine, mathematics, optics, astronomy, philology, arts, architecture, and calligraphy. Such progress was related to the philosophical bases of Islamic society. However, no consensus existed on these bases. Translations to Arabic of Plato, Aristotle, and other classical thinkers spurred fierce debate. Rediscovered Greek rationalism cast doubts on dogmas such as the creation of the world, God's omnipresence, and physical resurrection. Confrontation between two epistemologies—Qur'anic supernatural revelation versus

natural rationalism—spawned competing schools. Their rivalry was
to have long-term consequences. Conservatives stressed the universality of *shari`a*: they rejected any life dimension not ruled by religion
as service to God. The progressive school laid more stress on knowing
God than on serving Him: free-thinking reason, it taught, could, if correctly applied, reach the same understanding of the (visible and invisible) world as revelation. Their intellectualized religion attempted to
find a balance between reason and revelation: *kalam*. The most rationalist movement was the *mu`tazila*, which concluded that the Qur'an
was itself created and hence noneternal, thus opening the door for a
historical critique of religion itself. We are not too far here from the
point reached 1000 years later by the European Enlightenment!
Philosophical rationalism (*falsafa*) complemented the advances in science and technology and eventually served as the basis of Islam's
worldwide prominence. But although it became official doctrine in
827, the progressives' ascendancy did not last. From 847 on, an anti-
rationalistic reaction took the form of violent persecutions. In the
early 900s, Abu al-Hassan al-Ash`ari wrote that God was incompre-
hensible and far above mere creatures; human beings must simply
follow His commands without questioning them (*bila kaif*, i.e., "without how"). The "Ash`arite synthesis" became Sunni orthodoxy. How-
ever, the corollary of such absolute obedience was a fatalism that in
the coming centuries would undermine Islamic creativity.

Orthodoxy's long struggle eventually defeated what had been a
more pluralistic faith. The mystical (**Sufi**) path, Shiite revolutionary
esotericism, and `adab`, the rather agnostic literary culture, were
some of the defeated alternatives. There is not enough space here to
give Islamic mysticism the attention it deserves. The distance
between Creator and creature, and the absence of ascetic traditions,
seemed not to predispose Islam to the mystical Love of God, aspiring
to unite the soul with the Creator; yet there were always those who
remained unsatisfied with a primarily ritualistic and social religion.
Influenced by Christian, Gnostic, and possibly Buddhist examples,
Muslim mystics developed a gamut of spiritual and meditative techniques. However, when some openly affirmed their identity with God,
they scandalized the Orthodox and invited persecution. After al-Hallaj
was crucified in 922, mysticism became more "sober." Orthodoxy succeeded in integrating it as a minor branch of Ash`arism, but it did not
die. In the eleventh and twelfth centuries, Neoplatonism inspired Ibn
Sina (Avicenna) and Ibn al-`Arabi's heretical pantheism. From the
turbulent 1200s on, many Muslims looked for mystical teachers
reputed to have magical powers. Sufi masters (from *suf*, the woolen
cloth they wore) were especially popular among non-Arab converts,

although their ecstatic rituals were frowned upon by the more puri-
tanically minded. Secret doctrines, passed on from master to disciple,
developed into lineages of devotees of a specific path (*tariq*) and spiritual brotherhoods (*tariqat*). These schools were crucial to the spread
of Islam in Central Asia, China, Indonesia, and Africa.

As for **Shiism**, after Hussein ibn `Ali's death, a line of Imams followed
in his family; most died as martyrs. Political success against Sunni
authorities was rare, and persecution forced Shiites to adopt dissimulation tactics: only opportunism guaranteed survival. Shiism was more
susceptible to sectarian fragmentation than Sunnism. Schisms often had
their origin in questions of legitimate succession, but some involved esoteric (often Neoplatonic) doctrines to decipher the Qur'an's hidden mean-
ings. Isma`ilites or "Seveners" believe in the legitimate authority of the
first seven Imans. The majority of Shiites, however, were "Twelvers":
those who accepted a lineage of twelve Imams. The last of these Imams
disappeared under suspicious circumstances in 874, to return at the end
of time: Muhammad al-Mahdi, "the Expected" or the "Hidden Imam."
Expectation fed a type of messianism. After the Imams, jurists assumed
control of the community. Shiism vacillated between cautious quietism
and revolutionary activism, and false Imams appeared regularly. With
ups and downs, Shiism has survived; in 1978 a specifically Shiite brand
of Islamism led the first Islamist revolution of our times, in Iran.

Stage 2: The Arab Middle Ages

The second Islamic age knew destructive invasions and calamities,
yet a "rise and fall" dichotomy is too simple. While Islam's Middle
East center did indeed decline, expansion went on in Africa, India,
and elsewhere. The terms *Islam* and *Middle East* ceased to be coextensive. After 900, it became increasingly difficult to keep the empire,
with its far-flung provinces, united. The Abbasids entered into a long
decline, and with them Arab-Islamic culture. Ideological schisms
added to administrative fragility. Thus the Shiite (Isma`ilite) Fatimid
dynasty took over in Tunisia and later in Egypt (970–1150). In Baghdad a Shiite military clan, the Buyids, reduced the caliphate to a
merely ceremonial title, though the Abbasid dynasty continued formally until the thirteenth century. But the most unsettling factor was
Central Asian migration. From the 900s movements of steppe nomads
started, with no less devastating consequences for the Muslim Middle
East than for China and East Europe. Turkic tribes entered the Arab
world, both separately and in groups. They were more warlike than the
Arab elites, and made careers as slave soldiers, mercenaries, or praeto-
rian guards of caliphs and governors. Untrammeled by traditional
bonds, Turkish infiltrators soon concentrated real power (*sultan*) in

their hands, even though they nominally remained slaves. Eventually they constituted their own adoptive (*mamluk*) dynasties.

Seljuk Turks defeated the Byzantines in 1071 and established their rule over part of Anatolia, Syria, and Palestine. This was the backdrop of a Christian counterattack: the Crusades led to Islam's first significant territorial losses. The fall of Jerusalem (1099) allowed the "Franks" to keep a temporary foothold in the Holy Land, until Salah al-Din (Saladin) defeated them in 1187, restoring Sunni control. The Catholic *reconquista* of Muslim Spain and Portugal (*Andalus*), however, proved definitive. The thirteenth-century Mongol devastations were vastly more apocalyptic, however, than any crusade. Genghis Khan and his successors destroyed the remainder of the Abbasid Empire (as well as Russian principalities and Song rule in China). In 1258, Hulagu sacked Baghdad and massacred the inhabitants of the world's foremost metropolis. Egyptian Mamluks stemmed the Mongol tide at `Ayn Jalut in Palestine in 1260, but the destruction of Mesopotamian irrigation was irreversible and led to Iraq's long-term decline. Where the Mongols stayed on, in Persia for example, they constituted a thin ruling stratum that was soon assimilated into Islam. With civil wars raging and trade plummeting, the fourteenth century was at least as catastrophic for the Muslim world as it was for European Christendom. The 1348 Black Death was probably worse in the Orient. At the end of the century, Genghis Khan's descendant Timur Leng (Tamerlane) destroyed the first Turkish Ottoman kingdom, laid Persia waste, and nearly extinguished the Indian Muslim sultanate.

Stage 3: The Era of the Muslim Gunpowder Empires

The Rise of the Ottoman Empire

Restoration of Muslim power came in the fifteenth century, the start of the third era of Islamic history—but at the price of growing rigidity. Turkish Ottomans (practically coextensive with the Byzantines at their height), Persian Safavids, and Indian Great Mughals, as well as other smaller sultanates, formed "gunpowder" empires based on cannon, guns, and strong centralized governments, strong enough to keep European penetration at bay for centuries.[4] Only the cumulative political, industrial, and military revolutions of the late eighteenth and early nineteenth centuries made colonization by the West possible. Of these empires, the Turkish was the largest, strongest, and most durable.

Byzantine weakening in the Anatolian heartland, followed by the fall of the Seljuks, created room in the fourteenth century for the invasion of the Turkish tribe of Osman, son of Ertugrul (hence "Osman" or "Ottoman"). Their *ghazi* warriors waged guerrilla warfare, created the Turkish reputation for valor and tenacity, and soon started conquests in the Balkans, encircling the dwindling Byzantine realm. In 1389, the Ottomans destroyed the Serbs, but their first expansion was interrupted by Tamerlane. By the second quarter of the fifteenth century, however, the Ottomans had sufficiently recuperated to conquer dozens of Mediterranean and Black Sea Genoese and Venetian possessions. In 1453, they put an end to Constantinople. Conquest of Iraq, Syria, Arabia (with its Holy Places), and North Africa to Algeria followed in the sixteenth century.[5] Suleiman the Magnificent, most famous of the Ottoman sultans, successfully vanquished the Habsburgs in the west (where he allied with France) and the Persians in the east. In 1529, he was at the gates of Vienna. The Turkish Empire replaced the Abbasids and ruled most of the Arab world. Turks imposed Sunni supremacy and competed against the Safavids, who turned Persia Shiite. As a result of their long rivalry, Iran is now Shiite, whereas the rest of the Middle East is—except for a few redoubts—solidly Sunni.

Ottoman military success was to no small degree due to the janissaries, a levy of Christian boys, educated as Muslim soldiers and fiercely loyal to the sultan alone—a system that functioned well so long as janissaries did not turn corrupt. As long as the empire kept expanding, administering it was a relatively efficient affair. Then feudalization crept in. Military leaders who had received land grants against a promise of handing over taxes entrenched themselves as a new class of landed gentry, sapping an initially commercial economy.

The Decline of the Ottoman Empire

The Ottoman Empire enjoyed three centuries of expansion and survived three centuries of stagnation and decline: it thus proved extremely durable, and strong even in its death throes. In fact, it lingered until the end of World War I. But it frayed at its margins and was irreversibly fragmented. Despite accepting Islam and protecting literate culture, the new Turkish elite remained distant from the old Arabic-Persian one. The dichotomy between a traditional merchant and administrator class, and a new, ethnically alien, political-military stratum, enthusiastically Muslim yet lacking traditional religious sanction, was never overcome. Eventually a new equilibrium emerged, based on Sunni orthodoxy, that was dogmatic and remote from the piety of the lower classes, who had fled the insecurity of their time by retreating into mystical sects. The gap between urban and `ulama "High Islam" and exalted popular Islam grew permanent. Tolerance of nonbelievers decreased. The `ulama reached the conclusion

that, as the time of the revelation had receded, it would be more prudent to hew to the precepts of existing interpretive schools, which in
their wisdom appeared to have exhausted all possibilities of free
interpretation of sacred texts. Henceforth the "gate of *ijtihad* was
closed"; that is, individual interpretation was outlawed and "innovation" (*bid`a*) to be avoided. This theological turn doubtlessly weak-
ened Muslim ability to face the impending challenges that the West
was about to launch.

In part, decline followed geopolitical and economic factors beyond
Ottoman reach. The Middle East had traditionally profited from its
mediating position between the Far East and European markets.
However, Ottoman territorial advances interrupted that flow, spurring the European discoveries that would harm Middle Eastern trade.
The Turks lost control not only over the Mediterranean but also over
the Indian Ocean (once a "Muslim lake") to the Portuguese, Dutch,
and English. Spain's arrival in the New World produced a massive sil-
ver influx, which brought inflation and ruined Ottoman artisans. Economic crisis preceded military and social stagnation. From the failed
second siege of Vienna in 1683, the tide turned inexorably. In the eighteenth century, the Turks lost territory to Russia in the Ukraine and
to Austria in Hungary and Transylvania. At the same time, transoce-
anic trade was obviating the ancient caravan routes through Asia. In
the nineteenth century, Russia absorbed Central Asia's independent
Turkic khanates. Meanwhile, Ottoman losses in Balkans created the
"Oriental Question": which of Europe's great powers would inherit
former Ottoman territories? Once an asset, the Ottoman Empire's
geopolitical position now became a liability: the Ottomans survived
thanks only to jealousy among its enemies.

Internal weaknesses compounded the Turkish giant's ineffective-
ness. Its economy was unable to resist penetration of French and British capitalist manufactures. The Turks had no inventions, no
structural innovation, and little curiosity about Western life.[6] French and
other foreign merchants enjoyed juridical immunities ("capitulations")
and gradually took control of Ottoman trade, while the Ottoman elite of
a`yan (provincial feudal vassals) became an unproductive stratum of
profiteers. Decentralization had its counterpart in social-religious
fragmentation—the Ottomans' system of religious "tolerance in inequality." Islam was uncontested though stagnant: Sunnis were the majority that legitimated the whole structure. The Ottomans organized the
coexistence of the Muslim majority with *dhimmis* through a system where
each *millet*, or recognized religious community, enjoyed internal autonomy and functioned as a "nonterritorial nation," a corporative juridical
entity free in its internal regulation, and whose spiritual leader

answered to the sultan for his coreligionists' behavior. Thus the Greek Orthodox were represented in Constantinople by their patriarch, and the Jews by the chief rabbi.[7] Each community had its professional specialization: Sunnis were peasants and herders; Sunni Turks monopolized the military and the bureaucracy; commerce and finance were often left to the infidel Armenians, Greeks, and Jews. These minorities increasingly controlled contact with the West. Although sects harbored mutual prejudice and did not socialize much, the *millet* system kept the peace among these groups within a common structure. But not unlike Indian castes, they also constituted "social ghettoes." Minorities were economically and educationally advanced, politically vulnerable, and envied by the Sunni masses—the latter theoretically the Empire's backbone, but in reality its poorest and most exploited subjects. This was not a scenario for long-term stability.

Tensions increased and community relations worsened in the nineteenth century. In the era of nationalisms, minorities were less accepting of their subaltern position. Translating religious identity into national terms, *millets* grew into "proto-nations," their churches incubators of nationalists who militated for incompatible aims: greater communal autonomy, even independence—but also greater privileges *within* the empire.[8] This nationalization process was already complicated enough where minorities lived in compact blocks, but where they found themselves among other populations, communal conflicts, once kindled, defied resolution. While in the Middle East Jews and Christians were dispersed minorities (e.g., Armenians in eastern Anatolia), in the Balkans the vast majority—except for Albanians and Bosnians—had remained Christian. Here Turkish colonization was mostly limited to a thin stratum of Turkish *aghas* exploiting their *rayya* ("flock"). This was where the first anti-Ottoman revolts erupted.

Millet pluralism, once advanced for its time, became a liability in the era of European imperialism. The Ottoman elites initiated measures meant to modernize the empire. In 1856 the sultan abolished the *millets* altogether and introduced juridical equality. However, reform attempts were too little and too late; centrifugal nationalisms, in conjunction with external forces eager for spoils, had grown too strong. The attempt to graft an alien concept of citizenship on a society still rife with divisive religious definitions backfired. The religiously based Ottoman structure had been tolerant and open to all nationalities, but when nationalism finally infected it, coexistence among its communities became impossible. Incompatible group demands eventually tore the Ottoman Empire asunder. It may be too simple to say the empire's demise was unavoidable, yet few contemporaries believed in its viability as a traditional religious structure. Most observers, including Muslims, were opting for Westernization.

The Middle East Confronts the West _____

Stage 4: The Middle East under Western Influence

Napoleon Bonaparte's Egyptian expedition of 1798–99 and his easy victory over the Mamluks was the transition point to the fourth, and most traumatic, Islamic era. It was the beginning of a new type of foreign interference that would have fatal consequences for all Muslim regimes. The inability of the Ottoman Empire to modernize became the backdrop for the present Middle East. Sultans and viziers who tried to shore up the empire by military or administrative reform found vested interests in their way: rapacious pashas, corrupt janissaries, and backward-looking `ulama`. In 1807 Selim III paid with his life for attempting to found a new and more professional army. Only in 1826 was Mahmud II able to liquidate the janissaries. He opened military academies to study the West's "military secrets," starting the *tanzimat* ("regulations", i.e., reorganization) movement. In the mid-nineteenth century, reforming sultans abolished feudalism, introduced private property, replaced *millets* with citizen equality, reformed taxes and military service, and even dabbled in parliamentarism. Still they could not halt Western penetration. In the latter half of the nineteenth century, the Ottoman Empire was the "sick man of Europe." The reform movement abruptly ended in 1876 when Sultan Abdulhamid II restored absolutism. With `ulama` support, he closed the door to Western liberal ideas—although not to Western technology—and promoted himself as caliph. The proto-Islamist thinker Afghani helped the sultan create pan-Islamism.

One hundred years after Bonaparte, many Ottoman areas, as well as Persia, Egypt, Tunisia, and Morocco had, directly or indirectly, fallen under Western control. In 1830, France colonized Algeria. Beginning with Greek independence in the same period, the Ottomans had lost one Balkan province after another: Serbia, Moldavia, Walachia, Bulgaria, Bosnia-Herzegovina, and Albania, as well as Armenia, Georgia, and other parts of the Caucasus. Egypt became autonomous under growing Western tutelage. Aden and Kuwait were already held by Britain, Lebanon was autonomous under France; Tunisia became a French protectorate, and Libya was soon to become an Italian colony. When World War I began, the empire had been reduced to Anatolia, a small strip of East Thrace, and the Arab East. Foreign debt led to the impoundment of its customs revenues by the West; French and Italian merchants controlled a large part of Ottoman foreign trade; Christian missionaries opened schools and hospitals: German engineers supervised the construction of railways, canals, ports, and irrigation works; and colonists were settling Algeria, Palestine, and other areas.

The story was not much different elsewhere. After Napoleon, Mehmet Ali (Muhammad `Ali), an Albanian adventurer, made Egypt autonomous and started an ambitious modernization program. He made Egypt a major cotton exporter, although it lost its self-sufficiency in food. Mehmet Ali's industrialization schemes failed, and when he became too "bothersome," European powers intervened and checked his expansionism. The Suez Canal was dug from 1858, under British and French control. When Egypt became insolvent, the West intervened again. In 1882 the British smashed a nationalist revolt and installed a protectorate. Persia followed a similar evolution, somewhat later. After the Safavids, the Qajar dynasty (1794–1925) ruled a society with a more primitive economy than the Ottoman. Persia was squeezed between Russian and British imperial ambitions. The former conquered Azerbaijan, the latter Afghanistan. In 1907, they divided Persia into spheres of influence between themselves— despite an anticolonial "Constitutionalist" revolution.

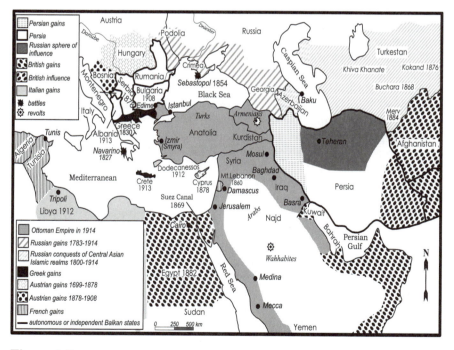

Figure 1.3
The Ottoman Empire: decline and the "Oriental question" through 1917

France and Britain were the main imperialist players in the Middle East, with Italy and Germany cast in minor roles. Little noticed, meanwhile, Russia not only claimed generous slices of Ottoman and Safavid territory, but in addition annexed the better part of Central Asia, absorbing that vast area's independent khanates. Manchu (Qing) China expanded westward, annexing Uyghur East Turkestan (Xinjiang or "New Province"). Between the two of them, Russia and China turned all Muslim communities into colonized minorities.

Intellectual Reactions to Western Penetration

Centuries of gradual decline had left Muslim society politically, militarily, and psychologically unprepared to fend off Western imperialism. The Islamic world's history from the middle of the nineteenth century on is that of an attempt to restore depleted forces, and to wrest initiative from the West. Western technological and military predominance first exposed the internal decay of Muslim empires, and then stimulated reflection upon it. Thinkers criticized Western supremacy, but also took issue with the Muslims' own impotence. The "diagnoses" and "therapies" they proposed in the late nineteenth century drew the fault lines for the Islamic world of the twentieth; their relevance continues today.

Ambivalence has always marked the Middle East's reception of the West. European science, technology, and industry were admired and prompted the wish for emulation. But the West also inspired repugnance, for Christendom's very success seemed to threaten Islamic identity, conditioned by the certainty of victory God had promised His followers. The Qur'an, after all, promised Muslims power on earth and instructed them how to achieve it.[9] Contempt for Christians had for a long time been part and parcel of the Muslim repertoire.

Three responses evolved: liberal Westernization, nationalism, and Islamic modernism. Relatively few in the Middle East opted for the first: constitutionalism and belief in human rights and individualism remained minority options. Most Muslims deemed such principles incompatible with some more important, overarching identity, whether Islamic, Arab, or Turkish.

Nationalism was more important. As the Ottoman Empire failed to provide protection to its subjects, the regime's legitimacy eroded, and opposition movements flourished. The Middle East never secularized as the West did—hence its nationalisms stand in tense relation with religion. Moreover, in a multiethnic empire, nationalisms were by definition corrosive. Nationalism had cost the Ottomans their Balkan provinces. Now it became a bone of contention between populations still within the Empire, in particular Arabs, Turks, Armenians, and (immigrating from Europe) Jews.

Arab nationalism started in the mid-nineteenth century among the Lebanese Christian intelligentsia, who saw it as a vehicle to escape *dhimmi* status and obtain equal rights as Arabs in a nationally—no longer religiously—defined polity. Palestine, then a forlorn corner of the decaying empire, was included in its claims and soon led to a clash with Jewish nationalism.

Turkish nationalism arrived later. Only in Anatolia did Turks constitute a solid majority. Oppositionist Turks were for a long time "Ottomanist," but Ottomanism was artificial and had limited appeal. Conspiring in secret societies, officers of the Committee for Unity and Progress staged the Young Turkish Revolution in 1908, and reinstated the 1876 constitution. However, after a brief moment of fraternization, the government became more dictatorial and central-ized, and imposed Turkification, alienating the Empire's other nationalities.

Meanwhile, attempts to modernize Islam had also come to the fore. Because Islamic reformers agreed that the cause of Muslim decadence could hardly be attributed to Islam, God's gift to humanity, they were led to find the root of evil in Muslim behavior. The solution, they held, was a return to a purer religiosity, free of age-old superstitions and creative in interpretation. Reformers rejected the blind imitation (*taqlid*) of scholastic traditions and the authoritarianism that pre-vailed in traditional education. They demanded a return to the Qur'an, and claimed for every believer the right to interpret the holy writ: *ijtihad*, the door medieval Islam had closed, was flung open. The three best-known intellectuals of this current were Afghani, 'Abduh, and Ridda. Today's fundamentalists and their progressive critics both take their cue from these early modernists.

Jamal al-Din al-Afghani (1838–97), a roving propagandist and con-spirer, created a Sunni identity for himself under the *nom-de-plume* al-Afghani ("the Afghan"); although he was most likely Persian. His travels in Islamic countries convinced him of the urgency of the "Western menace." In Egypt, India (where he criticized the then fash-ionable modernist Sayyid Ahmed Khan), and at the court in Constan-tinople, Afghani preached the need for a return to faith as precondition for an Islamic renaissance. An early anticolonialist, he called for *umma* unity against the West and under Ottoman leader-ship. Like most other reformers, Afghani did not reject Western technology—he wanted it to be imported cautiously, "disinfected" of the infidels' social and religious ideas. Modern science, he believed, was quite compatible with Islam.

Afghani was among the first to call for a clear Islamic policy. This led him to denounce the tyranny of the shah of Persia, the debauchery of Egypt's khedive, and Ottoman *tanzimat*, and to insist on the Qur'an as foundation of law. Exiled in Paris, Afghani collaborated with his Egyptian pupil Muhammad `Abduh (1849–1905). The two published their ideas in their periodical *al-Urwa al-wuthqa* ("The Indissoluble Bond"). `Abduh, however, was more moderate than his master, cultivated contacts with Western intellectuals, and saw Islam as civilization rather than as faith—an instrument of social peace and harmony, and thus a basis for integrating Muslims into the modern world.

`Abduh eventually rejected pan-Islamism as utopian, accepted the new borders drawn by the colonial powers, and made his peace with British rule in Egypt. In 1889 he returned to Egypt, became judge and *mufti*, and drew up laws that regulated private life, although without imposing complete *shari`a* rigor. These were later enacted in several Arab countries. In spirit he was close to the *mu`tazila*, the progressive rationalistic philosophers who had been defeated a millennium earlier.

Like his Christian counterparts, `Abduh and his fellow modernists had to reconcile the contradiction between revealed faith and objective science. This was hardly a new question, but took a different form in its Islamic context. For Christians, nineteenth-century historical criticism—based on Biblical philology and archaeology, advances in astronomy, Darwin's evolution theory, and the like—appeared to affect the literal truth of the Scriptures. Protestant theologians responded to that challenge by positing a symbolical, nonliteral interpretation. By understanding each of Genesis's six days of creation as signifying a geological era of millions of years, they hoped to save the Biblical narrative. This operation founded modernist Christianity. Religion kept its function as a social "cement" and continued to ground morality. Eventually, it was felt to lack spiritual depth, and churches were unable to staunch the hemorrhage of the faithful until new theologies emerged—existentialist and, importantly, fundamentalist. But this would unfold in the future.

In Islam, such historicization of faith was—and largely remains—taboo. According to Islamic orthodoxy, Prophet Muhammad, the perfect human being, is above criticism and the Qur'an was never created but always existed alongside God: its text is not susceptible to historical analysis, which may raise doubt as to its authenticity as God's word.[10] In interpreting, then, the commenter can never stray too far from the literal meaning regardless of internal contradictions, miracles, and seemingly absurd commands.

`Abduh "saw" in the holy text signs and premonitions of contemporary inventions and events (although he never embraced later extreme "scientific exegeses," which find in the Qur'an descriptions of nuclear bombs or interstellar voyages). But he could not modernize the juridical norms stipulated in the text and therefore viewed as immutable: penal laws, female attire, and prohibition of alcohol, for example. For the faithful the Qur'anic text cannot be modified or mitigated. `Abduh was also an important political modernizer. His Islamization of the concept of democracy (a Western invention) has not to this day exhausted its potential.

`Abduh influenced his country's future course. When Egypt attained independence in 1922, it opted for a secularist constitution and pro-Western foreign policy. Egypt was the Islamic world's most progressive state, and Islam was expected to accommodate itself to the "civilized" Western world. It was not to be: paradoxically, `Abduh also fertilized conservative religious opposition through his pupil Rashid Ridda (1865–1935). Unlike his tutor, Ridda, a Syrian established in Egypt, never experienced European culture close up. He reformulated `Abduh's thought in *salafist* vein; that is, he called for imitation of the *salaf al-salih*, the pious ancestors of the Prophet's time. From that pristine community, and following Hanbalism, the most rigorous of the four Sunni schools of jurisprudence, Ridda derived rules for Muslim behavior under conditions of modernity. He also wrote the first blueprint of an Islamic state. It was a curious mixture: its legislation would be modern and its caliph would preferably be Arab, a consensual (*ijma`*) leader embodying all the *umma's* strands and liable for dismissal if he deviated from religious duty. Ridda envisaged his caliph as a *mujtahid*, a creative renewer of Islamic tradition. But he never found his ideal candidate. In 1924 Atatürk's new Turkish government summarily dismissed Abdulmecid II (who two years earlier had succeeded in the function of caliph, when his cousin Mehmet VI Vahideddin had lost his position as last sultan) and abolished the caliphate, throwing the Islamic world into disarray.

World War I and the End of the Ottoman Empire

World War I was a watershed for the Middle East. Enver Pasha, strongman of the Young Turk triumvirate, led the Ottoman Empire to the side of Germany and Austria, against France, Britain, and Russia. In spite of some early successes (such as the battle of Gallipoli), he also led it to its ruin. The sultan-caliph's appeals to Indian and North African Muslims to revolt against Britain and France fell largely on deaf ears. Meanwhile, a British-supported Arab revolt against Constantinople, led from the Arab peninsula by the *sharif* of Mecca, Hussein, and his sons, drove the Turks from Arab lands. Britain promised the Arabs an independent realm. This promise was broken: under the terms of the

British-French Sykes-Picot Accords, the Entente powers secretly agreed to cut up the Arab East among themselves. To make claims even more incompatible, in the Balfour Declaration of 1917, Britain promised the Zionist Jews a national home in Palestine, a territory that Arabs regarded as part of their patrimony. By 1918, Palestine and Mesopotamia had fallen under British military control, and the sultan's power was now reduced to Anatolia. Before long, all of Europe's multiethnic empires collapsed and were replaced by national entities. For one group the breakup came too late. Russian-supported guerrilla attacks in East Anatolia had in 1915–16 become the pretext for the deportation and mass murder of Armenians.[11]

Turkey: The First Successful Anticolonial Revolution

While Britain and then France occupied the *Mashriq* (or Arab East), Greeks, surviving Armenians, Kurds, Italians, and Russians had designs on the Anatolian rump of the Empire. In the 1920 Sèvres Treaty, the Ottoman sultan was forced to sign away his empire. But while the Greeks were dreaming of restoring the Byzantine Empire, Mustafa Kemal, the hero of Gallipoli, inspired Turkish nationalist resistance against the occupiers. By 1922, the Turks had reconquered Anatolia and expelled the Ionian Greeks. The nationalists rose to power on a secularist program: Kemal abolished the sultanate and the caliphate, negotiated at Lausanne in 1923 a new treaty that recognized the sovereignty of the new Turkish Republic, separated state and religion, and guaranteed ethnic homogeneity by population exchanges of Turks and Greeks. Muslims became the quasi-totality of the population, but Islam disappeared from public life: Latin letters replaced Arabic ones, women were emancipated, veils and oriental dress were prohibited, and the bases were laid for independent industrialization. By the time of Kemal's death in 1938, the paths of Turks and Arabs had diverged forever. He received the title of "Atatürk": Father of Turks.

The Arab East in the Interwar Period

The period of direct Western colonization of the Arab East was relatively brief. Occurring after the heyday of imperialism, it was marked by inconsistencies among the colonial masters and frequent rebellions among the colonized. Three periods may be distinguished: (1) in the 1920s, the French and British, now rivals, consolidated their control over the region; (2) in the 1930s through 1945, competing German and Italian fascist imperialisms entered the fray; and (3) from the 1940s through the early 1970s, France and Britain fought rearguard battles to keep their colonies while the United States and the Soviets, although Cold War rivals, both supported Arab nationalism.

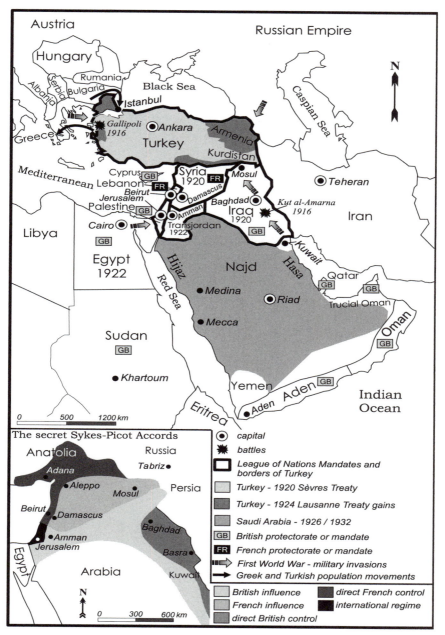

Figure 1.4
World War I and the postwar settlement

Initially the Middle East's importance remained primarily strategic—it was the route to India for Britain, and represented proximity to the metropolis for France. Later, oil became a central factor.

France and Britain had themselves installed as mandatory powers by the new League of Nations—the former over Syria and Lebanon, and the latter over Iraq and Palestine. Formally intended to lead Arab peoples to self-government, the mandate system as experienced by its "beneficiaries" was unadulterated imperialism. The Arab world was quite unprepared for the "surgery" that severed economically and culturally connected regions. Their many internal divisions notwithstanding, Arab peoples had been in a process of nationalization.

The West's broken promises caused bitterness and revolts—part of a worldwide postwar anti-capitalist revolutionary wave. In 1920 a pan-Arab assembly in Damascus offered Hussein's son Faisal the crown; shortly thereafter, the French took Syria by force. Resentments festered; the Arabs demanded immediate and total withdrawal. When the mandates eventually became independent states, their artificial character reproduced the old legitimacy problems. From the 1940s through the 1970s, inter-Arab interventions were the order of the day.

The 1920s

In communal affairs, the French and British both used nefarious divide-and-rule tactics. By using some minorities to police the Sunni majority—`Alawites in Syria, Assyrians in Iraq, and indirectly, Jews in Palestine—they strengthened the popular Sunni perception of their association with foreign interests. This complicated their coexistence.

Britain opted for gradual devolution of sovereignty. Egypt became independent in 1922, although Britain remained influential and continued to control the Suez Canal. Transjordan was detached from the Palestine mandate, and `Abdallah, another of Hussein's sons, was put on the throne. In yet another attempt at appeasing Arab anger, his brother Faisal was crowned king of Iraq. Ancient Mesopotamia, however, was an especially hard case of "demographic aberration." Baghdad, a sophisticated cultural capital, dominated the central zone at the confluence of the Tigris and Euphrates Rivers. Its Sunni inhabitants became Iraq's rulers. They looked down on the Shiites to the south, around the holy towns of Najaf and Karbala, who had borne the brunt of British repression. The Kurdish inhabitants of Iraq's oil-rich north were detested by all. In contrast to the case of India, British colonization of Iraq did not implant parliamentarianism; London preferred to build up a network of "reliable" tribal sheikhs. Tensions were also mounting in Palestine, where devolution was blocked by the Zionists, who insisted on a Jewish majority *before* independence. For their part, the autochthonous Palestinian Arabs refused to share their country with the incoming Jews.

The French were less open to the idea of self-determination: decolonization was consequently more difficult. Syria, a country no less divided than Iraq, became the cockpit of Arab nationalism. In order to better control it, France cut off Syria's Beqaa Valley and some other territories, "gluing" them to Mount Lebanon. Lebanon had a complex ethnic makeup—social and ethnic tensions between Maronite Christians and Druze had in 1860 led to a French protectorate. Adding the new territories threw more fuel on the fire, weakening the Christian predominance and making French overlordship more difficult to avoid. Syria never accepted the surgery.

This left the Arabian Peninsula, cradle of Islam, as the only area not yet colonized. While Britain controlled strategic ports and coasts such as Kuwait, Qatar, the Trucial States, Maskat, Oman, and Aden, the desert interior was considered too primitive to warrant Western occupation. Here *sharif* Hussein's dream of an independent Arab realm was finally realized—but not by him. In 1924–26 neighboring Najd conquered the Hijaz with the support of Wahhabite *Ikhwan* ("Brethren"), and exiled Hussein. Najd's tribal leader, `Abdul `Aziz ("Ibn Sa`ud," 1876–1953), a radical puritan, had renewed his tribe's historical alliance with the Wahhabites. The Wahhabites were followers of Muhammad ibn `Abd al-Wahhab (1703–92), an extremist preacher who had allied himself with the Sa`ud tribe. In the early nineteenth century the Sa`uds conquered and temporarily occupied the holy cities, destroying the tomb of Muhammad and other sites whose veneration they viewed as idolatrous.

By 1932 Ibn Sa`ud held most of the peninsula and proclaimed the absolute monarchy of Saudi Arabia. It became a fundamentalist prototype—a warrior community committed to spreading its puritan lifestyle. Inspired by the Prophet, the *Ikhwan* ("Brethren") Bedouin loyal to the Sa`uds settled in closed military communes and rejected any contact with modernity. Conflict between `*ulama*-led conservatives and modernizers has continued ever since, supported by competing branches of the sprawling royal house. In 1938, huge oil reserves were discovered in the desert, and the marginal monarchy became a strategic asset. During World War II, U.S. influence grew. The Arabian American Oil Company (Aramco) obtained unlimited access to the world's largest oil reserves. In return, the United States committed itself to military protection for the Saudis against foes and predators. The quid pro quo was vital to both sides, considering that Saudi Arabia, its huge swath of territory mostly devoid of population and defense, sits atop the world's largest oil reserves.

Qawmiyya (*qawm* = nation), or pan-Arabism, grew in the 1930s into the most popular ideology in the Middle East. Fascist regimes in Italy and Germany now inspired radical nationalists, who appreciated the revisionism of the brutal regimes that felt victimized by the Peace of Versailles. The Arab proverb "the enemy of my enemy is my friend" explains their behavior. Nazi anti-Semitism also echoed the Palestinian struggle against Zionism. More profoundly, *qawmiyya* paralleled the German type of irredentist nationalism—one that aspired to unite members of dispersed communities living in heterogeneous settings. In such nation-building projects, the basis of consensus cannot be found in common political values while the state itself is yet to be erected: collective identity is therefore projected on "immutable" group characteristics such as language and blood. In the Arab East, the main ideologues of the pan-Arab *Ba`th* (Renaissance) party, founded in the 1940s, were Sati al-Husri, Michel `Aflaq, and Salah al-Din al-Bitar. Pan-Arabism's heyday was in the 1950s and 1960s, when it reached power in several Arab countries; Egypt's Nasserism was a second pan-Arab line. Both suffered from four fatal weaknesses:

1. Monism: Pan-Arabism stresses what all Arabs have in common, such as language and traditions, but is blind to inter-Arab and regional particularisms. For example, Moroccans and Iraqis speak not just mutually unintelligible dialects, but their history has diverged for a millennium.
2. Intolerance of minorities: Jews, Kurds, Armenians, Berbers, and others were sometimes persecuted, and eventually developed their own nationalisms.
3. Authoritarianism: Wherever pan-Arabism came to power, it was centralist in form. First the Nazi *Führerprinzip* was adopted as a model; then Soviet communism, equally hostile to "bourgeois democracy," succeeded as external inspiration. The popular will would express itself through one national party, which led everywhere to dictatorship and monolithism, though with different degrees of brutality in repression of opposition, and sometimes masked by pro forma multipartyism. Eventually pan-Arab regimes were affected by the fatal wear and tear of regimes requiring ever-larger portions of their resources diverted to internal repression and external aggression.
4. Secularism: Secularism was a problem because of Arab nationalism's non-Islamic (namely, Lebanese Christian) roots. Qawmiyya never quite managed to position itself *vis-à-vis* Islam.

`Aflaq did not view Islam as a norm for social organization, but explained it as an "expression of the Arab spirit," de-emphasizing its universalism. However, Arab societies all had their "rockbed of religiosity,"[12] and this forced contradictory reflexes on nationalists, who felt compelled to publicly laud religion, although they were unwilling to accommodate its demands.

Qawmiyya had to compete with several rival ideologies. *Wataniya* (from *watan*, homeland) was a territorial concept, inclusive of all of a region's inhabitants but excluding those of other territories. It stressed local patrimony over wider loyalties—thus the Egyptian Taha Hussein emphasized his country's pharaonic past and saw Arab and Islamic influences as contingent; and the Lebanese Antoine Saadeh's "phoenicianism" extolled "Syrianness."[13] Saddam Hussein at different times used both ideologies, proving that *wataniya* and *qawmiyya* need not be mutually exclusive.

From the interwar years through the 1960s, Islam seemed (except for Saudi Arabia) absent from the ideological panorama—Islamic modernism was decidedly a minority view, and fundamentalism did not yet exist. But the reaction was brewing. In Egypt, modernity was usurping traditional religious space more rapidly than elsewhere. Hence radical reactions started earlier there. To fight Western influences, Hassan al-Banna (1906–49), a pious schoolteacher from Isma`iliyya, a town close to the English-controlled Suez Canal, founded in 1928 the "Society of Muslim Brethren" (*Jama`at al-Ikhwan al-Muslimin*). More radical than Ridda—for Banna only the Qur'an and a few *hadiths* were authoritative—he took the ideal of the Islamic society seriously. Here one sees for the first time political Islam's affirmation of politics as the central axis of combat for the Islamization of society. The Muslim Brotherhood grew into a sprawling organization— at once, a political party, scouting movement, and social club (sport would protect youth from temptations). The Muslim Brotherhood shunned neither patient educational work nor anticolonial violence, and grew into an authentic mass movement that began to worry the liberal national bourgeoisie of the *Wafd*.[14] Generally peaceful, in 1948 the Muslim Brotherhood distinguished itself alongside the regular Egyptian army in the *jihad* against the Zionist *yishuv*. The failed war against the new Jewish state destabilized Egypt. Its *ancien régime* repressed the Brotherhood and assassinated Banna, but this only fanned the flames. The shared frustration of nationalists and Islamists produced the 1952 Free Officers' revolution. Temporarily welcomed into the new regime, the Muslim Brotherhood soon clashed with its leftist secularists and was again repressed. Contemporary Sunni Islamism would spark from the Brotherhood's embers.

In addition to these ideologies, communism formed yet another strand, in the 1950s and 1960s mobilizing many proletarian and minority intellectuals in Egypt and Iraq, but never on a scale that would allow it to defeat rival ideologies. Identity in the Middle East remained an insoluble puzzle. Every ideology seemed to exclude as many people as it included: pan-Arabists could never integrate non-Arab minorities; regional nationalists had little to say to those seeking an overarching Arab civilization; Communists and Islamists possessed coherent programs, but their militancy frightened off more people than they attracted. The only consensus was that the future pointed toward modernization. Few observers saw the coming of a frontally antimodern politicized religiosity, and even fewer saw its hegemony.

World War II turned the Middle East—except for neutral Turkey—into a battlefield. The Axis strategy was to reach the region's oil fields through a two-pronged attack—one eastward, over North Africa to Egypt, the other southward, through Russia and over the Caucasus. Britain's 1939 attempt to appease the Arabs by distancing itself from the Zionist project had little effect. The fall of France in 1940 and Britain's weakness only inflamed nationalist passions in the Middle East. Britain and the USSR forced the shah of Iran, suspected of being an admirer of Hitler, to resign, and occupied his country. In 1941, a coup brought a pro-Nazi regime to power in Iraq. By the time the British deposed it a year later, the Germans had been defeated in El Alamein—Allied victory spared the Arabs Nazi occupation.

From World War II to Today

After sixty years of formal independence, the Arab world has achieved neither socioeconomic development nor popular empowerment. All its crucial dates are years of defeat. In 1948, the first Israeli-Arab War signaled the Arabs' inability to deal with the new Jewish state in their midst. Although inconveniently located on the Asia-Africa land link, tiny Israel would not by itself have prevented Arab unity. The injustice that accompanied the establishment of the state of Israel was not inherently beyond repair; the Arab world's inability to achieve an outcome it did not regard as shameful was the more insuperable obstacle.

The Suez crisis of 1956 symbolized the decline of European power and the ascendancy of pan-Arabism but the June, 1967, Six Day War was another defeat. Iran's Islamic Revolution of 1978–79 saw the emergence of an Islamist alternative to Arab secularism. Although it raised hopes for a psychological renaissance, it only led to more lost wars. The years 1990–91 brought Iraq's annexation of Kuwait and mass Arab enthusiasm for Saddam Hussein, only to be followed once more by humiliation at the hands of an international (essentially Western) coalition that restored the old colonial borders in the Gulf War. The year 1991 was also the year the Israeli-Palestinian peace process began—but for millions of Arabs this meant less a rational hope than one more shameful surrender to materialism, modernity, and foreigners. The decade since then has shown much more of the hubris of its leaders and naiveté of its masses, isolation, and growing Arab irrelevance in the era of globalization. All models seem to have been exhausted—except Islamism. Immune to rational critique, Islamism has grown most in the past decade and a half, and presents the only proposal to which neither the West nor Israel appears to have a response. The past five years have shown the undeniable *no* of the Islamic world, with 2000–01 the latest turn, bringing the breakdown of the Israeli-Palestinian peace process, the second *intifada*, and then 9/11. All obey a parallel logic: pain and anger reach a point where it seems the only way out is to inflict maximum pain on the enemy, even at the cost of one's life. Reactions such as Israel's partial reoccupation of the West Bank and Gaza and the Western invasions of Afghanistan and Iraq will not help unless the programs are simultaneously initiated that are no less radical to revolutionize the Middle East and end its social and cultural predicament.

1945–67: The Failure of Secular Arabism

In Palestine, the struggle between autochthonous Arabs (still a two-thirds majority in the aftermath of World War II) and the Jewish immigrant community made British control ever harder. Neither side accepted the other's legitimacy, and both rejected compromise solutions short of independence. The conflict came to a head in 1947. Jewish suffering in the Holocaust and the plight of Jewish survivors fed international sympathy for Zionism. Meanwhile, the Palestinians turned their conflict into a pan-Arab cause; the Arab world saw Zionist settlement as a doomed prolongation of Western imperialism. In 1947, the United Nations ordered the partition of the British Palestine mandate into two independent states—a decree that could only succeed if both communities were to accept it. Arab rejection led in short order to war, Palestinian defeat, Israel's declaration of independence and invasion of seven Arab neighbors, and their defeat. Instead of a Palestinian state, Transjordan annexed the West Bank, and Egypt occupied Gaza. An estimated 750,000 Palestinians fled to neighboring countries, where their presence continued to fuel the conflict. In 1949, armistice agreements were signed, but tension did not abate.[15]

Except for Palestine, the Arab world completed its decolonization after 1945. France left Syria and Lebanon after 1943. Transjordan became a kingdom, although under strong British influence. Libya obtained its independence in 1952; the French protectorates of Morocco and Tunisia then followed suit. Algeria, home to one million French *colons*, reached independence only after a long and bloody war in 1962; the *pieds-noirs* were repatriated. Britain liquidated its holdings east of Aden after the Suez debacle. Kuwait, Qatar, Bahrain, and the United Arab Emirates all achieved independence by 1971. Oman, never a colony, became dependent on Western help when its sultan put down a leftist revolt. Yemen, divided into a pro-Soviet South and a religious and monarchical North, united in 1990, after prolonged civil war and foreign intervention.

Although nominally independent, most Arab states remained artificial and economically dependent creations, surviving more by dint of repression than through their subjects' loyalty. They were also perpetually scheming against each other. The Arab League (1945) lacked coercive power, and the Cold War further hampered unification efforts. Saudi Arabia, the Gulf principalities, Jordan, and Morocco formed a conservative pro-Western block against the "club" of progressive, Soviet-looking, "Arab socialist," usually military-ruled regimes of Egypt, Syria, Iraq, Libya, and Algeria. Pan-Arabism, with its social basis among the petty bourgeois officer class, was the latter group's ideology. Its most charismatic exponent was Egypt's Gamal Abdul Nasser, who came to power after the Free Officers' coup in 1952. Progressive without being Marxist or anti-religious, Nasser wedded socioeconomic development to an ideal of social justice. His plans soon led to a showdown with imperial interests. In order to finance his ambitious Nile irrigation plans, in 1956 Nasser nationalized the Suez Canal, provoking a secret pact among Britain, France, and Israel. In a brief war, Egypt was defeated and the Sinai occupied; however, joint American-Soviet pressure forced a withdrawal. Nasser, his military defeat turned overnight into political victory, became the Arab masses' idol. Still, his United Arab Republic (UAR) project uniting Egypt and Syria (to begin with) proved unviable, and fell apart in 1960. Pan-Arabist Ba`thists came to power in Syria in 1963.

Instability was even worse in Iraq. All over the *Mashriq* (Arab East), anti-Western sentiment exploded in a series of revolts throughout 1957–58. These were suppressed in Jordan and Lebanon, but in Iraq, revolution abolished the pro-British monarchy, and Abdul-Karim Qasim (Kassem) led the subsequent left-leaning republic, based on participation by Kurds and Communists (the latter strongest among southern Shiites). However, as Kassem radicalized, he alienated the pan-Arabist Sunni petty bourgeoisie, and in 1963 he was killed in an army coup. In 1968 a second coup concentrated power in the hands of the pan-Arab Sunni-dominated Ba`th Party. The oil industry was nationalized; its income launched a combined welfare state–one-party dictatorship. Iraq crushed all internal opposition—Kurds, Communists, religious Shiites, and so on. In 1979, Saddam Hussein concentrated all power and established a personal tyranny.

Revolutionary promises were not kept in Algeria, either. The National Liberation Front had brought independence in 1962, but progressive rhetoric and sympathy from the international left notwithstanding, Islam crept back in, women's rights were rescinded, and—as in so many other post-revolutionary, postcolonial states—the heroic anti-imperialist generation became an inefficient and ever more corrupt bureaucracy.

After 1945, there were only two types of Arab regimes: conservative monarchies and one-party populist or military dictatorships. Western-type republics were rare: Israel and Turkey are not Arab; Lebanon's parliamentary system broke down. Authoritarianism ruled—often linked to one or the other minority, with a ubiquitous secret police, rubberstamp parliaments, controlled media, and prisons full of dissidents. Except for the special case of Saudi Arabia, Islamist regimes were still a new phenomenon. Mu`ammar al-Qadhafi seized power in Libya in 1969, initiating an atypical mix of Islamization and progressivism. He heralded a new trend.

1967–91: Incipient Islamization

Secular Arab nationalists attempted to annihilate Israel for the last time in 1967; 1990–91 witnessed the last military challenge that secular Arab nationalists launched against the West. Both attempts failed—between them lies a period when Arabs states achieved neither their external nor internal aims. Military defeat, poverty, mass unemployment, increasing pressure on scarce resources, and stagnating democratization produced a feeling that "all medicines have already been tried and failed." Four trends reflect the Middle East's dilemmas in this period, and the failure of its political models:

1. Israel grew in strength as Palestinian claims correspondingly failed.
2. Oil wealth did not produce economic development
3. Lebanon's civil war highlighted the impossibility of secular democratic transformation.

4. In the Iran-Iraq War, Saddam Hussein's near-racist appeal to Arab solidarity temporarily slowed Islamist impetus, but its sequel, the Iraq-Kuwait War, led to even worse Arab division.

As secular Arab states lost prestige, the Islamist alternative gained in appeal.

The Israel-Palestine Conflict

Misperceptions, demagoguery, and an unstable regional framework in which deterrence never reliably worked created a mix that spun out of control in 1967, when Nasser renewed his military threat against Israel. Israel did not really envision expansion, but feared a new Holocaust. The Arabs were ill prepared, but their honor had been put on the line. For the latter, the results proved catastrophic in the short term; for the former, in the long run. Israel took from Egypt the Sinai and the Gaza Strip; from Jordan, the West Bank; and from Syria, the Golan Heights. Israel survived and expanded, but was stuck with more then one million hostile Palestinians. In short order, it revisited its "democratic state" versus "Jewish state" dilemma that the 1948 Palestinian departure had apparently liquidated. On the Arab side, humiliation was total. Nasser survived politically and lived for another three years, but the worldview he incarnated had been mortally weakened. After Nasser, the Arab world never found another leader able to step into his shoes.

The Arab world refused any peace negotiation. It fell to Nasser's less charismatic successor, Anwar Sadat, to recoup the lost terrain. In October, 1973, Egypt and Syria launched a new war, the Yom Kippur War. Arab nondefeat (if not exactly victory) opened a psychological space for accommodation with the Jewish state. In a peace agreement that Sadat signed with Israel in 1978, Egypt retrieved its Sinai while sacrificing Arab unity. Although other Arab elites would eventually, very tentatively, follow Egypt's trailblazing, their moves were too dilatory and devoid of the popular support to prevent Israel's rightward move. Occupation had turned Israel into a regional Goliath facing a Palestinian David, the new international darling. Palestinian resistance, still largely nationalist and secular, was militarily ineffective and never threatened Israel, although its bomb attacks and airplane hijackings were spectacular enough to put the Palestinian question back on the international agenda. Eventually Fatah's Yasser Arafat, who grew into the national leader of the post-1948 generation of Palestinians, cautiously shifted to diplomacy. Again, Palestine Liberation Organization (PLO) peace moves were too hesitant to preclude Israel's radicalization.

Any peaceful solution between Israel and the Palestinians would necessarily entail compromise. By 1991, when a favorable constellation finally allowed official Palestinian-Israeli dialogue, the PLO leadership had shed a good part of its ideological baggage. Instead of liberating all of Palestine, they would accept a Palestinian mini-state (probably dependent on Israel). But their moderation had deeply split Palestinian opinion: a substantial minority clung to the original goal of destroying the Jewish state. Those who looked for coexistence, on either side, were secularists who understood peace as a precondition for development. Their opponents—the shrinking far left and the growing ranks of Islamists—saw "development" itself as a trap.

Tragically, similar erosion also affected Israel's peace camp. On both sides a fatal association linked honor and idealism with intransigence; concessions ("land for peace") with defeatism and exhaustion. Extremist—mostly fundamentalist—wings arose, willing to use any violence to derail rapprochement. In popular understanding, the ongoing violence was not the expression of a desperate opposition to peace, but reflected the adversary's "inherently evil" disposition. Eventually, the peace process came to appear as irresponsibly naïve. Civil war between Israelis and Palestinians reignited in conditions worse than before the peace process. After 2000, the atmosphere of lost illusions and bitterness was fertile soil for extremist proposals. The process was still in its beginning in the 1970s and 1980s, but its direction was already perceptible.

Oil

After 1967, the failure of Arab development became a public scandal. Today Arab stagnation contrasts with the economic success of such other former colonies as the "Asian Tigers." This is all the more paradoxical because the Middle East, dependent like most other Third World economies on the export of raw materials, contains the world's largest oil reserves; and after 1967 these were coming under Arab control. Earlier exploitation had been largely in the hands of the "Seven Sisters," Western corporations that paid a laughably low tribute. Early nationalization attempts, as in 1953 in Iran, had provoked blatant intervention.[16] In 1960, the Organization of Petroleum Exporting Countries (OPEC) was established; and by 1972, Iraq nationalized its oil. This example was soon followed by Saudi Arabia, Kuwait, and other producers, with which the industrialized West made mutually beneficial arrangements, which it now preferred to open conflict. The Israeli-Arab War in 1973 provided a pretext for quadrupling oil prices, triggering the first world oil crisis. The huge oil incomes were, however, not used to spur development and prosperity. Instead, Arab "oil sheikhs"

spent the money on luxuries, armaments, and "petrodollar" speculation. In some states, oil wealth was used to buy off popular political
demands. All this deepened the gulf between underpopulated but oil-
rich Arab countries and their populous but oil-destitute brethren (e.g.,
Egypt, Morocco, etc.). Oil income also allowed the importation of
"immoral" Western products and values, adding one more weapon to
the arsenal of Islamist arguments.

The Lebanese Civil War

The fratricidal 1975–89 Lebanese war was another painful example of Arab inability to solve or even alleviate an internal Arab crisis.
Since the 1940s, Lebanon was viewed as "the Arab Switzerland." The
image was deceptive. Lebanon's religious communities still controlled
the lives of their members. The Lebanese state had essentially reproduced the Ottoman *millet* system—only without the foreign Turks to
maintain equilibrium. A fragile equilibrium, based on the 1944
"National Pact" among Lebanon's multiple religious communities,
perpetuated Maronite preeminence; community-based power was mit-
igated by a spoils system that distributed public functions and the
like on the basis of a long-obsolete census. Lebanon's lack of a single
clear power center was unusual by Arab standards, and allowed for a
freedom of expression that made Beirut the intellectual cockpit of the
Arab world. However, the same logic also induced less lofty "broth-
erly" interference.

Behind the façade of conviviality, communal tensions were brewing.
Muslims were outnumbering Christians, but the Maronites refused to
share more power. The country's modernization and secularization
were soon proceeding in a very lopsided way: consequent social disloca-
tions and tensions exploded in civil war. The Palestinian refugees, most
of whom were Muslim, were the catalyst. After 1970, Palestinian commandos fleeing Jordan staged incursions into Israel across the Lebanese border, provoking Israeli retaliation. The Lebanese state, devoid of
strong institutions or an army of its own, was defenseless. In 1975 militia incidents sparked a 14-year cycle of open community conflict replete
with reciprocal atrocities. Initially the civil war pitted a nominally
rightist Maronite block against a leftist coalition of Muslims, Druze,
and Palestinians. Syria supported the pro-Arabist left; Israel supported
the Maronites, who stressed Lebanon's idiosyncratic makeup. However,
labels do not begin to clarify the complexities. Sunni elites often sided
with Maronites, who were divided into rival clans; poor Greek Orthodox
Arabs[17] sided with the left; Shiites—the poorest and most backward—
developed their independent militias. All despised the Palestinians.
Neighbors intervened to advance their own agendas. Syria cut down

the Palestinians in 1976 (spurring domestic Islamist unrest), as did Israel in 1978 and, more massively, in 1982, when it dismantled the Palestinians' military force and drove the PLO into exile in Tunisia. Unknown as yet, Israel's entry would bring about new Syrian occupation, of much longer duration. Meanwhile, tolerated by Israel, Christian fascists massacred Palestinians in the Sabra and Shatila refugee camps near Beirut. The United States and France intervened but instead of stabilizing the situation, they only inflamed Shiite resistance. In 1983 the first suicide bombers wreaked havoc on Western soldiers, who beat a hasty retreat. Israel withdrew into its unilaterally proclaimed "security zone," but civil war continued.

The 1980s were the formative period for Shiite radicalization, and a decade infamous also for the kidnapping of foreigners (and even more locals) for ransom or political concessions. Inspired and actively supported by the Iranian revolution, the Shiite Islamist resistance movement Hizbullah (literally, "the Party of God") conquered terrain in the "war of the camps." The civil war turned ever more complex and cruel: Lebanon became an early laboratory of the "clash of civilizations." In this microcosm, armed Islamist groups made their debut and gained legitimacy. Hizbullah became a powerful political party.

When Syrian ruler Hafiz al-Asad used the 1990 Gulf crisis to clamp a Syrian protectorate on the torn country, the bloodbath that had cost 200,000 lives and displaced or chased abroad more than one million finally came to an end.[18] A new political formula limited Maronite preponderance, and reconstruction could begin. But civil war had destroyed one of the Arab world's liveliest, freest, and—sectarianism notwithstanding—most secular societies. In one of the world's most heterogeneous neighborhoods, no recipe for coexistence had been found. Unlike the wars in Vietnam, Algeria, East Timor, and perhaps Bosnia, Lebanon's civil war was not a postcolonial conflict. Foreign interventions exacerbated but did not cause it; and its "solution" was 15 years of de facto recolonization—the defeat of pluralism in the Arab world. The failure of Arab society to generate a formula for viable coexistence based on secularism could not but strengthen Islamism.

From the 1980–88 Iran-Iraq War to the 1991 Gulf War

The Arab world's fourth crisis led immediately to the current upsurge of Islamism. Iran's 1979 Islamic revolution, which put an end to the shah's brutal modernization dictatorship, let loose a wave of enthusiasm that menaced all authoritarian regimes of the Arab world. By the late 1970s, their failure was already palpable. Inadequate schools dumped on the market every year thousands of unemployable youth with only a sprinkling of Western knowledge. The jobs, security, and consumer goods they craved were out of reach. As governability became more problematic, ever more repressive force was needed. The waves of global democratization of the 1980s and 1990s bypassed the Arab world. Rejection of Western models (including communism) and the religious turn became the visible symptoms of a social, economic, and cultural crisis.

Initially, the repressive character of the Iranian revolution was not evident, and it was possible to envisage a democratic and socialist outcome of what had begun as an atypical religious fundamentalist revolution. Founder and chief ideologue of the Islamic Republic of Iran, Ayatollah Ruhollah Khomeini exhorted Muslims all over the world to abolish their "treasonous" governments and establish authentically Islamic ones; co-religionists from around the Arab world responded to his call. Islamists briefly occupied even the Great Mosque of Mecca, accusing the Saudi government of corruption. (Their leader, Juhaiman al-`Utaybi, was duly beheaded, but underground agitation continued). U.S.-supported anti-communist Islamist guerrillas turned Afghanistan into a quagmire for Soviet soldiers, and volunteers from around the Islamic world joined the struggle. The fraternization and battle became a formative experience; upon their return these "Afghans" attempted Islamic revolution in their home countries of Pakistan, Algeria, and elsewhere. In 1981 Islamists killed Anwar Sadat in Egypt. A year later, Syria's Ba`th regime trembled under the impact of Islamist revolt. In Iraq, Iranian agents were agitating among the Shiites discriminated against by another Ba`th regime. Saddam Hussein unleashed a ferocious repression.

Such was the backdrop to Iraq's war against Iran. Saddam invaded Iran in 1980, using a minor border quarrel as pretext. His plan was to impose regional Iraqi leadership. Aggressively nationalistic and expansionist, Iraq expected a quick victory over the still-struggling theocratic regime in Teheran. Instead, World War I–style trench warfare dragged on for eight years, claiming at least 400,000 Iranian and 300,000 Iraqi lives. Thousands of Iranian children sacrificed themselves in "human waves" against Iraqi minefields. Khomeini did not start the conflict but once under attack, he viewed it as the perfect lever for exporting his Islamic revolution, and refused to negotiate before a "regime change" in Baghdad. To prop up what seemed the lesser evil, France, the United States, and the USSR armed Iraq. Kuwait and other Arab states gave financial support; Arab elites saw Saddam's imperialism as a lesser threat than Islamism, and hoped to use Iraq as a shield. By 1988 Iran was forced to agree to a ceasefire, its foreign dynamism broken. However, "victory" against Iran came with Iraq's ascendancy, and the ensuing chain reaction was to prove even more dangerous to the Arab regimes. Syria, Libya, Yemen, Egypt, and similar states differed from Iraq in their degree of violence, but hardly in their nature. All feared "regime change," and to survive they closed off routes to democratization.

The Arab world had unleashed a *jinn* it could no longer control. Within two years, Iraq invaded Kuwait—a new attempt to establish its hegemony, and an easy way to add to its oil wealth and liquidate its foreign debt. When Saddam defied the West and its international system, he instantly became the Arab masses' hero. In fact, his invasion came close to shattering the Arab system, and only an international "crusade" saved it. This intervention was unpopular, though, and humiliated the Arabs once more, further undermining the legitimacy of their regimes. Iraq was subjected to draconian sanctions that impoverished its population without breaking Saddam's regime. The image of starving Iraqi children was an added insult, which soon found its way into the rhetoric that a certain Saudi Islamist named Osama bin Laden levied against the supposed culprit, the United States of America.[19] The punishment he had in mind was death for all Americans.

ISLAM IN SPACE

2

Islam's Expansion Outside the Middle East

The narrative that has brought us to the most recent period in the Middle East must now be reversed to take in the enormous widening of Islam that has taken place over the last millennium, and that brought under its influence distant regions that came to play a key role in world affairs. Expansion in medieval and modern times created three wholly new Islamic areas: the Indian subcontinent, Southeast Asia, and sub-Saharan Africa. Together they are today home to two-thirds of all Muslims—and this leaves out a number of significant though demographically less important centers, such as the huge but sparsely populated territory of Central Asia, that harbored complex societies such as Transoxania (today's Uzbekistan), and the Muslim diasporas in China and the West. Analyzing these "newer Islams" beyond the Middle East core separately makes a certain sense. Keeping Islam's far-flung communities in the Middle East, Africa, and Asia united was impossible in premodern times, although communication was maintained through correspondence, the *hajj*, and by other means. As Islam spread it thus diversified, spawning multiple and rather different Islams. These regional variations become understandable if we pay attention to the earlier religion(s) Islam came to supplant, to the societies upon which it grafted itself, and to the demographic relation between Muslims and non-Muslims.

As we saw, in the Middle East where Islam replaced Judaism, Christianity, and other monotheistic or dualistic religions, the Muslim military elite did not, after the initial *jihad*, actively press for conversion. Islam spread through voluntary assimilation, and this became the model for all of *Dar al-Islam*. Rejection by a self-consciously superior, puritanic High Islam of more emotional or mystical, popular versions of Islam led to periodic purification movements, which often overlapped with the antagonism between nomads and sedentary populations. Western imperialist penetration strengthened the power of the urban poles over the rural and pastoral hinterland, but also shook Islamic self-confidence. In the Ottoman Empire most elites opted for Westernization, keeping their `ulama` under control. Thus, through various historical paths, Islam, once established, succeeded in keeping control over the Middle East.

In India, by contrast, Islamization was much more problematic, owing to the greater religious distance separating Muslims from Hindus, and to the latter's numerical preponderance. Although some areas eventually developed Muslim majorities, in most regions, Muslims remained foreign oppressors (or despised lower-caste converts). This fed defensive orthodox reactions on both sides. Moreover, the erstwhile Muslim elite lost power to British colonization, which started earlier and lasted longer than in the Middle East, forcing Indian Muslims to wage a double battle against Hinduism and the West. Secularization was no option for the Muslim minority, most of whom eventually embraced territorial separatism or "Muslim nationalism." Although successful in winning independence for Pakistan, that country was soon torn between two incompatible identities: state of Muslims or Islamic state.

In Indonesia (and, with some variations, in sub-Saharan Africa), Islam spread by peaceful infiltration. Royalty adopted Islam as a legitimating tool; later it served as an anticolonial ideology. Earlier religions, with their animistic and magical elements, continued to coexist with Islam, and syncretism facilitated further conversion. Here, the growth of Islamic orthodoxy, then, was a corollary of its role in anticolonial resistance, and of more intense contacts with the Middle Eastern core, made possible by modern means of transportation and communication.

Muslim India

India already had a venerable high civilization when Islam arrived on the scene. Productive agriculture and artisanship made dense populations and developed states possible. However, political disunity was the rule—religious culture alone provided a modicum of unity. With its colorful pantheon of deities emanating from one pantheistic essence and with its concept of an uncreated, cyclical cosmos, Hinduism could not be more different from monotheistic, linear Islam. Not surrender to divine grace, but individual effort through meditation, was Hinduism's way to escape from the "wheel of reincarnations" (*samsara*) and reach a higher state of awareness. Instead of Islam's equality of all believers under God, the caste system imprisoned every Hindu in his or her own professional and ritual niche, determined by the *karma* accumulated in one's former lives. Antithetical to such principles, Islam proved to be the first newcomer that was impossible to integrate.

The Islamization of India spread southeast from the Khyber Pass, the traditional entry point, near today's Afghan-Pakistani border. In 711, the Arabs had conquered Sind, Baluchistan, and Afghanistan, but kept the Indus River as a frontier. Only three centuries later did Mahmud of Ghazni, leader of a recently converted extremist Sunni state near Kabul, launch destructive incursions in northern Punjab. In 1175, Muhammad of Ghur defeated an alliance of Rajput princes and conquered North India, founding an Islamic theocracy—the Delhi sultanate.

From then on and until the British conquest, Muslims controlled most of the subcontinent. However, the Muslims settling India— Turks and Afghans of Persian culture rather than Arabs—confronted a double dilemma: an indigenous population following a religion so alien to Islam as to render impractical its incorporation as *dhimma,* yet so numerous that the choice between conversion and death was out of the question. The conquistadors' solution was to turn into a ruling stratum that did not assimilate (nor was assimilated by) the Hindu majority, keeping permanent religious and social distance. This was an ambivalent policy, leading to sporadic persecutions with wholesale massacres and the destruction of temples—and the intermittent acceptance of Hindus as quasi-*dhimmis.* Then again, good treatment of Hindu "idolaters" gave stricter Muslims a bad conscience. Coexistence was always difficult.

The Great Mughals

Five dynasties of Delhi sultans ruled over North India until the fifteenth century. They reached their maximum extent in the 1340s under Muhammad ibn Tughluq. In 1525 Timur's great-grandson Babur ("Tiger" or "Leopard") invaded India, cleaned up the Delhi sultans' last remnants, and established what would become one of

history's most glamorous dynasties, with a characteristic style that
mixed obscurantist fanaticism with cosmopolitanism. Babur destroyed
Hindu temples, built mosques and palaces, and then socialized with the
defeated Hindu grandees.[1] The Great Mughal Empire (*mughal* = Mongol)
reached new heights under Akbar (1556–1605). This contemporary of
`Abbas the Great of Persia and Elizabeth I of England ruled over per-
haps a hundred million subjects—the largest population anywhere,
except China. Employing mostly foreign Muslims of proven loyalty,
Akbar modernized and uniformed his administration, and introduced a
hierarchical bureaucracy of *mansabdars* responsible for their own military upkeep. His land classification, the basis for tax collection by
(largely Hindu) *zamindars*, survives today. Akbar was the "inventor of
India"—not only because he unified it for first time in 1000 years, but
also because he defined it as tolerant and pluralistic. A multiculturalist
avant la lettre, he tried to effect Hindu-Muslim rapprochement by conciliating native Hindu elites, diminishing their disqualifications and
their discriminatory poll tax, marrying their princesses, and including
Hindus in his government. A refined culture in architecture, miniatures,
and poetry flourished. Akbar was a tolerant mystic himself, but his syncretistic "Divine Faith" (*din illahi*) failed, provoking after his death an
orthodox Sunni reaction among the insulted `ulama. Henceforth ever
stricter separation between Hindus and Muslims would be the rule.
Reaction reached its height under Aurangzeb (1668–1707), the conqueror of nearly all of India, who destroyed temples, reintroduced *jizya*
and *shari`a*, and unleashed a Hindu revolt.

The Muslims were the first invaders India failed to assimilate;
conversely, Islam failed to convert India. The result was a very partial Islamization. The Muslim minority kept control through military
feudalism. Mostly Hindu peasants paid exorbitant taxes to maintain
luxurious, mostly Muslim, courts. Cities and courts were partly
assimilated, but the rural majority remained Hindu. High-caste Hindus embraced Islam for careerist reasons; then, from Mughal times
on, more low-caste Hindus and untouchables adopted Islam in the
hope of escaping discrimination. In flagrant contradiction to Islam's
principled egalitarianism among believers, however, a caste-type
division evolved among Indian Muslims, a division that distinguished *ashraf*, descendants of the invaders, from *ajlaf*, of convert
ancestry and viewed as inferior. Sufi mystics such as the Chisthis
played an important mediating role by stressing parallels with
Hindu pantheism, and may have been influenced by Hindu philosophy. (Another attempt at combining both religions was made by the
Sikhs, who were cruelly persecuted.)[2] Muslims constituted local
majorities in Sind, Punjab, and Bengal; everywhere else they lived as

dispersed minorities. With both communities keeping taboos against socialization, however, Islamization entailed the "denationalization" of its converts, rather than the "Indianizing" of new Muslims. The communities grew progressively apart until they had become two nations.

British Power and Islamic Reactions

Decline was swift after Aurangzeb's futile Islamizing efforts, although Mughal emperors continued to rule *pro forma*. By the mideighteenth century, the chaos was attracting renewed Afghan invasions. When Hindu Maratha princes and Afghans destroyed each other in the 1761 Battle of Panipat, the resulting power vacuum gave an opening to European maritime powers that used, often with the connivance of local elites, Indian *sepoys* to defeat other Indian forces. The British East India Company (EIC) had little trouble—starting from its first bastions in Calcutta (Kolkata), Madras (Chennai), and Bombay (Mumbai)—expanding its hegemony. Within half a century, three-quarters of the subcontinent was under the Company's control. However, EIC rule proved so corrupt and exploitative that the British government took over its responsibilities.

Communal antagonism worsened under British rule. Paradoxically, colonization may have been more traumatic for Indian Muslims than for Hindus. For the latter, indeed, foreign rule was "business as usual"; a national conscience developed only later. But the Muslims lost states they had controlled for centuries, and became marginalized. British economic policies in the first half of the nineteenth century, dictated by the motherland's industrialization, transformed India from exporter of artisan textiles into producer of raw cotton and materials. By introducing private property, the British ruined the Muslim rural elite. Cultural contempt added insult to injury. After the Napoleonic wars, England's antirevolutionary cultural climate left scant room for English officials to socialize with native colleagues; social distance between masters and servants grew. The era was one of evangelization of the "pagans" and of spreading the Utilitarians' rationalist gospel. Later, racism brought notions of the degeneration of India's culture and of the "white man's burden." British law replaced Islamic *shari`a* and Hindu indigenous codes, and English Persian. All this was not only bad for Hindus, but clashed even more with the respect to which Muslim ex-rulers were accustomed. The 1857 Great Sepoy Rebellion included both Hindus and Muslims and spread all over North India, endangering British rule. A reactionary Islamic element was apparent when the last descendant of the Great Mughals was proclaimed emperor. British troops had trouble dislodging him. After the revolt had been suppressed, India became a Crown Colony.

Although the combination of indigenous weakness and colonizer supremacy was not unique, India's lack of national awareness and its conditioning to foreign rule made it more vulnerable. Indian Muslims, never completely in religious control in a pluralistic society, experienced the more brutal loss of status. How to live as a Muslim outside the framework of Islamic rule? Three responses evolved: traditionalist, reformist proto-fundamentalist, and modernist:

1. Traditionalists: Conservative Sufis and `ulama who believed there was no need for substantial change either submitted to British rule or—like Sayyid Ahmad Barelwi—rejected coexistence altogether, and called for Muslim withdrawal to zones not yet under infidel rule, whence to prepare *jihad* to regain lost terrain that, they felt, had reverted to House of War status.
2. Reformists and protofundamentalists explained the Muslims' political losses as resulting from their nonobedience to Islam, provoking divine wrath. Although many were followers of the eighteenth-century conservative thinker Shah Waliallah, they also included pantheistic Chisthis and other Sufis. Remedy was sought in a purification of faith from superstitions (e.g., veneration of saints' tombs and other "Hindu influences"). Their ideal was one of an `ulama-led religious community.
3. Modernists eventually proved the most important stream. Muslim aristocrats and public servants tried to regain lost influence and prestige through accommodation. But this presupposed both Anglicization and modernizing Islam—hence the emphasis on education. While Britain was initiating schools for (mainly) Hindu youth in order to grow an indigenous Anglophone Indian elite—paradoxically the joint socializing of youth from distant parts created a modernizing intellectual stratum crucial to awakening a pan-Indian feeling—the Muslims' leading light, Sayyid Ahmad Khan, established in 1875 the competing Aligarh School, which combined Islamic teaching with Western scientific education. Khan believed in the compatibility of faith and modernity, and hoped that a new generation of Muslim elite formed in the "gentlemanly" mold could cooperate with the British. He is considered the spiritual father of Pakistan, although his symbolical reinterpretation of the Qur'an is no longer popular there.

Communalism Deepens Hindu-Muslim Alienation

British attitudes toward Muslims changed significantly after 1857. Initially considered a greater threat than Hindus (the colonizer feared the ancient ruling class might be tempted to regain power), Muslims came to be seen as a separate political community with its own interests and right to protection. Britain's divide-and-rule communalism, which privileged certain religious communities over others, flowed from this perception. Thus Britain switched to favoring Muslims against Hindus in distributing jobs. When representative institutions were introduced, Muslims were given separate electoral districts with disproportionate representation. The British nearly reinvented Muslim identity in India![3] From 1857 until 1947, Indian Muslims constituted a demographic and political minority, waging a triangular battle with both the British and Hindus. A dispersed community transmuted in a mosaic of culturally—and in certain areas, territorially—homogeneous blocks and redefined its collective identity from one in which Islam was one of several affiliations to one in which Islam became the essence—but there was no consensus over *which* Islam.

Britain's policy did not succeed in containing radicalization, although India, with its tradition of self-segregated identity groups, was ill prepared for independence. Cultural taboos reproduced social distance. Communalism only deepened the chasm. The era witnessed the gradual divergence of Muslim and Hindu communities, culminating in bloody partition. Established in 1885, the Congress Party, main vehicle of all-India nationalism, made Muslim relations with the Hindus more problematic. Like Muslims, Hindus faced a cultural dilemma: renaissance through emulation of Western models, or revitalization through return to religious tradition? Never explicitly Hindu, the Congress Party called instead for a religiously neutral state for all Indians that would transcend sectarian, regional, and caste divisions. But Hindus constituted the majority in the Congress Party, and Muslims saw it as a Hindu party. The younger generation of Muslim lawyers, civil servants, and journalists was gravitating to the idea of an independent organization, and in 1906, Ali Jinnah founded the All-India Muslim League. Without yet insisting on independence, Muslims demanded protection through separate electoral districts, which they achieved in 1906. Britain was stimulating subnationalisms and antagonism between India's communities.

There was no shortage of attempts at cooperation across the sectarian divide. After an initial phase during which both colonizer and moderate Indian nationalists hoped for an entente, Congress radicalized. By 1900, it was demanding total independence, which led to head-on collision with the British, who felt forced to retaliate against Congress revolutionaries. During the Great War, nationalist Hindu leader Mahatma Gandhi even secured Congress support for the *Khilafat* movement—the pan-Islamic, pro-Ottoman, anti-imperialist movement of Abdulhamid II. In return,

Muslims suspended cooperation with the British, throwing their support to the Indian nationalists. But the movement hardly survived the war (and lost its *raison d'être* with Atatürk's abolition of the caliphate). Meanwhile, for the first time the heterogeneous Indian masses became aware of their collective force.

While Indian nationalist consciousness grew in the interwar period, so did communal tensions. Every violent incident strengthened the separate identity of both victimizer and victimized, and appeared to prove the extremists' view that coexistence was impossible. Muslims feared becoming a minority in an independent India; Hindus feared that Muslims would retake control. Gandhi's moral authority was powerless to avert this evolution. Following the *Khilafat* failure, Muslims never achieved unity—neither with the Hindus nor among themselves—but split into two currents. One current, the conservatives' *tabligh,* preached a "return to personal piety"; the other, Muslim nationalism, demanded complete separation in an independent state: Pakistan.

Jinnah was to lead Pakistan to independence, although in the 1920s he was still willing to consider the autonomy of Muslim-majority provinces within an Indian federation. In 1930, however, the influential intellectual and poet Muhammad (Allama) Iqbal openly denied that all Indians formed one nation. In 1938, after Gandhi's nonviolent noncooperation and civil disobedience movement had forced itself as an inevitable negotiation partner onto Britain and Congress had won elections, demand for a state of their own became the Muslim League's official policy. Fear of "Hindu domination" now precluded any future cooperation. By 1945 the Muslim League commanded an absolute majority of the Muslim vote, and convinced its constituents of the "two-state theory" (although the project, advanced by Westernized Muslim intellectuals, was still secularist and aimed more at security of lifestyle than at state-controlled faith). World War II accelerated the inevitable outcome. The Congress Party boycotted the British war effort, unleashing fierce repression; the Muslim League cooperated with Britain, destroying what little Hindu trust was left. Britain partitioned its one-time "jewel" into an independent, mostly Hindu, India, and a Muslim-majority Pakistan, the latter cut off two pieces, 1600 km apart. Separation led to the mass flight of millions of Hindus and Muslims to the neighboring state: over half a million were massacred in the stampede. Centuries of uneasy coexistence had come to an end.

Pakistan

From its beginning, Pakistan—cultural frontier between the Middle East and India—has lacked a clear national identity. The "Muslim" nation is linguistically and ethnically heterogeneous. Sindhis, Baluchis, and Pashtos contest the Punjabis' predominance. Shiite, Christian, and Hindu minorities compound its complexity. Worse, two incompatible concepts vie for its soul. Is Pakistan the "state of the Muslim nation," as landowners, intellectuals, and officers have long propounded, with Islam the symbolic but noncommittal identity of the polity? Or should *shari`a* be the obligatory basis of an "authentic" Islamic state? The second option is favored by the traditionalist masses and followers of the *Jama`at-i Islami*, the party of Islamist ideologue Abu al-Ala Mawdudi, who would exclude non-Muslims politically, and have `*ulama* supervise public life. Because neither side scored a definitive victory, political vulnerability, instability, and military coups have become endemic. Prolonged constitutional crises brought first one dictator, Ayub Khan, to power, then another—Yahya Khan in 1969–71. East Pakistan seceded and became the state of Bangladesh, both of Pakistan's portions now inheriting the same problem. Territorial amputation alleviated but did not solve heterogeneity. Growing dependence on states such as Saudi Arabia made Pakistan even more susceptible to Islamizing pressures. In 1977, following the putsch of General Muhammed Zia ul-Haq, the Qur'an was introduced as Pakistan's constitution. However, Zia ul-Haq's Islamization project, pushed forward by radicalizing and recently urbanized masses, was cut short by his death in a plane crash in 1988.

The army's position remains ambiguous. Hostility to India has been constant; three lost wars against the Hindu enemy (focusing on the disputed territory of Kashmir), has left *revanchisme* very much alive. Throughout the Cold War, Pakistan was allied with and received military aid from the United States, and also channeled U.S. aid to the anticommunist Islamist Afghan resistance. Recently, the alignments have become blurred. Pakistan was swamped by millions of Afghan refugees, some of whom became involved in the drug and arms trade. In 1996 Pakistan helped the Taliban movement establish a fundamentalist regime in Afghanistan. Meanwhile, the United States and India have begun a cautious rapprochement. Both Pakistan and India are now nuclear powers; in 1999, they nearly stumbled into open warfare. In contrast to India, in Pakistan, democratic controls are defective. *Madrasas* and Islamist officers spread Islamist ideas and have infiltrated Pakistan's secret Inter Services Intelligence (ISI).[4] In 2000, a coup by Islamist-leaning Pervez Musharraf quashed the struggle between populist Prime Minister Benazir Bhutto, the first woman to head the government of a contemporary Islamic state, and her conservative nemesis, Nawaz Sharif. After 9/11, the country became the focus of cross-cutting military and diplomatic pressures.

To survive, Musharraf accommodated the United States against his erstwhile Taliban allies; but in the process he alienated anti-Western and Islamist forces at home (and lost further leverage as the United States began more clearly to gravitate to India). Pakistan is now a key player in the "clash of civilizations."

Bangladesh

The former "East Pakistan" and one of the world's poorest countries, Bangladesh suffered discrimination at the hands of its West Pakistani "big brother" before secession. The combination of a highly literate culture with extremely high population density, jute monoculture, half-feudal rural conditions, and propensity for natural catastrophes, made development the impetus for Bangladeshi independence. Since the 1960s, the Awami League, led by Mujibur Rahman (*"shaikh Mujib"*), militated for greater autonomy; but was repressed in spite of winning elections. In 1970 a cyclone killed half a million people, and West Pakistan's aid arrived too late to avert revolution. Indian support helped to defeat West Pakistan's efforts to crush the Bangladeshi secession. Politically, Bangladesh suffers from the same identity crisis as Pakistan. Initially, its nationalizing tendency appeared stronger than its Islamizing one, but stability has remained out of reach. Torn between its Bengali identity (shared with Hindu neighbor Indian West Bengal) and Islamic specificity, Bangladesh is dependent on India, although the relationship is troubled. There are still many Bangladeshi refugees in India, while a substantial Hindu minority lives in Bangladesh. In 1975, Mujib's attempt to concentrate power triggered his assassination, and set off a chain reaction of military interventions. Not until the 1990s did an uneasy democratization process resume. Bangladesh has a strangely low-key position within the Islamic world, which may not endure—in 2005 a series of bomb attacks struck the country, which may be related to state persecution of two radical Islamist parties, *Jagrata Muslim Janata Bangladesh* and *Jama`atul Mujahedeen Bangladesh*.

India's Muslims and the Kashmiri Conflict

India's reasonably functioning democracy is all the more impressive in light of the country's poverty, extreme diversity, and lack of shared identity. After Gandhi's murder, the Congress Party's Jawaharlal Nehru governed competently, investing time and effort in socioeconomic development. Nehru also oversaw the introduction of India's language-based federal system. Coexistence with Muslims has, all in all, been not too negative, in spite of some crises. But the 1947 partition left two open wounds. First, mass flight and massacres accompanied the territorial surgery; millions were resettled, but the trauma has been lasting. The second open wound is Kashmir.

With British prodding, the border between the two new states of secular India and Muslim Pakistan was hurriedly but peacefully decided upon. Independent princely states—areas of indirect rule where the British had left local maharajas in power—were the exception, however. Their rulers were allowed to choose between India and Pakistan. In two cases this caused problems. The Muslim *nizam* of Hindu-majority Hyderabad, in South India, opted for Pakistan, but his territory was quickly overrun by Indian forces. The case of Kashmir, with a two-thirds Muslim majority but a Hindu *raja*, proved more intractable. When the latter chose India, Pakistan invaded, provoking Indian counterattack. The war was suspended in 1949, when the United Nations brokered a partition that left India in control of the larger and richer part of the state. A referendum was agreed upon but never held. Two more wars were fought over Kashmir, in 1965 and in 1971, both ending in humiliating Pakistani defeat, owing among other things to the passivity of Muslim Kashmiris. However, from the 1980s on, India's rule (of questionable legitimacy) came to be more seriously challenged by an Islamist secessionist revolt in support of an independent Islamic state. This is being supported by Pakistan, which sees itself as protector of Muslim interests in India. In reaction to overtly terrorist Islamist guerrillas that recruited Kashmiri youth, India sent in its army.

Tens of millions of Muslims remained in India after 1947, either because they lived too far from Pakistan to move, or because they disliked partition. Numbering 137 million, they now constitute the world's third-largest Muslim concentration, equivalent to only slightly more than one-tenth of India's total population.[5] The position of Muslims in India is not easy. Descendants of erstwhile rulers, they are now on average poorer than other Indians, and are seen socially (though not officially) as potential traitors who dream of Muslim restoration. Prejudice and isolation reinforce each other. Religious conservatism is the predominant trend, with strict (though unpolitical) *tablighis* in the forefront. The *Jami`at al-`Ulama-i Hind* (Union of Indian `*ulama*) competed with the Muslim League on a federalist but anti-secularist platform stressing religiosity over political independence and the motto, "Better a strong Muslim Diaspora than a weak Muslim fatherland." India's Muslims nowadays identify with the Congress Party, which repeatedly violated its secularist principles to accommodate `*ulama* pressure regarding the status of Muslim women. In contrast to Hindu women, for Muslimas, not secular law but *shari`a* continues to rule personal relations.[6] But Muslim support has not stemmed the decline of Congress since the 1980s, or its transformation from a visionary social democratic party into a political machine. The emergence of Hindu nationalists promoting a "Hindu ethos" and demanding India's mutation into an expressly Hindu state threatened Muslims—the question of political disqualification of non-Hindus remained moot.

Southeast Asia

To an even greater extent than India, Southeast Asia is merely a geographical expression. Islam is mainly relevant in "maritime Indochina": in Indonesia, the world's most populous Muslim country; in Malaysia, which sees itself as an Islamic state; and in the Philippines, with its politically active Muslim minorities. Largely peaceful expansion through merchants and itinerant Sufis, combined with the syncretistic survival of pre-Islamic values, has produced a more mystical and accommodationist Islam, with less of a monopoly on its followers' thinking. More recently, however, significant modernist and Islamist trends have been in evidence. This evolution is related to Islam's role in the struggle against colonization. In fact, the archipelago's Islamization started rather late—first in Sumatra, whose oldest inscriptions date from the thirteenth century—and continues today. Tribal societies lasted much longer than in India. State formation, on the basis of irrigated agriculture, came later, with king-priests as intermediaries with the invisible spirit world. Animistic and magical practices survive everywhere. Current conflicts of collective identity reflect an incomplete cultural unification.

Spices, merchants, and pirates were the formative external influences. Indian merchants and Brahmins brought Hinduism and Buddhism, inspiring the Khmer in Cambodia, Srivijaya in Sumatra, and Majapahit in Java. Then the Mongol invasions shook up the political balance. Java had the best physical conditions for becoming the new political power, although no idea of "Indonesia" existed yet.

The first Muslim traders arrived between the twelfth and fifteenth centuries—not long before competing Catholic and Protestant missionaries entered the same arena. By the 1400s, Malacca had become the dominant intermediary and point of departure for Islamization. (The Strait of Malacca between the Malay Peninsula and Sumatra is the only sea connection for the Indian and Chinese worlds, and continues today to be a geostrategically neuralgic point.) Conversion commonly followed peaceable penetration by Arab and Indian traders, leaping from West to East, from island to island, and from the coast to the inland. Thus West Indonesia is today more strongly Islamized, whereas Christian missionary work was more successful in the Philippines, Timor, and the Moluccas. This atypical situation led to a rather different Islam—less austere and more mystical, with Hindu and other pre-Islamic survivals. "Purification movements" arose only later, in the framework of anti-Western resistance.

In the seventeenth century, the Dutch took over and expanded Portuguese trading-stations, acquiring a monopoly over the "spice islands" and extending their control over the Java sultanates. It was private colonization by the *Verenigde Oostindische Compagnie* (VOC, United Company of the East Indies) that, except where it interfered in spice production, on some islands, left social structures largely intact, provided the local aristocracy guaranteed delivery of tropical harvests. Conveniently, Chinese immigrants, squeezed in as intermediaries, became a lightning rod for persecution.

The Napoleonic wars led to a British interregnum. (They stayed on in Malaya.) Restitution to Holland in the post-Napoleonic restoration inaugurated significant shifts. The new imperialism transformed the economy and social customs. Intensified state-led imperialist exploitation included obligatory cultivation, provoking Islamic-inspired revolts on Sumatra and Java. This was the epoch in which Indonesia acquired its modern definition, as Holland conquered all the islands—sometimes against fierce resistance, as in orthodox Islamic Aceh (which withstood forty years of colonial warfare). In Javanese Banten, Prince Dipanegara revolted in 1825, with peasant and *kiyayi* (`ulama`) support, against Holland's cruel "cultivation system," which forced Javanese peasants to reserve part of their fields for colonial produce such as spices, indigo, tea, or tobacco, often resulting in the peasants' starvation. Later in the nineteenth century, the worst excesses were eliminated. Canceling obligatory deliveries and introducing capitalist production did little to raise living standards, however, what with unrelenting population pressure. (Half of Indonesia's population still lives on Java.) Exploitation continued on coffee and rubber plantations.

Anti-Dutch resistance bore a strong Islamic mark. The two natural candidates to lead the struggle were the Hindu-Javanese *priyayi* nobles, and the Islamic *kiyayi* village elite. The former were integrated into Dutch administration, leaving the latter—a local leadership with universalistic Islamic beliefs—as the last independent force.[7] Sultans had little control over religion, so transmitting Qur'anic (and magical) beliefs fell to *kiyayi*-led rural schools. Paradoxically, nineteenth-century European expansion actually strengthened Islam. Nautical advances also allowed more devout Muslims to make

the *hajj*. They returned generally more pious and—thanks to contacts
with Muslims from other regions—more orthodox than they went, and
became a force for Islamization. Islamic influence was further medi-
ated by networks of coastal merchants in Java, Sumatra, and other
Malay islands, who became carriers of an Islamic renaissance.
Naqshibandi and Qadiri Sufi orders to re-educate (*tabligh*) the
"lapsed" were another factor in this awakening. Islam soon became a
major motor of resistance, and started to worry the colonial masters.
The Dutch distinguished tolerance for Islam-as-religion, from repression for Islam-as-anti-Western-claim, and put obstacles in the way of
pilgrimage.

By 1900, unlimited exploitation had (at least theoretically) given
way to an "ethical policy," with more cultural interventionism but also
more help for education, and modest empowerment. As in India,
Western education produced a national conscience. Three political
currents evolved: nationalist (hoping to rebuild a national identity
from vestiges of Hindu court culture), communist, and Islamic. The
first two were led by *priyayi* descendants—civil employees, doctors,
engineers, lawyers, and intellectuals; the last was led by *kiyayi* and
merchants. After communist revolts were suppressed in the 1920s,
the Nationalist Party led by Soekarno became the mainstay of anticolonial opposition. Communists and nationalists may have been Muslims in private life, but publicly they adhered to a quasi-atatürkist
vision of a religiously neutral state. This ideal was vehemently
rejected by the Islamic current.

Political Islam in the Dutch East Indies—and subsequently, in
Indonesia—had two currents: one neo-orthodox reformist, backed by
devout merchants; and the other conservative traditionalist, with a
rural/`ulama* constituency. The modernist *Muhamadiyya*, strongest in
Java, stressed individual religiosity, approved of *ijtihad*, and opposed
"superstitious" practices such as the *wayang* shadow theater, suspected of carrying Hindu messages. Rationalistic, reformists placed a
nearly puritanical emphasis on self-control, personal virtue, and
social responsibility. From 1912 on, the related modernist *Sarekat
Islam* combined national and religious demands with practical initia-
tives in agriculture, hospitals, orphanages, and scouting. It became a
mass movement, but lost appeal after it started to radicalize. *Nahdatul
Ulama* emerged in the 1920s as a rural-conservative Islamic alternative, blending Sufi content with modern organizational methods.

Politicization deepened in the interwar period, polarizing existing
communities, pitting incompatible ideological movements against
each other, and envenoming coexistence; the Dutch reacted with
repression, inflaming nationalist passions. Then came the World War

II and Japanese occupation, exploding the myth of the "invincible white man." Japan tried to exploit Indonesian nationalism, as well as its Islamist movements, and promoted an interpretation of its war against the West as a *jihad*. In 1943, Japan created *Masyumi*, a controlled Islamic umbrella movement; but eventually both Islamist and nationalist movements escaped Japanese control, and in 1945 Soekarno proclaimed independence.

The Indonesia that thus came into being was an archipelago riven by social, geographic, and ideological divides—a "Pakistan harboring tens of internal Bangladeshes." Although Muslims formed the majority, most were only nominally so (the *abangan*), while a minority were orthodox *santri* Islamists embracing the ideal of the Islamic state (*Negara Islam*). With difficulty, consensus was reached on a national ideology of *pancasila,* or five principles: nationalism, humanism, democracy, social justice, and belief in God. An ambiguous agreement that "Muslims must live according to *shari`a*" provided the Islamists with a lever that, if applied, would have done away with freedom of religion, and allowed *santris* to put the Muslim majority in an Islamic straightjacket. Fanaticism, though, is not a very Indonesian trait and a compromise was achieved whereby Islamists, through the Ministry of Religions, administer *hajj, waqfs,* mosques, personal law, and *da`wa*, the "internal mission" to educate the masses in the light of Islam. This has resulted in little overt coercion, but in the long-term Islamization of public life.

The accord did not please the more extremist Muslims of the outlying islands. The secessionist *Darul Islam* movement, aspiring to an Islamic state, was not defeated until the 1960s. Soekarno had used political instability as an excuse to muzzle political parties; his brand of "guided democracy" steered Indonesia leftward with nationalizations, sympathy for the Partai Komunis Indonesia (PKI, then the noncommunist world's largest communist party), and hostility to *Masyumi*. Economic crisis, religious doubts, and fear of communist takeover sufficed to ally Islamists with the army. The latter launched a counterrevolution in 1965: Soekarno lost power and in the ensuing civil war, half a million communists were slaughtered. The new strongman, Suharto, effected a sharp rightward turn with economic liberalization and alignment with the United States, but with maintenance of rigid cultural controls, extending to the Islamists. *Pancasila* was reaffirmed; attempts were made to revive the pantheistic Hindu-Javanese inheritance; an "official," controlled Islamic party was tolerated; but *Masyumi* remained banned, as was propaganda for an Islamic state. Soekarno and Suharto thus both continued the Dutch policy of differentiating between religious and political Islam. By the late 1990s, however,

Suharto's modernizing dictatorship had become exhausted and corrupt. A return to Islam in private life was visible, as the rural `ulama and the urban *Muhammadiya* were both showing signs of strength. In the shadows, more radical fundamentalists were growing.

Sub-Saharan Africa

Africa is one of Islam's major frontiers. Hostile geography in most parts limited Africans to tribal structures, and for long periods prevented agriculture, thus slowing the rise of bureaucratic and military states. This delay made Africans vulnerable to the predatory practices of Arabs and Europeans. External economic interests in gold, slaves, wood, and ivory, and later in plantations and mining, were to determine their history. In return, the foreigners brought Christianity and Islam. Sub-Saharan Africa constitutes today the fourth great Islamic space—one that is gaining in importance, with between 111 and 400 million Muslims. The contested statistics point to both continuing rapid expansion and fierce Islamic-Christian missionary rivalry.[8] Africa's Islamization is reminiscent of Indonesia's: the personal example by traders, migrants, teachers, and mystics was more important than was conquest. Islam advanced along three axes: from Morocco through the Sahara to West Africa, from Egypt overland along the Nile to East Africa, and by Omani and Yemeni seafarers establishing settlements such as Zanzibar on the eastern coast. On the eve of European colonization, Islam was Africa's main "foreign" presence.

North Africa was among first zones to be converted and become part of the Arab world. Converted Berbers founded puritanical dynasties in the eleventh and twelfth centuries: Almoravids (*al-murabitun*) and Almohads (*al-muwahiddun*) ruled Spain and controlled caravan routes through the Sahara to the gold mines of West Africa. Trans-Saharan trade induced in West Sudan and the Niger region a succession of impressive states, including Ghana, Mali, and Songhai. Although still mostly polytheistic, these states welcomed colonies of Muslim traders and `ulama, whose literacy and (supposedly) stronger magic proved useful to the monarchs. As administrators, they became focal points for the conversion of other Africans. By the fourteenth century, Timbuktu was a world center of Islamic learning. Meanwhile, East African Christian realms such as Ethiopia blocked southward Islamic expansion, although Bantu culture came to be strongly influenced by Arabs; the conversion of Somalia and Eritrea was more the work of coastal merchants.

The slave trade inaugurated a new phase of Islamization. Slavery had long existed in Africa but intensified when traffic bound for plantations in the Americas stimulated the emergence of new states on the western coast (e.g., Dahomey, Ashanti, and others) that hunted human beings to be shipped abroad. In payment, their elites received guns from the European traders, which they used to consolidate their power and capture new tribes. Some slaves were Muslims—the first to bring Islam to the Americas. (The sultan of Zanzibar sold Black slaves to the Middle East.) Meanwhile, Islam expanded southward. The Hausas, some of the Yorubas, and many other nations converted. This process illustrates the link between trade and religion: with the decline of states such as Songhai, merchant corporations lost their protector and became more dependent on their own trust-based networks, which overlapped with Sufi brotherhoods such as the *Qadiriyya* and *Tijaniyya*. Common values were crucial; with their emphasis on honesty and puritanism, the Sufis performed useful ritual and social functions (e.g., conflict resolution) for the population, leading to numerous conversions.

Sufi orders were also instrumental in deepening Islamization. If the first stage of conversion was often superficial and latitudinarian, accepting "heathen" spirits, now turned *jinns*, was a way to smooth the transition. Next, *tariqas* and mosque schools began to press for more normative religious practices, opposed magic and alcohol, and favored the enclosing of women. In the eighteenth and nineteenth centuries, such protofundamentalist militancy led to various *jihads*, which founded strictly Islamic states in Senegal, Guinea, and elsewhere. Uthman Dan Fodio established the most famous of these, the Sokoto Sultanate of Northern Nigeria, in 1804. Forced conversions increased the number of Muslims. But colonial rivalry was heating up, especially between France and Britain. Integration into the capitalist world economy meant replacing Africa as source of slaves with African plantation production. Erstwhile top-slaver Britain turned abolitionist: abolition destabilized the slavery-based states, preparing the way for their colonization. The British defeated Sokoto, and incorporated it into Nigeria. Britain preferred indirect rule through local Muslim elites. The French gained control of most of West Africa, and left an even deeper imprint on its social structure.

By the end of the 1800s, the "scramble for Africa" accelerated into the division of the continent. While France was busy building its colonial empire on a west-east axis, the British followed a north-south arrow from Cairo to Cape Town. This nearly led to Anglo-French war where their paths crossed, but not before Britain had annihilated in the Sudan a militant Islamic state that stood in its way. A self-proclaimed *mahdi* had founded there in 1885 a strictly religious government, not unlike the Wahhabites of the Arabian desert.

It was defeated in the 1898 Omdurman Battle. The British then worked with less extremist *khatmiya* Sufis, although they had a hard time controlling ex-*mahdist Ansar*. The antagonism continues today in independent Sudan.

The colonial period lasted from 1880 to the 1960s. While African Muslims lost political power everywhere, Islam spread as never before. Colonization brought new Muslim minorities to East and Southern Africa. Indian migrants settled in Uganda and South Africa (where they met Muslim Malays whom the Dutch had imported earlier). Urbanization and socioeconomic dislocation followed colonization, rupturing traditional tribal and familial bonds and benefiting Islam with its universal message and latent anti-Westernism. In fact, Western colonialism evoked a variety of responses. Muslim-majority societies sometimes rallied to popular religious opposition leaders, but more often the struggle for decolonization was fought by Westernized and secularized elites. Muslims participated, but not necessarily *as* Muslims.

By 1960, nearly all colonies had obtained independence—within the artificial borders traced by the former colonizers. Rarely were their high hopes of liberty and development realized. More often, authoritarian or military regimes took control of inefficient state machineries that were incapable of building nations out of heterogeneous, often hostile tribes and territories plagued by epidemics, war, hunger, desertification, and international indifference. Africa's lot became permanent involution—a pervasive misery that Islam was best positioned to exploit. Islamization has thus been unceasing. Sufi brotherhoods remain a crucial force of social integration and conversion. States such as Mauritania, Senegal, and Somalia are now completely or largely Islamized, reproducing the same debates over the role of Islam in society we encounter in other longstanding Muslim countries. Other states, such as Tanzania and Malawi, have large, well-educated Muslim minorities. Finally, a third group of states consists of "borderline" or "hinge" countries, such as Sudan or Nigeria, that are evenly divided between Muslims and non-Muslims. This has been a recipe for internal conflicts.

ISLAM AMONG OTHERS

3

محمد

The Muslim Diasporas

The next population to consider is Muslims as minorities. About one-fourth of the 1.3 billion Muslims in the world are living under non-Muslim regimes. Many of them descend from Muslim realms that fell subsequently under non-Muslim rule, as in India. Others reside in communities in West African countries such as Guinea Bissau, Burkina Faso, Ivory Coast, or Cameroon, where Muslims are not (yet) a majority, but which are more or less contiguous with the rest of the Muslim world. Still others belong to residual Muslim communities that survived the withdrawal of Islamic empires. Finally, there are diasporas of Muslims who settled individually or with their families in other countries for a variety of reasons: political, trade (e.g., Middle Eastern merchants in China), labor (e.g., Turks and Moroccans in Western Europe), or professional (e.g., Indian and Pakistani Muslims in the United States). This chapter deals with such diasporas.

Russia

Europe's Muslims fall into two completely different groups: long-established Muslim nations in Eastern Europe and Eurasia, and recent Muslim immigrants in Central and Western Europe.

Descendants of Turkic populations and native converts to Islam live in Russia and the Balkans. Ottoman retreat and the retreat of

Islamized post-Mongol khanates left them under non-Muslim rule: ex-Yugoslav Bosniaks and Bulgarian Pomaks probably desend from converts from Bogomilism, a medieval Christian sect, whereas Tartars, Chechens of the northern Caucasus, and others are Turkic. The Russian case is especially complex because from the sixteenth through the nineteenth centuries, the tsars expanded their territory until it stretched from Germany to China and Japan. In the process, they annexed most of the Caucasus and predominantly Muslim Inner Asia. The tsars persecuted their Muslim subjects; then the Soviet Union inherited them. Atheistic communism aspired to create a proletarian, nonreligious, and non-nationalist "new man." In practice, the USSR oscillated between repression and accommodation. Official boards oversaw all religious activity; Stalin deported entire nations to distant parts of the USSR and fostered extensive Russian (non-Muslim) colonization. The breakup of the Soviet Union in 1991 turned Azerbaijan, Kazakhstan, and other central Asian Muslim-majority republics into independent states: but Moscow has not lost hope of eventually regaining control of this "near abroad."

Meanwhile, fragmentation left fifteen to twenty million Muslims (some 14 percent of Russia's population, and growing much faster than the non-Muslim population) within the borders of the USSR's largest successor state, the Russian Federation. Bashkirs, Tatars, Chechens, Daghestanis, and many other Muslims are divided into communities with widely varying degrees of autonomy or integration among ethnic Russians. Ethnic and religious factors cannot be disentangled here; the complexity is greatest in the Caucasus and to the north of it, as epitomized in the Chechen case. Urbanization and modernization are also in evidence. Tatars, for instance, are descendants of the Islamized Mongols who reached Muscovy in the thirteenth and fourteenth centuries, and live not only in Tatarstan, along the Volga, but also in the major Russian cities. Many Muslims feel discriminated against in Russia; and many Russians fear Islamism. In reality, however, only a minority of Russian Muslims are fundamentalist: seventy years of Communism have left Russia's nations rather secularized. Even though there is, among Muslims no less than among the Orthodox, a renewed interest in religion, the tendency is often liberal. Intermarriage with non-Muslims is common. In the big cities, Muslims are not noticeably different from other Russians.

China

Before turning our attention west, let us cast a quick glance further east to a relatively little known and isolated Muslim Diaspora.

Chinese Islam is quite old and diverse. It shares certain characteristics with Russia: imperial expansion incorporating Central Asian Muslim states that became continental colonies, plus the experience of communism. China, however, also has its "national Muslims." Although less than 2 percent of the population, China's twenty million Muslims have historically played a disproportionate role, especially in contacts with Central Asia. The Silk Road, after bringing Buddhism to China, became a conduit for Islam. Islam also reached China from overseas, through Arab and other merchant communities in port cities such as Guangzhou (Canton). From the Tang through the Yuan (Mongol) Dynasties (spanning the eighth through the fourteenth centuries), Muslims traders, among other foreigners, at times held high positions. They were generally tolerated under the Ming restoration (during the late fourteenth through the early seventeenth centuries). Then, between the seventeenth and nineteenth centuries, under the last dynasty, the Qing (Manchu), their position worsened.

Today's Chinese Muslims consist of two major groups: Chinese Muslims proper, and conquered Muslims from the nations of Inner Asia. The former, *Hui*, are the descendants of foreign immigrants and local Chinese converts. Although they now constitute a separate nation under Chinese law, they are racially, linguistically, and ethnically assimilated into the Han majority (who constitute 90 percent of all Chinese people). Structurally, their position is that of many old diasporas. Although long integrated into their new surroundings, and far from their mother community, they still intermittently feel her pull. *Hui* have settled all over China. In pockets of the northwest and southwest, they form majorities. Their sinicization has been periodically criticized by more orthodox Muslims, provoking reform movements, although the fairly decentralized and traditionalist "Old Learning" probably still commands a majority. From the sixteenth century on, *hajjis* and itinerant Sufi preachers from the Middle East and Inner Asia introduced the "New Learning," which was more ascetic and mystical, with ritual innovations and marked by a very different and tighter community organization. Some of these Muslims did not accept the Confucianist state, and in the nineteenth century instigated major rebellions that were suppressed. In fact, regulation by the always highly interventionist Chinese state has been frequent. China tolerated Islam as long as it posed no threat, but tried to play off one school of learning against another, backing those seen as most conformist over those that were revolutionary. A third proto-Islamist line, one of scripturalist reform, started to militate during the 1930s: the Muslim Brotherhood-influenced *Yihewanis*. Opposed to the veneration of saints' tombs, Chinese names, and pagoda-like mosques, they are, interestingly, the group that the Chinese communists have supported; their Sufi opponents were suspected of regionalism.

Since 1949, the Chinese Communist Party nationality policy, aimed at eventual assimilation of all minorities, has wavered between encouragement of local cultures, trying to bind Muslim elites to the Communist hierarchy, on one hand, and repression and pressure to amalgamate with the Han, on the other. During the Cultural Revolution, Islam was one of many persecuted religions. Since the 1980s, however, cultural controls have been relaxed, although this fails to solve the ambiguity between the Chinese and Islamic elements in *Hui* identity.

The other Muslim population is a mosaic of (mostly Turkic) peoples living in the huge but scarcely populated pastures and deserts of western China; *Uyghurs* are the most numerous. Although China controlled Central Asia during the Tang Dynasty, it was later lost, and only reconquered in 1759 by Qing emperors who incorporated it as *Xinjiang* (New Province). In the nineteenth century, Inner Asia was partitioned between Russia and China. Here Muslims have never been sinicized. Chinese rule spurred the growth of national awareness among the tribal populations, and provoked local revolts that mingled religious and ethnic elements. A string of autonomous Muslim warlords ruled here until the Communists reunified China in 1949.

China has vital strategic and economic interests here because of the region's mineral wealth, and the control China seeks over a new "Silk Road," to access the natural gas reserves of her Islamic Inner Asian neighbors. Although China recognizes the *Uyghurs* as an autonomous nation, increased contact with related Turkic peoples across the border, as well as ongoing Han colonization, are feeding separatism. Meanwhile, Chinese interests in Central Asia must balance the nationalism of the weakly integrated post-Soviet states, residual Russian imperial aspirations, and the pull of transnational Islamism.

Europe

Before World War II, few Muslims lived in Western Europe. The migration between Christendom and Islam was one-way because only Europeans visited and settled in the Middle East.[1] This changed after 1945. Recent Muslim immigrants (most of whom arrived after the 1960s) number between ten and fifteen million.[2] After decolonization, Muslims entered Europe in three waves. The first consisted of Muslims who had collaborated with colonial powers, feared reprisals after independence, and resettled in the metropolis; the pro-French *harkis* soldiers in Algeria are an example. A second, much wider wave consisted of guest workers. During Europe's epoch of economic expansion through the 1960s and early 1970s, which coincided with growing misery in the Middle East and North Africa, millions arrived to fill the least desirable jobs in the industries and services of the developed countries to the north. The new immigrants came from much poorer countries and were darker-complexioned, and their cultural distance from the European population was great enough for their stay to cause problems, for the host societies as well as for themselves.

Many Muslims found their way to the homelands of their former colonial masters. From Algeria and Morocco, immigrants went to France, Switzerland, and Belgium. From Turkey they went to Germany, Holland, and the Scandinavian countries; and from member states of the British Commonwealth such as India and Pakistan, they went to the United Kingdom. "Guest workers" sent money back home to their dependents, and planned their own return. Initially, their presence was thought to be temporary. As European economies fell into recession in the 1970s and 1980s, the Muslims' economic situation worsened and European states planned to deport the newcomers.

However, perspectives were even bleaker on the other side of the Mediterranean. Most immigrants therefore resisted repatriation and stayed on, surviving on social security and eventually bringing over their own families. A temporary population of single Muslim men thus became the permanent presence of immigrant Muslim families. In years to follow, one European country after another closed its borders to new immigrants—but by now, millions had already found their way in.

A third category of Muslim immigrant was political refugees from the Islamic world's numerous dictatorships: from Iran, Somalia, and Ethiopia, as well as Iraqi Kurds, Palestinians, and others. Numerically this third wave was much smaller than the second one; even so, it has been large enough to evoke xenophobic reactions. Massive migrations are part and parcel of globalization, as is the resentment they provoke. Muslims constitute Europe's largest immigrant population. Their population has grown thanks to a high birthrate; a second and third generation has concentrated in separate neighborhoods in which grave social tensions have been building.

Immigration to Europe

Once settled in Europe, Muslims had to deal with their identity. Since arriving, they have been perpetually split between assimilation and religious/ethnic particularism. In this force field, three vectors have been crucial: the attitude of the host society, the differences and similarities among various groups of Muslims, and the options that the immigrants have been developing for themselves.

Immigrants have been at the mercy of each country's immigration policy. The divergent French and British models stand out. France has had the longest experience with the Islamic world, and is home to proportionally the largest Muslim population (at least 4 million residents, more than 5 percent of the total French population). It also has a tradition of easily accepting immigrants, provided they assimilate and secularize. Muslims are welcome if they turn into Frenchmen and -women "like all the rest," including in the privatization of their religion. Because this concept is alien to the Islamic self-perception, conflicts have ensued, particularly among the second generation. After 15 years of polemics, in 2004, conspicuous religious symbols were outlawed in public schools—specifically, the headscarf (*hijab*), considered "religious propaganda in a public locale," was deemed to be at variance with the principle of separation of state and church. For Muslim parents, maintaining their daughters' chastity reflects not only ethnic values of honor, but also expresses obedience to a religious command. For the girls, external difference in dress sometimes signals the assumption of a distinct identity, a protest against outside pressure and rising racism.

Britain maintained its liberal immigration policy for Commonwealth citizens until the 1960s, when here, too, the gates closed shut. English-type integration follows the multicultural "ethnic community" model: British Muslims have the right to express their identity with official support and subsidy (monies, however, go to ethnic, not confessional, groups). The dominant Muslim tendency for self-containment over assimilation complements it. Holland, Belgium, the Scandinavian countries, and some Commonwealth partners overseas such as Canada and recently Australia have followed in Britain's steps.

Germany, along with Switzerland and Austria, long remained without any specific immigration policy, insisting that the guests were only temporary. Meanwhile, the number of Turks in Germany grew spectacularly. Berlin is today the third-largest Turkish city in the world (after Istanbul and Ankara). In the 1990s, the reunification of Germany brought de-industrialization and unemployment to the former communist German Democratic Republic. In their wake arose a neo-Nazi type of xenophobia. The social crisis that followed brought into the limelight the old question of Germany's national identity—an identity that had never been defined by common territory or values, but by language and the pseudobiological terms of ancestry and race. Reunification reawakened the identity problem and threw up the challenge of defining who did and did not belong to the nation—particularly if the millions of temporary, mostly Muslim workers had a claim.

Integration or Isolation?

For those who refused to "go home," the end of labor immigration after 1974 signaled the onset of reflection on the question, How to be a Muslim in Europe—by apartheid or assimilation? The question, in ever sharper form, now haunts the second generation of European Muslims—or Muslim Europeans.

Three facts must be kept in mind here. First, most Muslims arrived from Muslim-majority countries. Being a minority has therefore been an unfamiliar—and, in principle, illegitimate—experience. The Islamic tradition naturally appoints the "House of Islam" as the home of Muslims. While Muslims have historically migrated to non-Muslim areas, their destinations were nearly always less developed than the Muslim heartland, their point of origin. In contrast, now Muslims found themselves the weakest element within the society that had always been the most hostile to them. Second, instead of being one Muslim community, the diasporas are, rather, constituted of fragmented agglomerates of individuals belonging to a patchwork quilt of peoples. Apart from Islam, Moroccans, Turks, and Somalis have little in common. Community development occurred initially among compatriots. Only within the second generation have the gaps attenuated, and do Muslims of varied backgrounds come to identify themselves primarily as Muslims. It is more correct to speak of a European Muslim community today than it was a generation ago.

Third, most Muslims are poor and marginalized. Cultural antagonism embitters the competition with the native working class for scarce jobs. Also, most Muslims come from the lower classes of authoritarian societies and many lack any tradition of self-organization.

How, then, can Muslims live under non-Muslim sovereignty? Four types of answers have emerged.[3] The first one is rejection. When Abu al-Ala al-Mawdudi, the Pakistani fundamentalist leader, visited England in 1969, he was—like the Egyptian Sayyid Qutb in the United States before him—scandalized by what he described as Western decadence. He viewed this as a danger for Muslims; his prescription therefore combined combat, maximal separation from the surrounding rotten society, and a return to *Dar al-Islam*.

Others did not go as far. While they agreed with Mawdudi's critique of Western permissiveness, they viewed the weakening of family bonds, social solidarity, and self-control in the West as an opportunity to show Islam as a superior countermodel. The fate that had thrown the faithful into an "ignorant" milieu provided them a chance to criticize, propagandize, and convert—if not openly, then at least by example. The task at hand, then, would be to build a just and Islamic alternative society. Of course, many Muslims have simply taken comfort in their own traditions, without concerning themselves much with theological niceties.

Secularization is a third option. A new generation has come of age in the 1990s, and has already absorbed many Western values. Just as in the Middle East itself, in Europe modernity presents itself to Muslims as both danger and temptation. Finding a compromise between ancestral traditions and the demands of modern life is especially problematic for girls, particularly when confronting the question of freedom to choose a husband or pursue an independent professional career, problems that arise in particular in the mixed (ethnically and by gender) public schools that most Muslim children attend, Islamic schools being out of reach for most. Still, the promise of modernity attracts many. Here and there one encounters the embryonic contours of a more liberal Muslim middle class, although Muslims remain seriously underrepresented in all elites.

Will Islam in Europe make the same turn to a "secular religion" as Christianity and Judaism did before it? Some Islamic intellectuals (e.g., Geneva-based Tariq Ramadan) voice the idea of a new, specifically European Islam—reformist and tolerant without giving up its aspiration to convert.

However, most Muslims enjoy few friendships with "Whites" and socialize primarily among themselves; for them, the question of liberal Islam does not pose itself. Islamism becomes, for some Muslims who live in a non-Islamic environment, the last option. Exclusion pushes many to become more Islamic—a sign of their being different. Alienated from their community of origin, yet not fully accepted by the host society, more young Muslims than ever find solace in the ancestral religion. Obeying Islamic rules in the midst of an unprepared Western society invites visible sacrifices and risks isolating the believer. This is assumed as a *hijra,* although outsiders may take it as a provocation. Countries of origin such as Morocco or Turkey finance and staff mosques and clubs. Returning to Islamic religion is still far from radical Islamism. It is, however, a step that more and more young Muslims are making. Fundamentalist organizations such as the Egyptian Muslim Brotherhood and the Pakistani *Jama`at-i Islami* have branches in Europe and America, and have been successful in converting many immigrants. Saudi Arabia supports its own conservative Islamic institutions in Europe.

Reaction of the Non-Muslim Majority: From Integration to Islamophobia

Reactions within Muslim communities range from assimilation to self-segregation. In parallel, one may distinguish within the host society another spectrum, also spanning the gamut from acceptance to rejection. The first pole advocates Europeanization. The point of departure is compatibility, based on a certain mutual accommodation. This position has its roots in three groups: (1) Leftist intellectuals, faithful to universalistic values, who feel sympathy for the Third World and guilt for Europe's colonial past, and wish to make up for past sins; (2) Christian churches inspired by similar motives and by an ecumenism that favors dialogue between different faiths; and (3) bureaucrats linked to public education and social service apparatuses, who promote integration for reasons of governance efficiency and to prevent future problems.

From empty churches ceding space to mosques to states financing Islamic institutions, integration policies differ from country to country, but all are prodding Muslim citizens to self-organize in the hope that community institutions will serve as interlocutors with the authorities. Proponents of integration logically seek the cooperation of an "enlightened" counterpart within European Islam—educated, partly secularized, second-generation Muslims who know how to articulate their community's complaints and demands and are natural candidates to become its new elite. This official institutionalization of Muslim communities parallels the entry of Muslims into public and political life, where they are forming lobbies to advance their community's interests.

The growing presence of Muslims in Europe has thus consolidated Islam as a permanent thread in the societal fabric. Will the next step be the emergence of a Western Islam, just as there exists a Western Buddhism, and a Chinese Catholicism? This is a problematic proposition. The concept of either privatized religion or "Islamic *millet*" is alien to most Muslims. Besides, the question is not just how immigration will mold the minority's Islam, but also how Western civilization may itself change under the influence of a Muslim presence. On this level, resistances proliferate.

Rejection has been stronger than integration. *Anti-Muslimism* and *Islamophobia* describe the complex of negative attitudes toward Islam.[4] Such attitudes are older than the West's current encounter with Islam and older even than imperialism, although psychological constructions of an Orientalist type doubtlessly reinforced existing prejudices in the West. Mutual prejudices have grown deep roots on both sides of the Mediterranean. Historically more distant confrontations, such as the Crusades and the Siege of Vienna, feed back into this ideology. Yet, if Islamophobia manipulates old stereotypes, it is a new kind of ideological construction; what one witnesses here is an "invention of tradition" with growing popular appeal.[5] Islamophobia links two potentially threatening phenomena: (1) strategic security threats (related to oil, terrorism, the Palestinians, weapons of mass destruction); and (2) menaces of a demographic, social, and cultural order (supposed religious, racial, or cultural incompatibility; unemployment; crime). In Europe, impelled by its economic stagnation and the xenophobic reactions this feeds, demographic Islamophobia is stronger than strategic Islamophobia. In the United States, the reverse prevails. Europe—which in contrast to America, never saw itself as a land of immigrants—is challenged by the sudden influx of a group of newcomers who, nuances notwithstanding, remain clearly Muslim and hence "impossible to assimilate."

Rejection started perhaps with the poorly articulated rancor of the poorer native classes who stood in most direct contact with these newcomers. More than Islam, it is Muslims themselves who are seen as the threat. This rejection is tinged with ethnic and racial prejudice, and with economic competition over scarce jobs. Only later—from the late 1980s on—was Islamophobia exploited by far-Right populist politicians who expressed it in terms of a "clash of civilizations." Soon the supposed cultural incompatibility was joined by security concerns due to the growing list of attacks committed by or attributed to Islamic fundamentalists—and implicitly to their co-religionists in Europe. The Iranian Revolution and the civil wars in Lebanon, Palestine, Afghanistan, and Algeria were followed by Islamist acts of terror perpetrated on European soil itself—bombs in French trains and the underground, explosions in synagogues, and attacks on other Jewish targets. Tensions continued to fester throughout the 1990s, were further whipped up after the September 11, 2001, al-Qaeda attacks against the United States, and then exploded, literally, with massive terrorist attacks in Madrid in 2003 and London in 2005. Their international context will be discussed later, when we dissect the most recent Islamism (pp. 127–176) Here we note the relevance of Muslim radicalization for Europe's deteriorating majority-minority relations.

Lately, indeed, the discourse of "historical enmity" is being strengthened, and a vicious cycle has opened where Islamist and anti-Muslim propaganda reinforce each other. Islamic insistence on the *hijab* in French public schools, the struggle unleashed by Muslim groups in Great Britain to ban Salman Rushdie's *The Satanic Verses* (because its Anglo-Indian author supposedly insulted the Prophet Muhammad), and similar incidents put the Muslim minority in an unflattering light. The activities of fringe Islamist terrorist groups only reinforce the prevailing image of a retrograde Islam. Thus rhetoric has grown more virulent over the last decade, feeding xenophobic and far-Right violence against Muslims. The most shocking incident occurred in 1993 when German neo-Nazis attacked a Turkish pension in Solingen, killing five. In France, the *Front National* of Jean-Marie Le Pen, who promotes the obligatory repatriation of three million *Maghrebines,* won a sixth of the votes in the 2002 presidential elections. The *Front National*'s counterparts include the *Vlaams Blok* (since 2004, *Vlaams Belang,* Flemish Interest) in Flanders, the German *Republikaner,* and the Austrian *Freiheitspartei* (Party of Freedom). Similar movements are active in Britain, Holland, Sweden, and elsewhere. Attempts to organize antiracist solidarity movements with the Left, such as the French *beurs'* SOS Racism, are rather unimpressive in comparison.

To their rejection, European Muslims respond with the myth of the historical enmity of the infidel toward Islam. In their imagination, discrimination against Muslims in Europe mirrors non-Muslim indifference to the dead in Bosnia and Chechnya, Western complicity with Zionism, Judeo-Christian plots to recolonize the Middle East, and the like. Muslim conspiracy theories are no less counterfactual than those of the Islamophobes. Unsurprisingly, Osama bin Laden's message finds a sympathetic hearing among some of Europe's uprooted Muslim youth. However, in the end, demography primes culture— Europe's (post-) Christian majority and its Muslim and (partially) re-Islamizing minority are both bound up in the same vicious cycle of an aging continent. In order to keep up its productivity and guarantee an income to its vast nonproductive sectors, the old continent needs immigration, yet it hates the immigrants. The ambivalence remains.

America

America's Muslim communities share some characteristics with their European counterparts. With the exception of the nearly exterminated Native Americans, *all* inhabitants were immigrants to the continent. Some African slaves were Muslims, but the history of Islam in the New World really starts in the twentieth century with the arrival of Middle Eastern immigrants and with the conversion to Islam of many American Blacks. The United States currently has the continent's largest Muslim population—between four and six million— whose life experiences constitute a spectrum that ranges from immigrant integration efforts to Black self-segregation.[6] Canada has an immigrant community of some quarter million, mostly of Indian origin. Latin America has an estimated two million Muslims.

The United States: Muslim Immigrants and the Nation of Islam

Islam in the United States consists of two groups: immigrants from the Islamic world, and Blacks who converted. The immigration of merchants and laborers of Lebanese, Syrian, and Palestinian origin predates 1900; Yemenites and other Middle Easterners followed somewhat later. Although the newcomers spread all over the country, certain concentrations are still in evidence, as around the auto-manufacturing city of Detroit, Michigan. This first wave was well on its way to assimilation when the Asian Exclusion Law was revoked in the 1960s, opening the doors for a second wave. A significant number of Muslim professionals settled in the United States, many from the Indian subcontinent. Among these were Muslims whose religiosity would reinvigorate the country's existing Muslim community.

The other component of U.S. Islam consists of two or three million members of the Nation of Islam and its branches. Black Muslims are part of a wider Black social-religious movement that reacted against the accommodationist and pacific emancipation campaigns linked to the struggles of Martin Luther King. On the margins of the mainstream civil rights movement—which proposed to improve the Blacks' condition through action in common with progressive Whites, and ideally would lead to the Blacks' absorption into White society and values—there had always existed an alternative, autonomist tendency, opposed to accommodation with the former slaveholders, and emphasizing Black particularism.

At the turn of the twentieth century, Marcus Garvey had been that trend's most vocal exponent. In the 1920s, Wallace Fard Muhammad, who had for some time been close to Garvey, proclaimed himself to be the incarnation of Allah and started to preach the "Lost and Found Nation of Islam." Blacks, he explained, would achieve redemption by embracing their Moorish-African roots and thus overtake the Whites. This new religion—rather remote from normative Islam—gained some following in the ghettoes of the North. Wallace disappeared mysteriously in 1934. The mantle of leadership then fell on the shoulders of Elijah Muhammad, who went on to found a series of militantly anti-White and anti-Christian Black mosques. His was a vision of Whites as "devils" who had used Christianity as a trick to enslave the Blacks—returning to the Nation of Islam would allow Blacks to redeem their own lost sheep and inherit the earth.

A new radical turn occurred with the activism of Malcolm X, who called for total segregation and an independent Black state within the United States. Internal feuds precipitated Malcolm's assassination in 1965. In the meantime, a process of retrieval into Islamic orthodoxy of the Nation of Islam had already set in. In the 1970s, Elijah's son Warith Deen Muhammad, with the aid of Saudi instructors, transformed the radical sect into a recognized part of the Sunni world. Not all have followed this track. Louis Farrakhan leads a schism that holds fast to the Nation of Islam's original theology.

A figure with nationwide outreach, Farrakhan has become controversial because of his anti-Semitic statements. However, his commitment to social integration and emphasis on family values, which addresses particularly young, poor Blacks, cannot be doubted. For its thousands of participants, Farrakhan's 1995 Million Man March constituted a moment of commitment with responsibility. The Nation of Islam thus presents a multifaceted phenomenon. The rate of Islamization continues to be higher among Blacks than among other groups. However, Latinos and Whites are also converting to Islam—there may be 100,000 White converts to Islam in the United States.

Despite some similarities, the American scene differs from Europe's. The U.S. government never attempted to control its Muslim population as European governments have. There exists an extensive degree of Muslim self-organization, characteristic of the country's self-help tradition. Furthermore, most of North America's Muslims (except for Blacks) are not poor. There are Muslim doctors, engineers, and academicians, making a good part of U.S. Islam solidly middle-class.

The U.S. Constitution establishes an absolute separation between state and religion. Civil society's self-organization and nonintervention by the state are considered self-evident principles. Socially, the United States is a much less secular society than Western Europe, and the tendency toward secularization is counteracted by a contemporary return to religion. Islam is just one religion among many. Muslims have mosques, schools, and journals. The variety of currents and the diversity of messages are viewed as normal—at least within today's multicultural social diversity, which has become the dominant societal model. Its predecessor, the model of Judeo-Christian civilization, views the United States as the trans-Atlantic continuation (or culmination) of European culture, and recognizes its authentic roots as Protestantism, Catholicism, and Judaism. However, by basing the collective identity of the U.S. melting-pot nation on Anglo-Saxon superiority, the dominant culture discriminated against other religions and ethnicities.

Nowadays many other fragments of the nation are demanding recognition of their identities, leading to a proliferation of "hyphenated Americans": Irish-Americans, Polish-Americans, and among many others, Muslim-Americans. Incorporating new elements, including Islamic ones, has obvious advantages for social cohesion, but also has its drawbacks. From the point of view of society, celebrating and cultivating partial identities may create problems. Allocating public monies for compensation and reparation purposes has led to a proliferation of affirmative actions. This promotes a culture of entitlement and sometimes-exaggerated complaints and claims. Yet for those who do not view their own culture as just one element in a plurality of others, multiculturalism, with its cultural relativism and rejection of any hierarchy, implies a dangerous dilution of "the one truth." This is the case with Christian fundamentalists and Islamists, the latter an active and vocal minority within American Islam.

Islamophobia in the United States

The decline of the old white Anglo-Saxon Protestant (WASP) elite's supremacy has fed fundamentalist reactions, in particular in the conservative U.S. Bible Belt. Rejection of Islam is part of Christian fundamentalist ideology, and clashes with the widespread Islamophile trend in modernist churches. Protestant fundamentalisms also exist in Europe and Latin America, although they have not gained comparable public influence there. In the United States, however, fundamentalists control a great variety of churches, and include a significant parcel of the population. Not a few are Islamophobic, and share with their Islamic opposite number a Manichean vision of reality as realms of absolute good and evil. Based on their literal reading of the Bible, Christian fundamentalists reject modernity—no sex before marriage, abortion, alcohol, gambling, or other illicit pleasures. Permissiveness is blamed for the nation's presumed decadence and decline. Instead, they promote a return to family values, hard work, religiosity, and often, patriotism. They share as well a millenarian vision of Christ's imminent Second Coming. Catastrophes that will spare only the elect minority will announce God's Kingdom on Earth and the end of history.

Similarities and differences between Christian and Islamic fundamentalism will be analyzed below. Here we point out the religious, ethnic, and terrorist dimensions of fundamentalism's anti-Muslim animus.

1. **Religious anti-Muslimism** views Islam as false belief *par excellence* and proposes to convince Muslims of their "error." Therefore it adopts a theologically hostile approach to Muslims within the United States, and actively evangelizes abroad. Protestant fundamentalism makes the Second Coming contingent upon the prior conversion of the Jews, which conversion depends on their return to the Promised Land. This eschatological view leads to pro-Israel positions. Protestant fundamentalists in the United States constitute some of Israel's most enthusiastic supporters, just as fundamentalist Muslims are its most implacable adversaries.

2. **Cultural xenophobia** is one root of Islamophobia. Demonization of Islam and "the Orient" has in the United States the same sources as in Europe. Stereotypes are reproduced by popular culture, as in Hollywood movies from "The Sheik" Rudolph Valentino to the Palestinian terrorists of *Black Saturday*, and feed into existing xenophobic, anticommunist, racist, and anti-Semitic traditions. Since the end of the Cold War, such negativity has been primarily projected on Islam. (Demographic Islamophobia of the European kind is less evident in the United States, where illegal immigration is more diffuse and has a Latin, rather than Arab, color. Nevertheless, the belief in North American white cultural superiority, often mixed with isolationism, continues to be strongly held.)

3. Finally, the fear of terror. Since September 11, 2001, **"security Islamophobia"** has been more present in the United States than in Europe, which has suffered less from Islamist than from autochthonous terrorism (e.g., from the Basque ETA, the Irish IRA, the German Baader-Meinhof group, and the Italian Red Brigades). Since the United States has reached the status of the world's foremost power, it has become the preferred target of violent Islamists, who are opposed to both its geopolitical supremacy and its "decadent" cultural invasion.

Viewed from a global perspective, al-Qaeda's attack against the New York World Trade Center and the Pentagon was only the climax of a series of ever more audacious attempts against U.S. interests and symbols around the world. In its impact, however, 9/11 eclipsed all others because it violated U.S. territory and because of its horrific human toll. This act of war of Islamism's most extremist wing against Western civilization as such awakened a very strong reaction in U.S. foreign policy. In the United States, the "clash of civilizations" is understood as a threat coming from abroad, although with domestic repercussions. Attacks against mosques and Islamic cultural centers had been made before, as part of a nativistic antiforeigner trend. However, such incidents tend to proliferate in times of tension, and quite a few occurred in the wake of the September 11 attacks. President George W. Bush's visit to a mosque just one week later was an attempt to show that the U.S. government rejected the facile identification of all Muslims as inherently extremist and violent. Taken as a whole, however, U.S. Muslims have at their disposal more efficient resources to react than do their European counterparts. An active Islamic lobby (shading off into the Arab lobby) promotes equal treatment and tries to balance both Jewish and fundamentalist Protestant influences, especially concerning the issue of Palestine.

Mention should be made, finally, of **Latin American** Islam, whose principal centers are in Argentina and Brazil. Squeezed between the twin pressures of an antagonistic Catholic Church on the one hand, and a popular culture uncomfortable with Islamic puritanism on the other, Latin American Islam has long kept a low profile. Except for descendants of Indian and Malay indentured workers in the Guyanas, concentrated Muslim communities are the exception. The spreading out of *Turco* (mostly Lebanese and Syrian Arab) peddlers and shopkeepers was uncongenial to their survival as a solid community, although individual Muslim immigrants generally did well. In fact, most Arabs migrating to the Americas are Christians. Recently, there has been some Islamic awakening, but overall, Latin America remains the continent that is least responsive to Islamic concerns.

While Islam's reaction to the West in the West has been and continues to be mostly hostile, re-Islamization is one opportunity to construct plural identities, a trend that may lead to a reinterpretation of Islam that is more compatible with modernity, including re-evaluating taboo subjects such as democracy, equality for women, and coexistence with non-Islamic civilizations.[7] Moreover, Western Muslims' efforts address not just the West, but the wider Islamic world. In principle they might incubate a freer way of thinking that in Islam's core countries is still restricted and repressed. Nascent Western *ijtihad* could take up a privileged place. One must wait and see whether the rest of Islam will heed the call to dialogue.

THE OTHER IN ISLAM

4

Minorities and Women

Islam emphasizes the equality before God of all its believers. Three groups, however, have historically been selected for less-than-equal treatment: slaves, non-Muslims, and women. While slavery is by and large history, the position of women and of non-Muslims (and of Muslim dissidents) continues to be a main bone of contention between Islamic society and modernity.

Slaves

Islam attenuated but did not prohibit slavery, and introduced rules for the humane treatment of captives. Although males were routinely castrated in the main slaving centers, slaves enjoyed in general a much better life than they had in Greek-Roman antiquity, or much more recently in the Americas under "Christian" powers. Slaves were rarely exploited in plantation-type agriculture, but served either as guards or soldiers. (Sultans considered them as more loyal than Muslim aristocrats; some grew into *Mamluk* slave aristocracies that eventually controlled states and developed their own dynasties.) Others—eunuchs and concubines—served as domestic personnel. Theoretically, neither Muslims nor *dhimmis* could be enslaved, so Muslims had to come by their slaves through war or purchase. In the Golden Age the human

merchandise was most often Slavs, Central Asian Turks (prized for
their martial qualities), or Africans from *Bilad al-Sudan*, the "Land of
the Blacks." In the later Middle Ages, however, conversion of the first
to Christianity and of the second to Islam turned provisioning problematic, leaving only Black polytheists as a reliable source. In the sixteenth
and seventeenth centuries, Ottoman expansion kept the slaves coming
from the Caucasus, but eventually this source also dried up. Abolition
prevailed in the Ottoman Empire in the nineteenth century, mainly
under Western pressure; much later in Arabia. Nowadays, slavery sub-
sists semi-clandestinely in isolated regions such as Mauritania.

Non-Muslims

Muslim treatment of non-Muslims is a topic of polemics. Some have
idealized Jewish-Christian-Muslim coexistence in the Abbasid Middle
East or medieval Spain to the status of a golden legend of "tolerance
being part of Arab culture." Detractors have painted a countermyth,
the black legend of intolerant Islam.[1] Both versions have their political usefulness, and both are exaggerated. Generalizing across fourteen centuries and three continents is a problematic proposition, so
great is the variation in situations. Comparatively speaking, the experience of non-Muslim minorities was far from negative.

Like all sacred books, the Qur'an contains exhortations to both militancy and tolerance. Verses enjoining tolerance include "Unto you your
religion, and unto me my religion" (106:9), and "There is no compulsion
in religion" (2:256).[2] From the outset, Islam confronted the dilemma of
Judaism and Christianity, its "ancestral" religions, which it could neither deny nor accept as equal partners without calling its own veracity
into question. The result was a permanent tension between fanaticism
and pluralism. A reasonable treatment prevailed most of the time,
although it would be anachronistic to refer to this as modern tolerance.
In exchange for disarmament, paying the *jizya*, and certain disqualifications (distinctive dress, prohibition against building new churches, etc.),
dhimmis enjoyed wide autonomy and could enter nearly all professions.
However, acceptance was frequently tinged with contempt, opportunity
with insecurity. Tolerance was best in periods of the greatest Muslim
power but tended to diminish over time, *vis-à-vis* both *dhimmis* and
heterodox Muslims. Strictly speaking, the latter were apostates—a
crime punishable by death, although real theological persecutions
were rare. The pressure was more commonly on orthopraxis (right
behavior) than on orthodoxy (right thinking).

The Ottomans went furthest in formalizing the status of minorities in *millets*, the self-governing community churches of the Greek

Orthodox, Armenians, Jews, and others. In the long term, however, institutionalized internal fragmentation put the Empire at a disadvantage against Europe's more homogeneous ethnic-territorial states. By the nineteenth century, some minorities controlled substantial segments of the Ottoman economy. Thanks to their familiarity with the religion and proficiency in languages, they became the intermediaries and interpreters in French, Austrian, or Russian service, through whom Western influence flowed into the Empire. After the edicts of 1854 and 1869 that practically abolished the discriminatory effects of *millets* and established civil equality, ecclesiastical authorities lost control over their congregationists, and the minorities modernized more rapidly than their Sunni neighbors. Some became ostentatious, overbearing, or nationalistic. Some demanded greater community autonomy, others special privileges, still others independence. Sunni majorities increasingly saw them as diasporas of opportunistic aliens in collusion with the infidel foreigners. Tolerance evaporated as community tensions increased. This deterioration has continued through the present. Coexistence is today far more difficult in the Middle East than it was in earlier epochs. In Saudi Arabia there is no official room for Christians and Shiites; in Pakistan, they are subject to pogroms. In Shiite Iran, Sunnis and Bahá'is are the victims of discrimination. And nearly all hate Jews. The West has long since overtaken Islam in tolerance.

A particularly nasty aspect of intolerance in the Islamic world, indeed, is its growing anti-Semitism. Though theological antagonism has from the beginning been present (and mutual), Jews were generally well integrated—Muslim Spain, Fatimid Egypt, and the sixteenth-century Ottomans are rightly considered showcases. In other areas and eras, the Jewish lot under Islam was less rosy, probably worst in Yemen and Persia. The nineteenth century brought emancipation and modernization, but also growing hatred. However, modern anti-Semitism only entered Muslim (especially Arab) minds in the last century, in connection with the Palestine conflict. In the 1930s and 1940s, Nazi influence introduced racial anti-Semitism. Although Jewish communities have since virtually disappeared from the Arab East (most having moved to Israel), anti-Semitism has only grown uglier, with conspiracy theories attributing Israel's success to the "inherently evil" Jews.

Women

Whether as sensual harem odalisque or victim of genital mutilation and oppression, Muslim women have long been objects of Western (male) fascination and fantasy, symbols of an unreachable Otherness. Although the images are exaggerations, "woman" and "sex" are not in fact neutral categories in Islam, but objects of much attention and extensive, if not always unambiguous, regulation. In contrast to Western modernity, committed (at least in theory) to civil equality between men and women, Islam places woman in subordination to man. Such inequality, found in most premodern societies, reflects the social reality that gave rise to Islam. Biological realities dictated a labor division that allocated to women the task of maternity; fecundity considered a group resource not unlike that of cattle, wheat, or money. In comparison to sedentary societies, the nomadic Bedouin tribes offered women a slightly better position, and the Qur'an further improved on it. In fact, women's position was initially better under Islam than in most other traditional civilizations. Women were, and are, not chattel, but juridical persons with a right to possess property.

The groom pays a *mahr,* or bride price, upon marriage; this remains the wife's property in case of divorce. Women have clearly established inheritance rights (half those of man); polygyny is limited to four spouses; in litigation, the testimony of two women is equal to that of one man; husbands have a limited right to physically chastise their wives. These rules were probably more progressive than the seventh-century peninsular Arab society that gave birth to them. However, their inclusion in the Qur'an and perpetuation in *hadith* has created problems. For although Islamic societies developed in myriad forms and are subject to global influences, for pious Muslims, textual norms remain unassailable. Initially women performed a variety of secular and religious functions. Documents portray *muslimas* as companions of the Prophet, political leaders, religious interpreters, Shiite martyrs, mystics, `ulama, waqf* managers, entrepreneurs, and many other positive role models (though also as witches, whores, or slanderers). Over time, however, women's position declined. Sayings attributed to Muhammad, such as "a people whose affairs are ruled by women will not prosper," or that women are spiritually and intellectually inferior, were used to justify their exclusion.[3] Islam's erstwhile asset has become a liability. Now that the Islamic world is affected by global pressures for emancipation, the debate on the role of women has become one of the main sites for the "clash of civilizations."

Sexual Segregation

In order to "protect" men from sexual temptation, the practice of segregation started early. So as not to be distracted, men pray separately.

The practice of imposing the veil or *hijab* (scarf), viewed currently in fundamentalist circles as the hallmark of the observant *muslima*, may have started as a Byzantine sign marking off "free" women from slaves and concubines. Originally no more than a matter of etiquette for the Prophet's own wives, the *hijab* subsequently reached the point of complete sexual segregation.[4] In Pakistan and Afghanistan, *purdah* (literally, curtain) requires covering a woman's entire body and face whenever she leaves her home. Within her own home, she uncovers only in front of her husband or *mahrams* (relatives whom she cannot marry). Traditionally, the ideal woman would through all her adult years leave her home only twice: on the day of her wedding, and on the day of her funeral—completely veiled on both occasions.[5] But this ideal woman was urban and well-to-do, the wife of someone who could afford to relieve her of the burden of work. Rural Muslim women's lifestyle would generally be more arduous, but also more equal.

The deterioration in women's status has continued in recent times. Though socioeconomic factors in Muslim women's subordination parallel those of women in other pre-industrial and traditional societies, in some ways the Muslim woman cannot be compared to her counterparts in traditional China, Hindu India, or medieval Christendom. Her more extreme isolation and more strictly controlled sexuality cannot be reduced to material factors, but follows from a psychological contradiction between, on one hand, the strong association of woman and sexuality, and on the other, the dependence of male honor on female chastity. Loss of such control is then viewed as both danger to social order and attack on masculine identity—a contradiction that can only be resolved by locking away the object of desire.

Many authors have pointed out that in the Middle East, women are considered as objects of masculine lust, and that sex is primarily associated with the female. In contrast to Christianity, Islam approves of sex in and for itself. Islamic sources speak of coitus as an act of harmony with the cosmos. Celibacy is forbidden; there is nothing in Islam to recall the asceticism characteristic of Christianity. Sex means reproduction, and precondition of parental pride (with a strong preference for male offspring), but sensual pleasure is viewed as legitimate in itself.[6] However, sexuality is also a dangerous antisocial and chaotic force; hence its "imprisonment" within the confines of marriage (and consequently the rejection of contraception, abortion, homosexuality, and other "perversions"). In practice, moreover, marriages are economic alliances between families rather than bonds between couples. Most marriages are arranged, often without the future spouses ever having met. Although consent is necessary, forced marriages still occur, as does the wife's seclusion in that part of the house especially appointed for her but prohibited (*haram*) for all men save her own husband: the harem. Nonetheless, the vast majority of marriages have always been monogamous because Islam conditions polygamy on equal treatment among all of a husband's wives. Most men could never afford the upkeep of multiple spouses and their children. Polygamy is still practiced in the Arabian Peninsula but has been outlawed in Tunisia and Turkey.

In the Islamic view, sexuality emanates from the woman. She is seen as active, possessive, and irresistibly attractive. Women are associated with *fitna*, the destructive force of seduction. This is the same word used to describe the fratricidal civil wars that tore the Islamic community apart after the time of Muhammad. Sex outside marriage is equated with debauchery and corruption. In order to maintain his wife's virtue, a husband must therefore keep his wife sexually satisfied, lest she gratify her desire outside the marriage and destroy the family's honor. Adultery is a crime against religion, traditionally punishable by a hundred lashes or death by stoning—penalties that Islamists are eager to restore. The transgression's severity, however, necessitates the testimony of four male (or eight female) witnesses. Transgressing the rule of purity—and even the mere suspicion of having done so—constitutes a social disgrace for a man and his family that only the death of the "criminal" woman can expiate. "Honor crimes" still occur, and law and social custom tend to pardon the perpetrator.

At the same time, no social stigma or juridical sanction attaches to male adultery, provided it happens outside of the home. Male sexual desire and prowess are considered normal and admirable. Traditionally a man could sexually satisfy himself outside of marriage with a slave or concubine; this has become in our days an unfeasible solution. This leaves prostitution, which is illegal, although only the prostitute risks punishment. Gender segregation has led to the growth of separate male and female social spheres. Outside the circle of their intimate relatives, women socialize only with other women; their sons and husbands only with other men. At least, this was the situation until modernity's destabilizing forces started to break established patterns. Three conclusions follow. First, Middle Eastern and many other Muslim societies were traditionally marked by strong sexual tension. The origin of this is debatable, but separation of the sexes was perpetuated from generation to generation. The ever unreachable Other explains much of the fascination with the "promiscuity" of modern Western society, which has created a strong ambivalence among many Muslims and, on the part of the fundamentalists among them, aggressive rejection.

Second, woman's role in Islam reflects the values of tribal society, not strictly religious values. Qur'anic rules circumscribing women's behavior are few and open to interpretation. However, Islam, in lieu of transcending tribalism, built some tribal values into its authoritative sources, and then exported them to the societies it conquered, influenced, or converted. Hence, societal norms are interwoven with religious commands. The area of overlap is wide and questionable enough to allow contemporary feminist Muslim thinkers to proffer more liberal and woman-friendly reinterpretations of the sources.[7]

Third, contact with the West and the modernization of Islamic society and economy have led to much more intensive and less controlled interaction between men and women than was customary in the traditional world of Islam. This causes psychological confusion: one more stimulus for Islamist reactions.

The Challenge of Modernization

Colonization, and then independence, created a new set of problems. Urbanization, attending school, employment, physical and social mobility, and the like expose young women to ever more contact with men outside of their *mahrams*. While this contact was traditionally kept to the absolute minimum, public transportation, coeducational colleges, factories, and offices make it unavoidable. Modernity breaks the simultaneously protective and oppressive cocoon. A new psychological assertiveness is in evidence, expressed in demands for freedom to learn, work outside home, choose a spouse, control her own body, and participate politically. However, for the erstwhile masters—men—these new women constitute a threat. Muslim men lose certainties without gaining correspondingly. Educated and assertive women are competitors in tight job markets as well as challengers of the structure of domination itself. The modern Muslim woman has come to symbolize a number of "dangers," and is seen as conspiring with non-Islamic minorities and with the West.

There have been two reactions: (1) religious and secular modernists approve of woman's emancipation, provided necessary precautions are taken to safeguard their chastity, the social order, the dignity of the nation, and religious dictates; (2) Islamists regard women's entry into the public realm as an affront to the God-given social order, and hence attempt to undo their emancipation. Class antagonism also plays an unspoken role, because emancipated women are often from the educated and privileged classes, in contrast to their fundamentalist counterparts. Nowadays, however, ever more women are joining Islamism.

Liberal and nationalist Arab and Turkish authors first demanded equality for women in the late nineteenth century, arguing that their second-class position deprived society of valuable human resources. `Abduh opposed polygamy on the grounds that the condition of equal treatment extended also to the realm of feelings, and that polygamy was thus humanly impossible to fulfill. Muslim women from Egypt and other countries proposed models for full female participation in public life without "descending to the level of promiscuity" that Muslim observers imputed to the West (too-short dresses, mixed dancing, etc.).[8] Moderate feminists cited feminine role models from the *hadiths*, Sufism, and female leaders. Nationalist regimes such as the Ba`thists took radical measures to emancipate women; consequently, their position is better today in Syria (and was better in Iraq under Saddam Hussein) than in Egypt or Jordan, to say nothing of Saudi Arabia. More recently, feminists such as Egyptian doctor Nawal El Saadawi and Moroccan sociologist Fatima Mernissi have broken taboos by opening discussions on intimate subjects such as sexuality; however, their reach is limited to literate elites. A strict Islamist such as the Pakistani Abu al-Ala al-Mawdudi, on the other hand, insisted on total *purdah*, to control "indecency."

Islamism and Women

The status of women is at the center of the culture wars under way in the Islamic world. Islamist discourse contrasts Islam's respect for woman with the indignity she suffers in the West as the object of lust and commerce. Hers is the sphere of motherhood and of transmission of Islamic values to children—a biological determination that limits her public role. Female participation varies widely among Islamist movements, from outstanding in the social, propagandistic, and even military fields (e.g., in Shiite Islamism), to complete exclusion in Taliban Afghanistan. Western fashion is rejected everywhere: "sexual exhibitionism" (as commonly portrayed in Western media) would immediately brand a Muslim woman a whore, destroy her reputation, and place her in physical danger. For while the visible woman projects for many men the mirage of easy prey, for Islamists she symbolizes corruption. Hundreds of women have had acid thrown into their faces or been attacked merely for showing their hair.[9] The less attention a woman calls to her sexuality, the easier her access to the public space—hence hair cover and modest overcoats (for Shiites, the *chador*). The Islamist "uniform" discourages flirtation, emphasizes inviolability, and marks a woman as devoted to God. Moreover, the ostensibly defeminized woman is a vital weapon for Islamist movements. In 1978, female participation in mass demonstrations was crucial in the victory of the Islamic revolution in Iran; in the 1980s, Lebanese Hizbullah women were among the first suicide terrorists; in the Israeli-Palestinian arena, Hamas sisters have followed in their footsteps since the 1990s. Female support for a cause that appears only to perpetuate female oppression remains, however, something of a mystery in Western eyes.

One of Islamism's constant demands has been for men and women to occupy separate spaces in the public sphere. Sexuality must be channeled into the religiously sanctioned domestic and matrimonial sphere of privacy. Treatment of women varies, however, among Islamist regimes. Thus, while both in Iran and in Taliban Afghanistan, prostitutes were executed and public expression of sensuality (e.g., makeup) prohibited, the scope of permitted public activity differs dramatically. In Iran, women are juridical persons and citizens with voting rights; work in the professions; and take part in most public functions, in politics, and even in sports (duly shielded from male eyes).[10] In Afghanistan, on the other hand, each woman was legally submitted to a man and wore the *burqa,* covering everything except the eyes. Girls were forbidden to go to school, their mothers to work outside the home. Women could appear in public only in the company of a male chaperone.

On women's issues, therefore, Islam accommodates a gamut of positions. Like many other societies, the Islamic world traditionally viewed sexuality as an uncontrollable and disruptive natural force. (According to an Arab proverb, "Whenever a man and a woman meet, Satan is third among them.")[11] Women's segregation and the strict control of their sexuality were among the external means of dealing with this demon, but modernization has made such a strategy ever more problematic. Modern society internalizes these controls. The Islamic gaze is not used to Western permissiveness and is sensitive to its defects: divorce, fatherless children, alcoholism, violence, and suicide are among the symptoms of "Western decadence." The puritanism of Islamism is one way of dealing with this tension.

PART II

Today

ISLAM AND (POST)MODERNITY 5

What Is Fundamentalism?

The Islamic world today is in turmoil, and its consequences affect the rest of the world. Although many contradictory currents tug at them, Muslims worldwide are generally returning to religion. Within this trend, a growing minority identifies with a politicized, anti-Western, and antimodern reading of their religion, called Islamism. Among the Islamists, a minority endorses the use of violence and terrorism against the West to attain their goals.

Fundamentalism as such is a religious movement that started a century ago among American Protestants. Although journalistic use has given it wide acceptance, "Islamic fundamentalism" is thus an incorrect neologism; this label also applies to similar movements in other religions. Alternative terms, however, are little better. *Intégrisme*, a word that French authors prefer, copies a Catholic phenomenon. "Political Islam" and "Islamic revivalism" are acceptable, but limited. Others simply use "radical" or "militant" Islam. In Arabic *islamiyya* is used, simplest and best: **Islamism**. (*Al-usuliyya al-islamiyya*, a literal translation of "Islamic fundamentalism," is also used.) This book uses both terms interchangeably.

Fundamentalism in the West is an illegitimate grandchild of modernity. Modernity is associated with the twin political and economic transformations that began in Europe a little over two centuries ago: the French Revolution and the Industrial Revolution. The former, and the Enlightenment before it, had put religion on the defensive with their criticism of clerical abuse and hypocrisy, and with scientific criticism of the biblical narrative. Industrialization and urbanization dissolved traditional social bonds, hierarchies, and certainties. Just as the world was becoming more unpredictable, faith was losing credibility. As faith lost appeal, atheism (and alternative religions) gained ground. The most successful new faith was faith in science: if it did not promise eternal life, it demonstrably seemed to make life on earth better and more comprehensible. The mainstream Protestant churches (and later, Roman Catholicism) tried to defend themselves with modernism. The modernist reaction "proved" there was no real breach between science and the Bible, but came at a price: the personal Creator now became a distant Cosmic Watchmaker with little interest in His creation. This led to a widespread sense of spiritual abandonment, vacuum, and loss of community.

Malaise grew throughout the twentieth century, as the promises of reason, science, and technology started to disappoint. Formerly sheltered and controlled, individuals now had to make an array of sometimes agonizing choices. The modernity that had brought penicillin, an end to slavery, mass literacy, the computer, and space travel was increasingly also blamed for world wars, pollution, weapons of mass destruction, divorce, and broken families. Disenchantment prepared the way for fiercer antimodern reactions. Besides, entire social strata were suffering rather than benefiting from modernization—farmers losing out to mechanization, shopkeepers battling supermarkets, servants and other personnel whom centralization and the decline of nobility were turning redundant, geographically peripheral populations, and all those (mostly conservatives) who had kept an edge over the poor by dint of prestige symbols. For all of them, modernization meant not emancipation, but decline. Those longing for the "good old times" became susceptible to ideologies promising a return to certainty—secular nationalisms and fascism, and religious fundamentalisms. Fascism died an ignominious death in 1945, but fundamentalism is alive and kicking.

If religious modernism is the child of modernity, fundamentalism—which from the late nineteenth century on started to react against modernism—must be its rebellious grandchild. Fundamentalism is an antimodern product of modernity. In Protestantism, it calls for a return to the "fundamentals" of faith (such as the Bible's inerrancy), commitment to a virtuous and frugal life of hard work and family values, and rejection of permissiveness ("sin"). The myriad denominations into which American fundamentalists are subdivided fall outside our scope. Suffice it to say, they had and have remarkable success in their outreach and have grown to include a significant segment of the U.S. population. What all have in common is their critique of secularism.

What makes this discussion relevant to current Islam is that modernization did not limit itself to the West. Its taking by storm the rest of the world has fomented similar reactions everywhere: modernist children, fundamentalist grandchildren. Colonization forced modernization upon the nonwestern world in ever faster and more brutal ways, and without the self-determination and empowerment that it brought in the West. Imperialism entailed oppression—subordination of the colonized society, culture, and economy to the interests of the colonizer. Non-Western societies caught in this maelstrom of Western expansion were forced to reflect on the causes of their defeat, and devise strategies to escape their predicament. The first to do so, in the early eighteenth century, were the Russians, since then split forever between Westernizers and slavophiles. In the nineteenth century, Chinese intellectuals wavered between Neo-Confucian and Western ideals before finally embracing Marxism; Japan opted for defensive modernization; and Hindus, for a middle way. And the Islamic world, traumatized by Western penetration, experimented with a variety of approaches, all of which failed—until it recently turned to fundamentalism. Indeed, despite local variations, there are only two ways of rationalizing defeat: either the civilization of the colonized is, apparently, incapable of withstanding the challenges, or the autochthonous forces are not correctly using their civilizational resources. Each option has strategic consequences. Followers of the first option, the modernists, concluded that in order to retake control of their own destiny, their societies would have to discard tradition and Westernize. Followers of the second option, the traditionalists, reject Western modernization and opt to return to their own roots. Followers of a third way seek to use the best of both orientations: adopt Western techniques, keep one's own culture. Islamic fundamentalism, or Islamism, may be considered a special case of this third formula.

The Three Waves of Islamism

For the Islamic world, colonization meant not just the loss of political and military control, but also the humiliation of a lifestyle that views itself as intrinsically superior to any other. In the Middle East and in

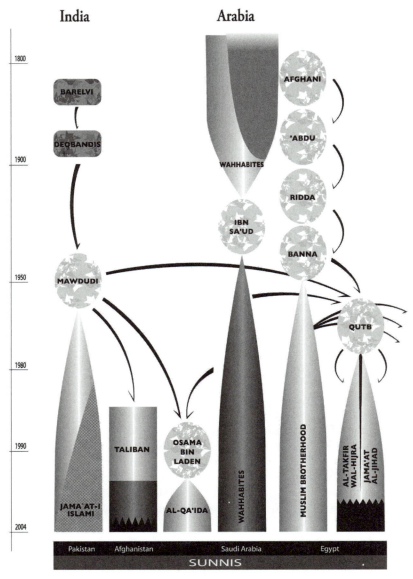

Figure 5.1
The genealogy of Islamism

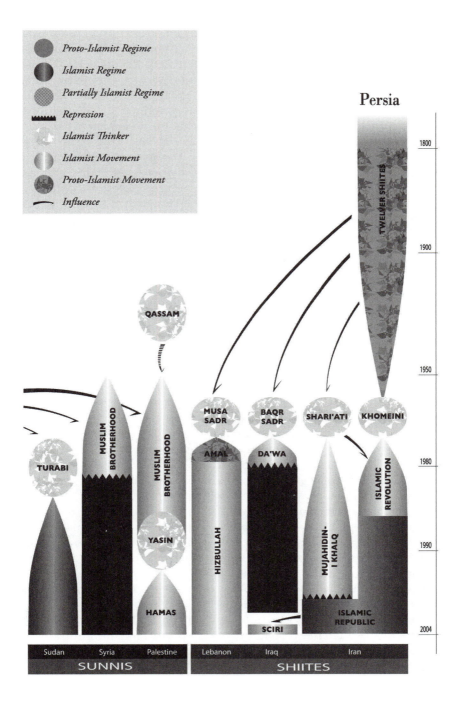

Proto-Islamist Regime
Islamist Regime
Partially Islamist Regime
Repression
Islamist Thinker
Islamist Movement
Proto-Islamist Movement
Influence

Persia

1800

1900

1950

1980

1990

2004

TWELVER SHIITES

QASSAM

TURABI

MUSLIM BROTHERHOOD

MUSLIM BROTHERHOOD

YASIN

HAMAS

MUSA SADR

AMAL

HIZBULLAH

BAQR SADR

DA'WA

SCIRI

SHARI'ATI

MUJAHIDIN-I KHALQ

ISLAMIC REPUBLIC

KHOMEINI

ISLAMIC REVOLUTION

Sudan	Syria	Palestine	Lebanon	Iraq	Iran
SUNNIS			SHIITES		

93

Muslim South and Southeast Asia, the modernizing option manifested itself in Islamic modernism and secular nationalism. In most places, antiscientific traditionalism was easily defeated. Religious modernism may not have run its course, but has had difficulty translating itself into a coherent political program. It is also fair to say that with a few exceptions such as Turkey and Syria, self-contained secular national-ism as a development strategy (though not as a sentiment) is today moribund in the Muslim world. Pan-Arabism and local Arab patrio-tisms in the Arab world, and neo-Persian Pahlevi nationalism in Iran established dictatorships that exploited and oppressed their own popu-lations. In Pakistan, secular nationalism was never an option; in weakly integrated Indonesia, it has from the outset had to contend with the double challenge of regionalism and of Islamic universalism. One should not exaggerate the secular component of these nationalisms—even in their "canonical" version (articulated by a Greek Orthodox Christian, the Syrian Michel `Aflaq), pan-Arabism reserved a special role for Islam as "supreme expression of the Arab spirit" and never attacked it frontally. The intermediary religious option, represented by the modernist Islamic reformism of `Abduh and his disciples, is still very much alive in Pakistan and Indonesia. In the Middle East, how-ever, where it has been instrumentalized by the pseudo-secular state (as in Egypt), modernism has been overtaken by events.

Secular national experiences in the rest of the Arab world reached their zenith in the 1950s and 1960s. As described earlier, the legiti-macy of the statist national development model was weakened by the Arab regimes' impotence against Israel in 1967, by their political ineptitude in dealing with Lebanon's fratricidal war, by squandered oil revenue, and by the decadence of the pan-Arab option in the Iran-Iraq War. What has emerged from these (moral no less than political or military) defeats is an Arab world in crisis. In the breach opened by this crisis, Islamism grows: an antimodern, antisecular, and anti-Western political ideology whose aims are to convert each Muslim into an observant believer, to transform a merely nominally Muslim soci-ety into a religious community organized around service to God, and to establish God's rule over the world. Although Islamism appears to be the dominant, or at least most visible, tendency in today's Islam, it is a new phenomenon. It has evolved over the last few decades in reac-tion to globalizing modernization.

Islamist ideology has crystallized from the 1950s and 1960s on. In Sunnism this occurred through the writings of Pakistani author Abu al-Ala al-Mawdudi and Egyptian ideologue Sayyid Qutb; in Shiism through those of the Iranian ayatollah Ruhollah Khomeini. We may divide fundamentalism into three partially overlapping generations.

The first hit the international scene in the 1970s and 1980s. A second wave in the 1980s culminated in the Iranian Revolution, the assassination of Anwar Sadat, and the appearance of Lebanon's Hizbullah. Yet activity was still limited mostly to Shiite areas in the Middle East.

The last decade of the twentieth century witnessed the start of a third wave, characterized by expansion and much stronger internationalization. Islamism spread rapidly in the wake of the 1991 Gulf War, then became a threat of global proportions with the Algerian civil war, Hamas in the Palestinian territories, the wars of Bosnia and Chechnya, the Taliban in Afghanistan, al-Qaeda's international terrorism, and the rise of Islamist parties and movements in Pakistan, Indonesia, the Central Asian Republics of the former Soviet Union, and elsewhere. The invasion of Iraq in March 2003 may have strengthened this wave. These events are not Islamism's last gasp: Islamic fundamentalism will be with us in the coming years if not decades.

1967–1981: THE FIRST ISLAMIST WAVE 6

بسم الله الرحمن الرحيم Qutb's Egypt and the Sunni Jihad

Today's main fundamentalist Sunni movements are inspired by Egypt's Muslim Brotherhood and the ideas of its principal ideologue, Sayyid Qutb (1906–66). Egypt is thus the best place to start our discussion. Fulcrum of the Middle East and center of the Arab world, Egypt is a very poor country in the grips of an inexorable population explosion. Geography and history created a fairly homogeneous nation that is 90 percent Sunni (the remaining 10 percent being Coptic Christian). This is where Muslim reactions to Western predominance first took shape. `Abduh and Ridda, forerunners of Islamism, formulated their Islamic reform here. With its militant nationalism, Egypt gained its formal independence early, in 1922. It had an active and relatively liberal civil society; but its monarchy depended on British support, and proved corrupt and inefficient—not a force for modernization. The Muslim Brotherhood comprised the right wing of the opposition to government. After the assassination of its founder, Hassan al-Banna, in 1949, it joined the antimonarchical and anti-British revolution of 1952, and then rallied to the new, left-leaning Free Officers' regime.

This flirtation did not endure, though. In 1954, after an attempt on the life of President Gamal Abdel Nasser, the government suppressed the Brotherhood, executed some of its leaders, and jailed others,

Sayyid Qutb among them. His nationalist and pan-Arab course made Nasser a hero in the Arab street from Casablanca to Baghdad. Domestically, though, his socialist state development strategy came at the cost of individual liberties. Egypt turned into a repressive society that abrogated political and religious rights and freedom of expression in the name of the national interest. In 1967 Egypt was for the third time defeated in war against Israel, and again lost the Sinai Peninsula. This defeat became a symbol of the bankruptcy of secular Arab nationalism, and signaled a profound ideological shift in favor of an alternative project—Islamism. Qutb did not live to see the change. Accused again of conspiring against Nasser, he was hanged in 1966.

Sayyid Qutb is Islam's most important fundamentalist thinker, the one who led it in a new direction that was neither traditionalist nor modernist. His life exemplifies the traits of the "marginal man," traits that would be seen again and again among his latter-day followers. A sensitive young man, he had received a traditional religious upbringing, although he was also comfortable with secular culture. Then he went to work as an inspector of education. An unfortunate stay as student in the United States between 1948 and 1951 became his turning point. In California, Qutb was disgusted with Western society's open sexuality, humiliated by its racism, and scandalized with the sympathy for the Zionist cause he encountered everywhere. One may speculate that his violent rejection of Western culture arose from a deeper ambivalence than he realized. However, his rejection of the lifestyle that his generation linked with the West—the one that today's generation associates with globalization—was absolute. His American experience brought Qutb back to religion. Back in Egypt he became a "born-again" Muslim, joined the Muslim Brotherhood, became an activist, was arrested, and spent the better part of the rest of his days in prison. There he evolved into Islamism's most extreme thinker.

Mawdudi's Influence

Qutb was strongly influenced by the writings of Abu al-Ala al-Mawdudi of Pakistan. Mawdudi (1903–79) was educated in the ultraconservative *deobandi* school. In the 1940s and 1950s, he developed five principles that Qutb would later make his own: anti-apology, anti-Westernism, literalism, politicization, and universalism.

The first principle, anti-apology, is related to fundamentalism's self-referential logic: Islam proves and justifies itself, and hence is in no need of either external validation or harmonization with other ideologies. The Qur'an is true because it says that it is God's word. Because Islam is perfect (having been given by God), it needs no adaptation—only the right application. Mawdudi stands in the Indian Islamic tradition: that of an Islam perpetually on the defensive. He imputed the Muslims' political weakness not to their being overly religious or traditionalist, but to being insufficiently so.

Because, as Mawdudi taught, Islam is totally self-sufficient and is different from, incompatible with, and superior to any other religion, one must maintain a barrier between Islam and the non-Muslim world. Islam needs no apology but must counterattack.[1] Among the enemies, the West stands out. Mawdudi criticizes Western intellectual colonization, the corollary of political and military conquest. His anti-Westernism is total, based on its humanism (i.e., its "worship of Man"), which for Mawdudi is the same as *shirk*, or "attributing partners to God"—the supreme sin. Its consequence is depravity (particularly in the sexual sense). Qutb could well identify with Mawdudi's violent rejection.

Literalism is common to all fundamentalisms, whether Islamic or any other. The holy writing must be understood in its literal form (though it may also hide esoteric content over and beyond its evident meaning). Fundamentalists ridicule modernist attempts to soften "hard" verses. If the text sounds illogical, counterintuitive, or antinatural, this only shows the limited capacity of human reason.

Whereas literalism has parallels in Judaism and Christianity, politicization is more specific to Islam—or at least finds its most emphatic expression there. Of course Islam has always had a political aspect. Ideally it does not differentiate between the spiritual and temporal realms. More correctly, Islam sets out to subjugate the latter to the former, and to force the world into the service of the transcendent. This ideal, however, was seldom realized in Islam's history. Even today, it is correct to state that for most Muslims, Islam is a system of cultural symbols rather than a political ideology. After the partition of British India, Pakistani moderates hoped to establish a state based on Islam as a cultural identity. Radicals protested that Islam must not be reduced to a series of mores and customs but demanded an exclusive and total commitment. Hence society would have to be organized around Islam's commands. No one was more radical than Mawdudi, who insisted upon a primarily political Islam. His Islamic (as opposed to Muslim) state would have the Qur'an as constitution; legislation would be limited to the interpretation of *shari`a*; and its president would be a devout Muslim surrounded by an all-Muslim council. Non-Muslims would return to *dhimmi* status, and enjoy only local political rights.

Last, universalism. Everything in Islam, Mawdudi warns, is valid for all human beings. He thus cleanses it of any national, ethnic, or regional connotation, just as he rejects all mystical, magical, and "superstitious" forms of popular Islam. Because it is universally valid,

Islam must be imposed on all. "Very explicitly, for the entire human race, there is only one way of life which is Right in the eyes of God and that is al-Islam," insists Mawdudi.[2] Hence Islam would have to use any available means to shake up the whole world, until *jihad* has entirely Islamized it. Mawdudi wished to convert India to Islam, as a first step to the conversion of all humanity. He only halfheartedly accepted the idea of Pakistan as a separate national home for Indian Muslims.

Sayyid Qutb's Ideology

Qutb viewed the Divine revelation as an internal, immediate, irresistible, and essentially incommunicable irruption of the transcendent.[3] God's presence is the absolute Other whose demands bear only absolute obedience. He accepted Mawdudi's analysis but expanded it to apply his concept of *jihad* to Muslim society itself. Qutb rejects not only the West's "dissolute" and "blasphemous" lifestyle, but equally its government. For democracy, the Western product par excellence, resulted from the Enlightenment's erroneous anthropocentric premise that Man belongs to himself. Habermas's subjectivity principle (i.e., human beings as individuals distinct from their collectivity, and endowed with critical reason that allows them to know themselves, have inherently, because of their human nature, the right to self-determination) is the scaffold on which the whole building of modernity is erected—free thought, human rights, individual liberty, popular sovereignty, and so on.[4] But Qutb rejects this basis: sovereignty does *not* belong to Man but to God alone. The human being is no less *makhluq* (creature) than the rest of creation and has but to serve the Creator. Following Ibn Hanbal, Qutb views man's goal as neither to know nor to love God, but to serve Him. Thus Islamism's first principle is *hakimiyyat Allah*, God-Government.

Since God transmitted once and for all the form of government to Muhammad, there can be no doubt about the principles of political organization; they can be all deduced from the sacred sources. The faithful should model their actions on the Prophet and his Companions who founded the ideal Islamic community—hence *salafiyya*, the imitation of the precursors, the pious *salaf* of Islam's first and greatest generation. Qutb's call for restoration of original Islam is a program for the return to an earlier and better situation. He shares with other fundamentalists a backward-looking utopia. Like them, he is unaware that he is himself the product of the modernity he aspires to overthrow.

Qutb's second step is to lament how the world has lapsed into a new *jahiliyya*, the state of ignorance and false belief that prevailed before Muhammad. The Prophet and the first believers made the necessary efforts (*jihad*) to reverse this situation—they built a society ruled to the last detail by God's will. Since that blessed time, however, much has deteriorated. Qutb observes how even in formally Muslim societies, God's law is disrespected: *shari`a* no longer rules, education focuses on worldly and Western knowledge instead of religious studies, and a shameful ostentation of sensuality has supplanted modesty and self-control. Nor is the situation better in the political field. Instead of an Islamic government that would keep God's command of *taghallub* (the supremacy Muslims are enjoined to keep in the state) and spread Islam to the corners of the earth, an oppressive foreign-inspired government is worshiping the nation instead of God, and lets immorality invade society. The unavoidable conclusion is that such a society, in spite of its nominally Muslim majority and despite preserving some gloss of Islamicity, is no longer Islamic but has reverted to *jahiliyya*. No wonder God abandons those who first abandoned Him: humiliation, poverty, and Israel's victory over vastly superior Arab armies are among His punishments.

This last point remained implicit in Qutb's thought. He died before the catastrophe of the June 1967 War. However, those who let themselves be persuaded by his reasoning perceived in the following years a series of added signs of *jahiliyya*: Anwar Sadat, Nasser's successor, shifted Egypt to a pro-Western position, opened the country to foreign investment, and tried to rescind the economic controls and subsidies that supported the poor. Hotels, banks, and nightclubs (the Mac-Donald'ses of the time) multiplied. While the rich followed Western fashion and female tourists in miniskirts shocked local sensibilities, Egypt's destitute majority barely eked out a living.

In the 1973 war, Egypt had shown sufficient force against Israel for Sadat to travel to the Jewish state and talk peace. Evidently he concluded that Arab honor had been saved, and that his country's development would benefit from peace with its neighbor. However, he offended millions of Egyptians and Muslims around the world, who saw Qutb's dire predictions vindicated. What to do, then? In the third, prescriptive aspect of his theory, Qutb sets out to specify the believer's duty to establish a just order based on God's law: corruption of the current "pseudo-Islamic" polity has reached the point where gradual reform by educational and propagandistic means, as the Muslim Brotherhood preached, would no longer suffice. One must follow a new strategy. At this point radical Islamism wavers between two options: withdrawal or revolutionary action.

The first path suggests "reborn" Muslims shield themselves from their fatally flawed surroundings and "start over," creating their own isolated religious utopia. The choice reminds of the Prophet's *hijra* from Mecca to Medina, which had also been an act of separation from evil. Attempts to establish puritanical countercultures in the desert were nothing new—Ibn Khaldun had observed a similar dynamic in the fourteenth century, and Wahhabites repeated the pattern in the Arabia of the 1920s. The hope was always that religious nuclei would radiate throughout the whole of society. Qutb, however, opted for a second alternative: *jihad*. Where *jahiliyya* is so powerful, only the most forceful response, going well beyond mere defense of the faith, is in order. The second path, then, is that of militant violence against society's very base. An absolute and irreversible commitment will drive the faithful to revolutionary action for the sake of Islamic transformation. And in God's service, the believer may be called upon to sacrifice his or her life and become *shahid,* or martyr—"witness" for God.

Qutb thus demanded *jihad* not just against pagans and infidels but also against a government that was Muslim but not Islamic, and hence illegitimate. He based his reasoning on the theology of the medieval theologian Ibn Taymiyya (1263–1328), an extremist Hanbalite born shortly after the massacre of Baghdad and deeply aggrieved by the decline of Islam. Ibn Taymiyya attributed Islam's weakness to the seeping in of theological novelties, and called for stricter boundaries between believers and infidels. Living under a pro-Mongol, heretical but formally Muslim government, Ibn Taymiyya was also the first to theorize *jihad* against false leadership. He declared such *jihad* to be no longer a collective duty that a restricted group could execute in the name of all, but an individual obligation incumbent upon every Muslim. Qutb updated Ibn Taymiyya's justification for struggle against a Muslim authority that no longer fulfilled its Islamic obligation—essentially a brief for tyrannicide.[5] The only missing link was to determine the authority that could legitimately declare the ruler an apostate. In the Sunni framework, anyone in the community called by God will do. In fact, it did not take long for followers to start practicing Qutb's precepts.

Egypt between Jihadist Terror and Islamizing Accommodation

Nasser's repression split Egypt's fundamentalists. Most Muslim Brethren abandoned revolution and committed to moderate educational and political activity, hoping to turn society around in the long run. Hassan Hudhaibi, one of the Muslim Brotherhood's "regretful," declared that only God was able to judge a person's (or the whole *umma's*) Islamic faith. No mere mortal could arrogate himself such judgment. Meanwhile, however, the martyred Qutb was assuming iconic status, and a Qutb-inspired minority was growing increasingly radical. Qutb's *Milestones* has become obligatory reading for generations of extremists. In between long hours of forced labor, Egypt's prison system became the fundamentalist "university," preparing its "graduates" for their revolutionary careers.[6] Egypt's pro–United States turn under Sadat, economic liberalization, peace with Israel, and isolation within the Arab world were a boon for fundamentalist propaganda. Followers of Qutb attacked the Muslim Brotherhood's "cowardly" and "accommodationist" attitudes; the `ulama were denounced as hirelings of a pharaonic *jahili* regime. While some small Islamist cells withdrew into their closed communities, others opted for direct action and started to assault symbols of Western decadence (e.g., bars, hotels, movie theaters); symbols of regime power (e.g., police headquarters); and symbols of religious pluralism (Copts were singled out for atrocities). Although Islamists were at first not unsuccessful in mobilizing economic protests—hunger triggered serious riots in the mid-1970s—they were more likely to resort to isolated terrorist action. The efforts of the *Takfir wa-l-Hijra* ("Excommunication and Hijra," led by Shukri Mustafa) and the *Jama`at al-Islamiyya* to destabilize the regime failed, however. Islamist violence provoked a retaliation that crushed the would-be revolutionaries. But the reaction did not come before they had eliminated the man they held responsible for Egypt's descent into sin: Anwar al-Sadat.

In 1978, negotiations with the "Zionist entity" (extreme opponents of the Jewish state avoid referring to it by name) led to normalization of relations in return for withdrawal from the occupied Sinai and a promise of autonomy for the Palestinians. Both pan-Arabists and Islamists cried treason; one year later, formalization of the peace further exacerbated the public mood. Sadat now declared himself in favor of separation of state and mosque. Opposition grew, and so did repression by the regime. During a military parade in 1981, Khalid Islambouli shot Sadat.[7] The assassin belonged to the *Jihad* group. He had been granted approval for his plan from `Umar `Abdul Rahman, a blind sheikh whose complicity was rather exceptional in view of the generally docile attitude of the `ulama. The assassination sent shock waves through Egyptian politics, and reaction was ferocious. Hosni Mubarak, Sadat's successor, ordered his police to destroy fundamentalist organizations. Islambouli was hanged, as was Muhammad Abdul Salam Faraj, the movement's ideologue. Scores more were condemned to long prison sentences. After his release from prison, `Abdul Rahman moved to the United States, where in 1993 he masterminded the first attack on the New York World Trade Center.

Mubarak, however, could not forestall Islamist revolt in Asyut in Upper Egypt in 1981. In fact, Egypt has for two decades been regularly rocked by bloody Islamist attempts to destabilize the Mubarak regime. Egyptians waver between identifying with their role as leader of the Arab-Islamic world and taking refuge in their own millennial Egyptian identity. Nasser's pan-Arabism had led to disappointment, but so had Sadat's emphasis on local patriotism. Mubarak searched for a middle way: Egypt cooled its friendship with Israel and returned to the Arab League, but deepened its economic and military dependence on the West. Attempts to implement International Monetary Fund (IMF) demands for further economic deregulation fueled new violent protests that fundamentalists tried to capitalize on. Egypt's participation in the 1991 Gulf War alongside the United States was not popular. In the 1990s, attacks increased—against not just the regime but also against progressive Egyptian intellectuals and Copts. The most brutal and potentially successful strategy by far, however, was the massacre of Western tourists—the visible incarnation of Western culture, vulnerable targets, and critical sources of national income.

Although it is difficult to gauge support for political Islam, it clearly goes well beyond the membership of extremist parties, and even of the Muslim Brotherhood. The greater the problems and frustrations, the more popular becomes the slogan, *Islam is the solution*. Like other Islamic countries, Egypt is in the midst of a conservative return to individual religiosity, a trend that is apparent in the growing number of bearded men and covered women. To take our narrative fast forward: by the late 1990s, harsh repression of extremist activists had essentially broken the back of the jihadists—but Islamism had only grown.

The Egyptian government combined elimination of Islamist radicals with a strategy of soft-pedaling its repression of the much more massive Muslim Brotherhood, and made concessions to Islamist cultural demands, which appear to also be the preference of an important segment of the population. *Shari`a* is being partly introduced, freedom of expression curbed, homosexuals persecuted, and anti-Semitic sentiments in the state-controlled media given free rein. Official Islamization has led to rather surprising moderation on the side of the radicals. In 1999 *Jama`a Islamiyya* announced suspension of its terror campaign. Arguing that introducing *shari`a* legislation was somehow turning Egypt into an Islamic state, erstwhile extremists in jail criticized their own earlier actions and accepted parliamentary party politics, thus opening the way to their rehabilitation. Meanwhile, the Muslim Brotherhood has also begun emphasizing gradualism and civil society values. *Ikhwan* leader Hassan Hudhaibi reminded his followers in 1969 that they should be "missionaries, not judges."[8] In terms of Egypt's own popular Islamic icons, "Banna is down, `Abduh up!" The whole process recalls social-democratic reformism within Marxism (though without the democratization of the revolutionaries' own institutions).[9]

All this has not necessarily been good news for Mubarak's authoritarian regime. Revival of the (officially still banned) Brotherhood has also meant that pressures to liberalize the political system have only become stronger, fueled also by secular opposition and human rights activism. Egypt's autocrats have found it increasingly troublesome to crack down on their opposition. From the 2003 Iraq War on, the United States stepped up pressures on Egypt to liberalize its system. In 2004, street protests grew to the extent that Mubarak had to allow multiple candidates for the 2005 presidential election. Although intimidation and vote-rigging easily assured him his seventh (!) "victory" (feeding popular skepticism about Egypt's "democratic turn"), the Muslim Brotherhood carried the next parliamentary elections. Thus the authoritarian (if not exactly dictatorial) Mubarak government survives, precariously, on a combination of repression, clientelism, and a rather popular cultural "illiberalization" that is eating away at civil rights.

The First Wave of *Jihad* in the Sunni World

We must now retrace our steps and see how from Egypt, the Arab world's center of gravity, Islamism irradiated abroad. This was where the first fundamentalist wave to sweep the Islamic world had its origins and its most forceful manifestation. South and Southeast Asia, with the largest Sunni populations outside the Middle East, were still relatively calm in the 1970s and 1980s. But in the Arab world itself, Qutb's ideas were already resonating—in particular in the Fertile Crescent. Few regions in the world rival the ethnic, religious, and political complexity of the Fertile Crescent. Yet in the 1970s, the communities that tore each other apart, although defined by religious markers, were still relatively untouched by religious strife. Lebanon, for instance, was (until the rise of the Shiite Hizbullah) a relatively secular society. So were, surprisingly, Israelis and Palestinians. In the 1970s, paradoxically, only officially socialist Syria was on the verge of fundamentalist revolution.

In Syria and in Iraq, nationalist Ba`th dictatorships put a mask of uniformity over extremely heterogeneous societies. In **Syria** in particular, where the Sunni majority was more or less excluded from power and the Muslim Brotherhood had established radical branches since the 1940s, Islamists posed a serious challenge. Syria is fragmented along three axes: ethnically, between Arabs, Kurds, and other communities; economically, between city and countryside; and religiously, between Sunnis, strongly present among the urban middle class, and a variety of rural sects (including the Druze, Isma`ilites, a profusion of Christian churches, and others). Particularly interesting are some million `Alawites, or *nusairis*, an extremist Shiite sect whose secret beliefs are thought so heterodox as to no longer count as truly Islamic in Sunni eyes. Like his father Hafiz, current President Bashar al-Asad and a good part of Syria's power elite are `Alawite, and not by coincidence. The French gave this despised minority arms and privilege; then Ba`th secularism pulled them into its orbit, and since 1966 they have controlled the levers of power. Until today, the `Alawite minority dictatorship has hidden behind a veil of pan-Arab rhetoric—a rhetoric all the more relevant because Syria lacks natural borders and a historical identity of its own. Seen from Damascus, Lebanon, Jordan, and Palestine flow easily into "Greater Syria."

Since acquiring independence in 1943, Syria has been a nation where violent repression became any ruling faction's answer to political instability. The army was the arbiter. Well-to-do Sunni merchants gravitated to the Brotherhood, poor peasants to Communism or Ba`th. When the latter came to power and started a leftist economic program, the Sunni bourgeois felt threatened. Without a parliamentary safety valve, the Syrian Muslim Brotherhood radicalized much faster than did their counterparts in Egypt. Local animosities and clamor for an Islamic state intensified in 1976, after Asad's opportunistic intervention in Lebanon on the side of the Maronite Christians, against Muslims and Palestinians. The Brotherhood reacted with terrorist *jihad*. By the late 1970s, mutual massacres were polarizing the army itself. The regime was tottering, and in 1982 an Islamist revolt broke out in Hama. Asad reacted by leveling the city, at the cost of some 20,000 lives. The Muslim Brotherhood was broken. Surviving Islamists reorganized in the subsequent years. Some accepted help from Saddam Hussein, the Iraqi dictator hailing from a rival Ba`th wing, but they were seriously weakened. By 1991, Asad (who had by now established a protectorate over Lebanon) had the situation sufficiently under control to offer his foes a "magnanimous" pardon. Over the next years, the regime consolidated its hold on power. In any case, the growth potential of Sunni extremists seemed more limited in Syria than in Egypt, making unnecessary cultural concessions such as those made by Mubarak. In fact, civil society hardly existed anymore, and Bashar's smooth succession in 2000 illustrated that "everything was under control". Initial expectations of a *glasnost* of the essentially one-party Ba`th dictatorship were soon quashed, and the regime has so far survived post-9/11 international isolation, post-Iraq War pressure from the United States, and, most ominously, withdrawal from its profitable protectorate over Lebanon in 2005.

In **Iraq** too, the power that rhetorically belonged to the whole nation was in the hands of a minority—only here the minority was Sunni. This circumscribed the growth of an indigenous Sunni fundamentalism. Iraq is no less artificial a nation than Syria, and Saddam Hussein's Ba'th regime kept it together with a brutality that far eclipsed that of his cousins in Damascus. Besides unruly Kurds, Islamists constituted certainly the main threat to his regime; but the chasm between the oppressed Shiite majority and the privileged and co-opted Sunnis pre-empted any hope of an inter-Islamist rapprochement. Opposition, then, centered on Shiite fundamentalists. However, as we shall see in the following, they were led by an ideology that was immune to the blandishments of Mawdudi and Qutb.

Other Sunni countries, too, began to feel the pressure of Islamism in the 1970s. In **Pakistan**, Zia ul-Haq, an admirer of Mawdudi, had taken over and started to impose *shari'a*. Banks were forced toward an interest-free economy, and *'ulama* commissars "parachuted" to ensure judicial compliance with Islamic law. Transgressions such as theft, illicit sex, or alcohol use were met with Qur'anic flogging and amputation.

The Maghreb was still devoid of serious Islamist turbulence. In **Morocco**, the absolutist monarch Hassan II ruled by a combination of nationalism, patronage, and *baraka*, the charisma of the Prophet's descendants. In **Algeria**, natural gas revenues provided the increasingly corrupt National Liberation Front elite the wherewithal to buy a few more years of internal calm. Only in **Tunisia** did fundamentalism threaten to engulf the regime. *Al-Nahda* (The Rebirth) arose in reaction to that country's strong Westernization, which was promoted by the old dictator Habib Bourguiba. When he was deposed in 1987, only state violence prevented Islamist agitation from getting out of hand; Nahda leader Rachid Ghannouchi had to flee.

In **Sudan**, a huge country torn by an interminable racial and religious civil war between the Arab-Islamic North and the Christian and animist Black South, Islamization started in 1981–83 when ruler Ja'far al-Nimeiri went over from Arab nationalism to Islamism. Imposition of *shari'a* in the South sparked renewal of the civil war after a ten-year lull. After the 1989 coup led by General 'Umar Hassan Ahmad al-Bashir, religious pressures intensified. Sudan became the second country to officially adopt the formula of the Islamic state.

World attention, however, was riveted on the first—on Iran and its Islamic revolution. In Iran, Iraq, and Lebanon, radical Shiites seemed to throw down a much more dangerous gauntlet.

THE 1980s: THE SECOND ISLAMIST WAVE

7

Shiite Interlude

The second stage of development in Islamic fundamentalism was marked by two factors: the movement's monumental growth, and its unmistakably Shiite face. Newspaper readers in the West may never have heard of Qutb or Mawdudi, but they could no longer neglect headlines about ayatollah Ruhollah Khomeini or Hizbullah. Yet Shiism also soon posed limits to Islamic revolution, and in its third stage in the 1990s, Islamism assumed new and emphatically Sunni forms.

Who Are the Shiites?

In order to understand both the impetus and the limits of the second Islamist wave, we must understand Shiism. Fifteen percent of Muslims are Shiites. Although Iran is the only country to have a Shiite regime, Shiites constitute majorities in Iraq and Bahrain, and are Lebanon's largest religious community. They form also substantial minorities in Saudi Arabia, Pakistan, Afghanistan, Azerbaijan, Turkmenistan, and India.[1] Nearly all of these are countries in Persia's historical sphere of influence, for in the sixteenth and seventeenth centuries, Persia was the first and only country to impose Shiism.

Shiites and Sunnis read the same Qur'an and follow a similar *shari`a*. Yet to understand the deep schism separating them, we have to go back to the discord that surrounded Muhammad's succession in the seventh century. `Ali ibn Abi Talib, Muhammad's cousin and son-in-law, insisted on the rule of succession within the Prophet's immediate family so as to guarantee the purity and infallibility of the successors. However, he was defeated by opponents who rejected his "elitist" apostolic succession in favor of a more "democratic" one; any good Muslim could be a candidate and be acclaimed as caliph (substitute of the Prophet) by community consensus, as long as he belonged to Muhammad's Quraish clan.

Three times, `Ali was overlooked in favor of candidates of the opposite faction, who soon showed a marked talent for power politics. `Ali, on the other hand, stood for the *umma's* "clear conscience," committed to the idealism of unadulterated faith. But he was no politician, and when he finally became fourth caliph, he alienated both the Quraish and his own, more extreme and conservative followers, who broke with him to form an egalitarian and ultra-puritan sect, the Kharijites.[2]

Soon afterward, in 661, `Ali was assassinated in Najaf, Iraq, by a disappointed follower. The new caliph, Mu`awiyya the Ummayad, owed his power more to arms than to consensus. Many continued to believe in `Ali's dynasty, now represented by his two sons, Hassan and Hussein. The caliph bribed Hassan with the promise of a future succession, but then reneged. He had the pretender killed, and made sure of his own son's succession. The latter, Yazid, embodiment of evil in Shiite memory, went on to challenge `Ali's younger son Hussein, who had inherited his father's stubbornness. Hussein refused homage, and then left to confront the usurper's army. Only fifty loyalists stayed with Hussein, who obviously had no chance. All were massacred in Karbala. Although Hussein's voluntary sacrifice seemed futile at the time, it actually saved Shiism, for it racked his surviving sympathizers with guilt and shame, and made them vow to never again betray `Ali's just cause. Thus Hussein became the prototypical Shiite hero. His martyrdom is re-enacted and commemorated each year in passion plays. With plaintive songs and self-flagellation, the faithful expiate their sin, and symbolically turn past defeats into future victory. Shiism henceforth vacillated between, on one hand, quietism and half-hearted accommodation with the powers of an unjust world (recognizing these powers de facto without accepting their legitimacy), and on the other hand, millenarian activism to confront evil and better the world.

To Shiites, Hussein was the Third Imam ("one who stands in front of his congregation," the Shiite equivalent of caliph). From his family descended another nine imams. According to tradition, all died as martyrs except the last of the twelve, who supernaturally disappeared in the ninth century. This "Hidden Imam," it is believed, will return at the end of time as *mahdi*, a kind of Messiah to usher in a reign of universal justice—a *Weltanschauung* quite different from Sunnism's "pessimistic realism." For Sunnis, the world does not have a positive evolution. Each succeeding generation grows more distant from the Prophet's eternal message in a sort of spiritual involution. Sunnism developed a meticulous ritualism designed to sanctify the humblest act. This procedure is reminiscent of Orthodox Judaism, and stands in contrast with Shiism, which is fraught with idealism and obsessed with suffering and the presence of evil. Shiites became Islam's excluded, drawing to themselves persecution, humiliation, and pain. As in Catholicism, suffering is viewed as expiation. Sunni scripturalism and puritanism, on the other hand, remind one of Calvinism.[3]

Although much more exuberant than Sunnis, Shiites never condemned *mu`tazila* rationalism. Fatalism, often erroneously attributed to Muslims, is absent from Shiite theology, which lays stress on free choice, individual responsibility, and the eventual victory of good over evil. It is easy to see how Shiism came to attract the disenfranchised, minorities, and revolutionaries. Yet its anti-authoritarianism also caused plenty of internal splits. Today 85 percent of Shiites are "Twelvers," followers of the lineage of the Twelve Imams. Since the "occultation" of the last one, authority passed to the Shiite clergy, who built up much wider prestige and influence than their Sunni counterparts (the `ulama`), and have over the last centuries grown into a powerful hierarchy. Other currents are the "Seveners," or Isma`ilites, who cling to another chain of succession. They stop at Isma`il ibn Ja`far, son of the Sixth Imam, who predeceased his father. From this branch grew a variety of other esoteric sects with Gnostic and neo-Platonic influences.

Popular Shiite belief in the magical and semidivine powers of the Imams made it possible to tap into sources of energy among followers. A conspiratorial element is never far below the surface, and Shiite history has repeatedly seen the emergence of leaders who claimed to be the Imam or his *bab* (gate, or messenger), challenged caliphal power, and occasionally succeeded in their bid. Thus we may recall, in the tenth and eleventh centuries, the Fatimids established an Isma`ilite regime based in Cairo. In the end, however, they succumbed to a process of decentralization similar to that which undermined the Abbasids in Baghdad. In 1169, Nur al-Din, opponent of the Crusaders in Palestine, restored Sunni power in Egypt. Sunni propaganda soon reduced Shiites to a despised minority. Isma`ilite sectarians continued their militancy after military defeat. The *nizaris* specialized in assassinating Seljuk Turkish leaders (according to tradition, after drugging themselves with hashish, hence the word *hashishiyin*, assassins). Most of these early terrorists were killed.[4] Shiism was beginning to look like a losing proposition—until it obtained a new lease on life in Persia.

Persia between Shiism and Modernization _____

The association among Iran, historical Persia, and Shiism dates to the early sixteenth century. The fall of Baghdad in 1258 created an ideological vacuum in the Sunni world. Sufism and Shiism flourished, providing the backdrop for the emergence of the Safavids (1501–1736), a Sufi sect of Azeri (Turkic) orgin that became important as the dynasty that imprinted Shiism on the Persian national character. Whatever the political calculus of the first Safavid emperor, Shah Isma`il—perhaps a desire to accentuate difference from the Sunni Ottomans—he was driven to claim descent from the Shiite Imams. In order to impose Shiism, he had to import Twelver `ulama missionaries from Lebanon as political commissars. Yet whether because of Shiism's national appeal as opposition ideology against Arab supremacy or because of its association with the dualistic and spiritual rationality inherent in Zoroastrianism, the experiment proved successful. The Safavids were in essence the founders of the Persian nation. Their empire had its heyday in the early seventeenth century, when `Abbas I the Great built his capital in Isfahan. But Persia was engaged in permanent struggle against the Sunni Ottomans, whose conquest of Iraq's Shiite Holy Places was to have long-lasting political effects.

The Safavids weakened in the eighteenth century, abandoning first their semidivine pretensions, then their political charisma, and finally their power. Decades passed before a new dynasty, the Qajars (1779–1921), consolidated its grip; in the interim, the *mullas* (Shiite clergy) grew stronger. Qajar shahs never enjoyed the religious prestige of their Safavid predecessors; as prudence dictated, clerics would move to holy places outside their temporal power, from where they felt safe to criticize their monarchs. Even after Wahhabite puritans temporarily conquered the Shiite shrines (destroying them in 1806), the mystique of Najaf and Karbala was not broken.

Inside Persia, the shah's opponents sought protection in the immunity granted to mosques, which became inviolable sanctuaries of political resistance. Moreover, freedom of rational interpretaion had never been restrained in Shiism as it was in Sunnism; latitude grew even more in the eighteenth century when *usuli* theologians defeated the literalist *akhbaris*, who argued that Shiites could not develop new thought until the Hidden Imam returned. The victory of the *usulis* strengthened the hand of the *mujtahids*, the high Shiite clergy whose highest rank came to be known as *ayatollah* (God's sign). Moreover, the Persian clergy enjoyed economic autonomy, because they were the ones to levy the *khums* (the religious fifth tax, comparable to the Christian tithe) and were in charge of administering religious foundations, mosques, schools, and welfare. Thus Persia's `ulama* had a much stronger position than their Sunni Ottoman counterparts. This is why Turkey produced an Atatürk but Iran a Khomeini.

By the turn of the twentieth century, the *mullas*, holders of the most traditional values, had become imperial absolutism's most vocal opponents. European penetration in the late nineteenth century strengthened their resistance. Persia was located between the British and Russian arrows of expansion; eventually the two Great Powers divided it into their respective spheres of influence. Imperialism thus stimulated an alliance between the *mullas* and the pious conservative *bazari* class, against the shah and the foreign infidels.

The Constitutionalist Revolution broke out in Teheran in 1905–06 and showed where real power lay. Strikes forced the shah to promise a parliament and civil rights, but the `ulama* demanded God's sovereignty rather than the nation's. Their threat to go into exile produced a constitution that gave the clergy veto power over legislation—nationalist agitation had produced Islamist counter-radicalization! In 1911, the Qajar shah had his most dangerous cleric, Fadlollah Nuri, hanged. But World War I soon ended both constitutionalism and the Qajar regime itself.

While Turkish, Russian, and British armies occupied Persia in 1914–18, regional revolts threatened its integrity, especially the ethnically non-Persian regions, which were influenced by German agents and then by the Russian Revolution. Colonel Reza Khan repressed a communist revolt, grabbed power, and restored central control. A secularist admirer of Atatürk, he had himself crowned emperor in 1925. Founding the Pahlevi Dynasty was meant to appease the `ulama*, who associated republicanism with secularism. *Mujtahids* returned from Iraq, which had meanwhile fallen under British rule, and established themselves in the Holy City of Qom.

However, Reza Pahlevi soon initiated a brutal modernization. His educational and juridical reform, *waqf* secularization, prohibition of *chador* and beard, and forced sedentarization of the tribes made him look like a copy of Atatürk—or resembled a rehearsal for the project, forty years later, of Reza's son, the last emperor. Persia was renamed Iran, "Land of the Aryans," in order to distance Persians from the Arab world. In 1941, the British and Soviets, suspecting Reza of pro-Nazi leanings, deposed the shah, and put his young son on the throne. The clergy immediately forced Iran's women to veil themselves.

The Last Shah: Forced Modernization against Popular Shiite Opposition_____

After 1945, Iran embarked on a leftist nationalist course. In 1950, Muhammad Mossadeq came to power on the crest of a small and disparate coalition of entrepreneurs, communists, and `ulama, united only by an interest in economic protectionism. When he nationalized the oil industry, all were pleased; but when he went on to give women the vote, he enraged the clergy. Ayatollah Abul Qasim Kashani, leader of the *Mujaheddin-e Islam,* lobbied for *shari`a*-based legislation. Although there is no clear proof that he had a hand in the CIA-engineered 1953 coup that restored the shah with absolute powers, there is no doubt that cultural and social prerogatives mattered more to the *mullas* than did political and economic rights. Young Reza Pahlevi projected a religious image while trampling political liberties. The clergy, except for one young *mujtahid,* Ruhollah Khomeini (1902–89), adopted an apolitical stance.

Iran now joined the Western camp, where it assumed the role of pro-United States regional police officer. In the 1960s, the shah launched his White Revolution, an ambitious modernization project of land reform and women's emancipation as levers of industrialization. In the end, however, only a tiny stratum of landowners and *nouveaux riches* profited from a process that drove millions of peasants into already overpopulated cities, feeding the hostility of the poor and of the anti-Western intelligentsia alike. Protests started in 1963, once the *mullas* came out against plans to empower women and non-Muslim minorities. Repression was bloody, and Khomeini, already Iran's most outspoken cleric, was exiled. Although the shah's regime survived for another 15 years, its social base crumbled. When the Islamic revolution broke out in 1978, neither oil nor his artificial imperial ideology could salvage it.

Significantly, the most influential opposition ideologies that developed in the interval had Islamic colors. Doubtlessly, the most important was Khomeini's, developed in exile in Najaf. Khomeini, now ayatollah, revived Shiism's founding myth: Karbala. Good Muslims, he said, should abandon their neutrality and emulate Imam Hussein's resistance against the oppressor, the shah—the latter-day Yazid the Usurper. Paralleling Mawdudi and Qutb, Khomeini called for an Islamic state, not merely a state of Muslims. However, Khomeini had his own Shiite blueprint of Islamic government, based on *vilayat-e faqih*, the vice-regency (awaiting the return of Hidden

Imam) of the *faqih* (or master jurist of *fiqh*). In this manner the law would be guaranteed to agree with *shari`a*.

Khomeini went on to become Iran's leading revolutionary strategist and leader, and the man who molded its public persona in the country's postrevolutionary stage. But he was also the revolution's main ideologue. What his theory lacked in subtlety it made up for in programmatic vigor. His edict, "Make every place a Karbala, and every day `Ashura," translated the 1960s' anti-imperialist slogan, "Let there be many Vietnams," in Shiite imagery.

`Ali Shari`ati (1933–77), the other great theoretician of the Islamic revolution, is a much more complex and attractive figure. He was an unsystematic thinker who mixed Marxist, Third World, and Shiite mysticism to produce an eclectic Islamic liberation theology. During his Sorbonne studies, he absorbed the teachings of Marx, Sartre, and Fanon. Back home, he joined Mossadeqism, as did other progressive Islamists such as Sadeq Qotbzadeh (later executed as a traitor) and Abdolhassan Bani-Sadr. His popular course on Islamic sociology at a Teheran college embarrassed the regime and in 1973 landed him in jail. He was only released in 1975, left for Britain, then died suddenly.

From Frantz Fanon's critique of imperialism, Shari`ati borrowed the key concept of psychological decolonization, the precondition for a return to the authenticity of the colonized. His favorite Qur'an verse was "Allah changeth not the condition of a folk until they first change that which is in their hearts" (13:11). He rejected Marx' atheism, believing that to resist imperialist invasion, the "wretched of the earth" (in Shari`ati's Qur'anic terminology, the *mustazafin,* or miserable) need spiritual values no less than economic resources. He similarly rejected determinism, arguing that humanity has a divine sparkle that would allow it to build a just society.

Shari`ati reinterpreted Muhammad and the Imams as revolutionary role models. His ideal egalitarian society betrays mystical and pantheistic influences; because God is identical with the people, socialization of the means of production signifies that everything belongs to God. Thus Islam becomes a declaration of rights that abolishes man's exploitation by man. For Shari`ati, only Islamic transformation could lead to the fraternal classless society of the new theomorphic person. This, however, would demand a return to authentic Islam—to the "red Shiism" of `Ali and the masses, not to the subverted "black Shiism" of the corrupt *mullas*. With such sophisticated and intoxicating theories, Shari`ati obviously had more success with intellectuals than with the masses; among the traditionalist `ulama he was even more unpopular. In political terms, the intellectuals' Islamism could not compete with Khomeini's brand of popular Shiism.

The *mujaheddin-e khalq* (People's Holy Warriors), a leftist Islamist group, took their inspiration from Shari`ati. Together with the more secularist *Fedaiyin-e khalq* (People's Martyrs), they waged an urban guerrilla war against the shah. They were no more successful than Sunni students in Egypt or Syria, however, in kindling revolution.[5] Torture, disappearances, and executions by the Savak, the shah's secret police, continued until 1977. Then newly elected U.S. President Jimmy Carter tied further U.S. aid to Iranian respect for human rights, and the shah felt impelled to allow cautious liberalization. But releasing a limited number of political prisoners (who promptly demanded reestablishment of the constitution) was no longer satisfactory. The accumulated pressure exploded in popular protests. The shah had unleashed an Islamic hurricane; before a year had passed, it had blown him away.

The Islamic Revolution

The 1978–79 Iranian Revolution has been the only Islamic revolution to overthrow a secularist regime and, with support of the vast majority of the population, install an Islamist one. It is also one of history's largest revolutions, comparable to those in France in 1789, in Russia in 1918, and in China in 1949. Like them, it went through a series of increasingly radical phases, devoured many of its children, and in the end failed—but not without drastically transforming domestic and international politics. It is too early to say whether this revolution also created a model for future convulsions in the Islamic world. At first glance, the Iranian experience appears too idiosyncratic to be emulated by other societies.

Antigovernment demonstrations and strikes started at universities in 1977, and by early 1978 had spread to the bazaar and to Qom's seminaries. Repression created student martyrs; commemorative ceremonies forty days later were the occasion for new and larger demonstrations in which even more people died, and forty days later, unrest would spread again to other cities. Within months the shah's regime was exhausted. By the time the shah tried to appease the opposition by promising a new constitution, it was too little and too late. From his exile in France, Khomeini was demanding the shah's head, and a new regime. In the holy month of *muharram* in December, protests climaxed with millions of workers, civil servants, and women marching in the streets and demanding abolition of the monarchy and the appointment of Khomeini as new leader. Khomeini exhorted his followers to use a non-violent strategy, insisting that the moral force of their sacrifice would break the regime's morale: "Soldiers, by shooting your sisters, you are shooting the Qur'an." A parallel power structure in mosque committees began challenging official authority and, in January 1979, the shah fled. The army remained neutral. One month later, Khomeini returned from exile to take the reins of power.

The shah's regime fell because it benefited only a privileged elite, and had long ago lost its legitimacy in the eyes of its subjects. Iran was ripe for a revolution. For a revolution to succeed, at least three conditions must exist: a coalition of popular forces, a program of demands or an ideology that galvanizes the masses, and a revolutionary leadership capable of exploiting the revolutionary conjuncture. These conditions were present in the late 1970s in Iran, but have nowhere else in the Islamic world been met since the Iranian Revolution. Three disparate oppositions coalesced around Khomeini's anti Western platform: the traditional clergy, supported by *bazaris* and *mustazafin*; the Islamic and secular Left, students, and communist workers whose strikes shook the oil industry; and the liberal minority. Khomeini made wise use of his charisma as *mujtahid*. For the poor he embodied millennial hopes; many saw in him the Hidden Imam. To the more educated, he left his plans vaguer. But in the end, all accepted him.

The Islamic Republic

Once in power, what were Khomeini and his followers going to do? The outcome, an unprecedented theocratic polity mixed with democratic republican traits, surprised many. In September 1979, a constitutional assembly was elected by universal suffrage. Khomeini's Revolutionary Islamic Party won the popular mandate to remake Iran. The new regime thus reflected Khomeini's theory, which, with minor modifications, continues in force. Legislative and judiciary powers are concentrated in the Supreme Guide, the *faqih*—Khomeini himself being, of course, the first incumbent (after his death, he was succeeded by his close ally Ali Khamenai). The responsibility for day-to-day administration rests with a president and government responsible to an elected *majlis* (parliament). Political parties are legal, but candidates need prior approval of a screening commission, which evaluates their Islamic credentials. Although multipartyism reflects the democratic side of the coin, theocrats are the senior partner in this equation. Laws are scrutinized by the Council of Guardians, which can veto any that it finds inconsistent with Islamic norms. In the late 1990s, this commission, half of whose members are `*ulama* (and which was initially presided over by Khomeini), would block the liberal and democratic proposals sponsored by reformist President Mohammad Khatami.

"Imam" Khomeini introduced the rigorous Islamization of law and social rules, which included a dress code requiring women to cover their hair in public and a long list of prohibited "immoral" activities and their respective punishments. Nevertheless, the new regime was not completely illiberal. Freedom of expression, for instance, although not unlimited, compared favorably to that in most other Middle Eastern countries. In twentieth-century Iran, the worst disturbances were linked to women's emancipation. Yet millions of *chador*-clad Iranian women had chased the shah out of the country; and now they had the vote. Female participation in public, professional, and political life, although segregated, is pervasive. Women may hold any political office, save the presidency. Neither were the non-Muslim minorities reduced to *dhimmi* status, as some radicals demanded. Assyrian and Armenian Christians, Jews, and Zoroastrians enjoy a certain freedom of expression and (as in communalist British India and Lebanon) have reserved seats in parliament. Similar tolerance was not, however, extended to Sunnis or Shiite heretics such as Bahá'is.[6]

With its emphasis on "the wretched of the earth" and its brutal purges of the shah's worst profiteers, Iran's revolution initially seemed, at least to sympathetic observers on the Left in the West, a strange creature, with its reactionary surface hiding a progressive essence. Plans were drawn up to expropriate illicitly accumulated riches, and to nationalize industries and public services. This promise was only partially fulfilled, but reassured Western liberals. In reality Islam recognizes the right to private property and is far from hostile to capitalism.[7] Yet, in a system that intended to base policy upon *shari`a*, economic policy remained an enigma. *Shari`a* sees five kinds of human action: obligatory, recommended, neutral, disapproved, and prohibited. Most economic activities are in the neutral zone, and permit a variety of interpretations. Khomeini did not support the more egalitarian views.

If 1978 was Iran's Bastille Day, and 1979 saw its Declaration of Rights, then 1980–83 corresponds to the revolution's Reign of Terror, with purges and the firing squad instead of the guillotine. Once the shah was gone, only anti-Westernism remained as an ideological glue.[8] Britain, Russia, and the United States had controlled Iran's course for decades. Now their cultural values were discarded, along with their political influence. In Khomeini's view, the poison of Western ideas posed the gravest peril—he used the neologism *gharbzadegi* (Westoxification) for this to-be-extirpated plague. Divine and popular sovereignty were incompatible. In 1979, the extremist Students of the Line of the Imam occupied the U.S. embassy in Teheran, provoking a first-order diplomatic crisis with the Great Satan (Israel being, in Iranian Islamist parlance, the Little Satan). On both sides of the divide, radicals benefited. In the United States, Ronald Reagan defeated Carter in the 1980 presidential election. In Iran, those who did not embrace the line of the Imam were marginalized. Abdolhassan Bani-Sadr, a moderate Khomeinist and Iran's first president, was in a classical postrevolutionary quandary over the choice between the development of state and economy or the purity of ideas and export of revolution. Did the revolution need theologians or mathematicians? Bani-Sadr lost out to the more rigorously puritan `Ali Khamenei (the current Supreme Guide and leader of the conservatives). *Pasdaran* (revolutionary guards) were committed to suppressing opposition. After Bani-Sadr's fall, Khomeini destroyed all opposition—"atheists" (i.e., communists), "hypocrites" (i.e., *Mujaheddin-e khalq*), and liberal `*ulama,* who were executed along with prostitutes and drug dealers. Between 1981 and 1983, between five and ten thousand opponents were liquidated, after which the Khomeinists' power monopoly was never again challenged.

Henceforth the "morality police" were in charge of controlling not only political but also social behavior: Western dress, songs, books, music, and movies; adolescent flirting; birth control; adultery; prostitution; extramarital sex; and homosexuality were all punishable offenses. Iranian society was being maintained in a state of permanent mobilization and enthusiasm. Friday sermons and religious studies were obligatory. But as the new generation was subjected to relentless fundamentalist brainwashing, the level of education fell.

By the time of the Iran-Iraq War in the early 1980s, the revolution was on the verge of collapse. Although Iran survived the first attack, its army was disorganized. Then Khomeini started to use the war to promote his Islamist universalism, and combined it with appeals to Iranian patriotism. He exhorted his nation with symbols of martyrdom. Eventually Iran staunched Iraqi advances with human waves of the *basij*: thousands of adolescents and children threw themselves onto Iraqi mines. *Mullas* explained to the bereaved parents that viewing youth as a special stage worthy of protection was a Western concept. They affirmed that every girl older than nine and every boy over sixteen was adult enough to make the sacrifice in *jihad*. Burying thousands of mutilated young bodies, Iran fell into the thrall of a death cult. Relatives of the martyred received pensions from the Foundation of the *Mustazafin* and Martyrs, which grew into a veritable economic empire that administered the shah's confiscated properties.[9]

International Impact

A good part of the hope (and alarm) that the Iranian Revolution raised was because of its potential to inspire similar uprisings in other countries. Inside and outside of the Arab world, the revolution was greeted as a blow to the West that proved that, given mobilization and leadership, profound change was possible. Overlooking its excesses, many admirers of the revolution shrugged off the details (such as human rights violations) in favor of its overall frame: its challenge to the twin devils, the United States and Israel. Hence the similarity in support for Khomeini and for Saddam Hussein one decade later. For Khomeini, Islam's scope was universal; exporting the revolution was part and parcel of his ideology. Iran's constitution envisions a pan-Islamic state and commits the Islamic Republic to support just struggles. In fact, Iran does selectively support Islamist causes wherever it sees fit. It sent hundreds of *pasdaran* to South Lebanon, to help local Shiites in their struggle against Israel. Revolutionary Iran competed against conservative Saudi Arabia for the mantle of Islamic legitimacy; tensions between both regional giants occasionally reached dangerous proportions.

In 1987 spontaneous political demonstrations organized by pilgrims during the *hajj* in Mecca led to massacres between Sunni Arab and Iranian Shiites. Echoing Wahhabite extremists, Iran viewed the Saudi princes as corrupt sultans; it plotted against Sunni authority with Shiites in Hasa, Bahrain, Kuwait, and elsewhere in the Gulf, and Iraq. However, the chasm between Sunnis and Shiites was deep, and the perceived Iranian threat urged peninsular Arab states to join forces in the Gulf Cooperation Council. Khomeini (who had been very anti-Sunni during his exile) now emphasized what both Islamic branches shared, although his newly found ecumenism could not overcome Sunni antagonism.

Nowhere was Islamic revolutionary expansionism clearer than in the war against Iraq. Although Iran was not the aggressor, it soon used the conflict to reach out to its Iraqi Shiite brethren, and to the Holy Cities, Najaf and Karbala. Khomeini called the war a *jihad,* and demanded Saddam's removal as precondition for peace; but his attempt at regime change did not work. The Iranian leaders underestimated the fear they had instilled abroad. It was precisely the revolution's crusading character that evoked the international reaction that Saddam was able to manipulate for his own purposes. As the war dragged on, it degenerated into trench carnage until mutual exhaustion. In 1988, Khomeini accepted armistice and the bloodletting finally ended. There was no doubt that the Islamic revolution had suffered a moral defeat.

Post-Thermidorean Iran?

Normalization of the revolution—the Iranian Thermidor—started in the late 1980s. It was caused not only by war losses and dislocation but also by the inevitable processes of institutionalization, loss of ideological fervor, and routinization. The population was saturated with sermons, the *pasdaran* were losing ground, land reform stalled, and exploitation of the poor returned, along with corruption—and with it came deep disappointment. In the privacy of their homes, outside the reach of the morality police, the well-to-do were enjoying Islamic forbidden fruits.

One of Khomeini's last acts was the publication in 1989 of the *fatwa* condemning to death for blasphemy Salman Rushdie, the Muslim Anglo-Indian author of *The Satanic Verses*. Iran thus adopted one of the causes of European Islamists: although Rushdie was a British citizen and outside of Iranian jurisdiction, Khomeini agreed that *shari`a* had universal jurisdiction for all Muslims, whereas national borders (including Iran's) had only relative value. The crisis between Iran and the West deepened, and by the time the "Imam" died, it had become a pariah state accused of sheltering terrorists. It inspired more repugnance than imitation, and seemed to have lost its revolutionary impetus.

When the octogenarian *faqih* expired, no one was legitimately appointed to replace him. Political continuity was guaranteed, however, as Khamenei took over as supreme leader, although without his predecessor's authority. The more politic `Ali Akbar Hashem Rafsanjani became president. He was hailed in the West as a pragmatic moderate, although he did not make good on such expectations. In the 1990s a struggle broke out between the conservatives—yesterday's radical fundamentalists—and today's reformists, whose preferences were closer to the West's, and who in earlier years would have been considered conservatives. It was during Rafsanjani's tenure that the respected *sayyid* Mohammad Khatami started to defy the system from within. Social norms, political liberties, and closure against or opening to the outer world became controversial, as did the economy, which improved or worsened with the price of oil, Iran's main source of income.

It would be inaccurate to speak of a struggle between clergy and laity, because the *mullas* are practically everywhere—and are no less divided among themselves than is the general population. The struggle does, however, have a generational character. The revolutionaries' sons and daughters grew up with no memory of the shah. As the *ancien régime* ceased to be a point of reference, the children of the new regime started to demand Western-style freedom and prosperity. Yet it would be shortsighted to suspect an anti-Islamic reaction: most Iranians want religion to remain in its place of honor in public life. What they reject is the politicization of religion and the clergy's quasi-monopoly over politics and intrusion into their private lives. Reformists would reintegrate Iran as a normal state in the world, preferring dialogue over a clash of civilizations, and not rejecting globalization out of hand. In the camp of modernization, the will to export the Islamic revolution is no longer evident. Between "Islam as political norm" and "Islam as cultural identity," modernizers tend to the second model.

Khomeini insisted on an *Islamic* republic—neither *democratic* nor *Islamic democratic*. The people followed his recommendation, and the result was a hybrid, neither complete freedom nor a clerical dictatorship. Constitutionally guaranteed freedoms were often not respected; still, they allowed a civil society to emerge. Elected government continued to have far greater legitimacy than in any pro-Western Arab country. What was at stake for civil society was to increase its terrain and emancipate itself from the heavy hand of the church-state, not to de-Islamize society. In the 1990s, demonstrations in favor of economic, cultural, and political reform implicitly questioned the legitimacy of the Islamist regime. Then in 1997, Khatami came to power with the votes of the professional classes, women, and youth.

Khatami set a cautious course toward liberalization, and opened some room for public debate on the campuses and in the media. However moderate his attempts, though, he could not avoid a backlash from the fundamentalists close to Khamenei. For in spite of representing 70 percent of the electorate, the reformists did not control many resources or power levers. Worse, their moral superiority was more apparent to sympathizers abroad than to rivals at home, who considered themselves morally more idealistic and authentic than their challengers, and who had on their side the law, the forces of order, the uneducated, and the traditionalist silent majority. New protests in Teheran in 1999 and other cities provoked brutal repression: most progressive media were muzzled, belying optimistic predictions of a post-Islamist epoch waiting in the wings.[10] Because there were no viable alternatives, Khatami was reelected in 2001. However, the enthusiasm was gone.

Nor have the years since 9/11 internationally helped the Iranian reformists' cause. In view of Teheran's support of terrorism and because of its nuclear ambitions, the George W. Bush administration declared Iran a member of the Axis of Evil. The consequence was to strengthen the fundamentalists' hand, and dissidents' room for maneuver continued to dwindle. The U.S. invasion of Iraq created new troublemaking opportunities for the ayatollahs' regime. And at home, the clerical establishment succeeded in thwarting all attempts to legislate liberal change. In 2004, it canceled the candidacy of most reform candidates; reformists responded by boycotting parliamentary elections, but the attempt backfired when more than half the population cast their ballots anyway, clearing the way for a malleable *majlis* cleansed of progressive representatives. Henceforth, the conservatives were in the ascendancy, though still split between technocrats and Islamist extremists (many former *pasdaran*) who had spearheaded attacks on the "Westernizers" and now controlled the security services. The latter current advocated "revitalizing the revolution," and released a populist backlash against the newly rich post-revolutionary elite—a course that earned them the support of the poor. Reformists entered the 2005 presidential elections divided, many still insisting on a continued boycott. In the ensuing runoff, the extreme Islamist candidate Mahmud Ahmadinejad won a surprising victory over more traditionalist clerical competitors. He lost no time launching a cultural counterrevolution at home and a more assertive international course.

Indeed, the "neo-Khomeinist" idealists of the Right who now again control Iran apply a more aggressively Islamic foreign policy, openly calling for a war of civilizations against the West, eradication of Israel, and development of Iranian nuclear power. All this add to concerns in the United States and Europe, but international isolation and the threat of sanctions are rekindling nationalist sentiment, and thus strengthen Ahmadinejad's home base—from his viewpoint, a virtuous circle.

Hizbullah

By the 1990s, Iran had lost its reputation as vanguard of the "Islamist International." Whatever the eventual outcome of its domestic tug-of-war, the results may be limited, as Islamist leadership passed back to extremist Sunnis. Before analyzing the most recent stage, however, we must pay attention to another Shiite group that made headlines in the 1980s: Hizbullah. In the 1970s, Shiites were the largest of Lebanon's seventeen recognized communities; they were also the most backward and least represented. Most Shiites were poor peasants concentrated in Jabal `Amil in the south, close to the border with Israel, and in the Bekaa Valley close to Syria. Economic and political crises forced many to find a precarious refuge in Beirut's slums. One person was responsible for transforming this humble and passive community into Lebanon's most assertive political force: Imam Musa Sadr, an Iranian descended from Shiite `ulama brought over in the sixteenth century by the Safavids to convert the Persians. In 1961, he left for his ancestral Lebanon and inspired his coreligionists to organize and defend their own interests. He taught that tyrants who oppress Shiites were latter-day Yazids, that *jihad* pleases God if it is struggle against the injustice of the mighty against the weak, and that He will help those who help themselves. Sadr's efforts led to formation of the *Amal* (Hope) group. By the early 1970s, Shiite activists were clashing with Palestinian commandos who fled from Jordan to Lebanon, from where they harassed Israel.

The Shiites liked neither Jews nor Palestinians, but when civil war broke out, they joined the Islamic-progressive block that contested Rightist-Maronite hegemony. Pressed between Maronites, Druze, Sunnis, and Palestinians, Mussa Sadr reorganized Amal as a Shiite self-defense militia. He did so with the financial help of Libyan leader Mu`ammar Qadhafi, who considered his country's oil riches the patrimony of all Muslims and distributed gifts to anti-Christian and anti-Zionist groups. However, the two leaders quarreled on one of Sadr's visits to Tripoli in 1978. Qadhafi had Sadr shot on the spot, then declared him "missing." Many Shiites, however, refused to believe that he was dead and, repeating an earlier pattern, awaited his return.[11] Nabih Berri, a much more Westernized secular leader now took control of Amal. Berri was much more interested in democratizing Lebanon, abolishing its consociational political system, and obtaining proportional representation for his community than he was in creating an Islamic state. Shiite fundamentalists disapproved and, encouraged by the success of the Iranian revolution, formed Hizbullah, "the Party of God." The founders of Hizbullah were two radical Shiite Islamists, Muhammad Hussein Fadlallah and Hussein Mussawi. Together with the Afghan *mujahidun*, Hizbullah was among the first Islamist movements to define itself primarily through armed struggle against a foreign occupier.

Israel's invasion of South Lebanon and Beirut in 1982 gave Hizbullah its opportunity. While Israel succeeded in expelling the PLO, it also created a power vacuum that was soon filled by hostile groups who turned Lebanon into a test case of the clash of civilizations. It did not take long for ferocious Shiite resistance to enter the fray. While Syria nodded assent and Iran helped militarily, Shiite "martyrdom operations" chased the United States out of Lebanon and, more slowly, pressed on Israel. The latter withdrew in 1986 behind its security barrier. Shiites continued fighting Christians and Palestinians in the infamous War of the Camps in West Beirut. Acts of ethnic cleansing on both sides turned Lebanon into a patchwork of homogeneous community territories.

After Syria pacified Lebanon and established its protectorate, the Party of God won elections in the following phase of reconstruction; meanwhile, it continued its low-intensity war against Israel, masking its Islamist face as a national liberation movement. In 1992, Israel assassinated a relative of Mussawi; a few months later, Hizbullah (probably in collusion with Iran) bombed the Israeli embassy in Buenos Aires, killing twenty-nine people. It was not the first time enemies fought Israel abroad, but it may have been the first time Islamists did. Attacks continued for several years. Ever more audacious, the Shiite guerrilla fighters eventually became more efficient than any Palestinian faction. Israel's reactions were furious but ineffective; after a Shiite rocket barrage in 1996, Israeli retaliated by accidentally killing a hundred Lebanese civilians, setting off an international outcry. With Muslim "martyrs" killing ever more Israelis, demoralization set in. The Islamist example doubtlessly inspired the second Palestinian *intifada*, which broke out in September 2000. Barak's new government had just completed Israel's withdrawal from Lebanon, after eighteen years of occupation. However, Hizbullah did not cease its attacks.

Iraq's Shiites

Shiites now constitute a 60 percent majority in Iraq, and have recently become the most critical factor in determining that country's future and with it, that of the post-9/11 U.S. campaign to bring democracy to the Middle East. Their background and significance in the 1970s and 1980s warrant consideration here. Iraqi Shiism is of course bound up with the presence of Najaf and Karbala, yet Shiite demographic preponderance dates only to nineteenth-century sedentarization and conversion of Sunni Bedouin tribes roving in the vicinity of these Shiite Holy Cities. Initially concentrated in the South, millions of Shiites have moved into Baghdad. In spite of their current strife, differences between Iraqi Sunnis and Shiites are relatively minor; they share social mores, and intermarriage is common. In the twentieth century, however, each Arab community chose an opposite political path. Sunnis monopolized power and started to discriminate against Shiites.

This process began long before Saddam Hussein. After 1918, Iraq was carved out of Ottoman provinces that had fallen under British control. Britain crushed a Shiite revolt, and thereafter favored the Sunnis. The Sunnis embraced pan-Arabism—most other Arabs also being Sunni—while Shiites emphasized Iraqi particularism. Many Shiites secularized, and quite a few turned communist. The 1958 anti-Western revolt was primarily *watani* Iraqi; however, when Sunni Ba`thists grabbed power in 1968, the Shiites were once more excluded. Saddam's regime was secular and rested on clan-based clientelism—*vis-à-vis* Shiites it was hostile, sometimes racist. The

Sunni state held power through the army (although most privates
were Shiites); toward the Shiite elite it combined carrots and sticks.
Among the sticks, Saddam had many of the prestigious Shiite lineages of Hakim and Sadr eliminated.

By liquidating any and all political opposition, Saddam left the Shiites no alternative but the mosque. Community leadership passed to
the men of religion. Although Iran is near, and both countries share a
long Shiite history, Iraqi `ulama` are not necessarily pro-Iranian.
Khomeini developed his theory of the *vilayat-e faqih* while in exile in
Najaf; but he convinced only a few Iraqi ayatollahs of the superiority
of his new theocratic proposal: most remained followers of the less
exalted and more quietist Twelver tradition. Still, the 1978 Iranian
revolution had some effect on the restive Iraqi Shiites next door. But
Shiite terrorist attacks were just the pretext the Ba`thist regime
needed to launch a bloody purge. Muhammad Baqr Sadr, Iraq's prime
Shiite leader and chief of Da`wa (*Hizb al-Da`wa al-Islamiyya*, the
Party of the Islamic Appeal) was assassinated in 1980. Torture and
executions weakened Da`wa; some fled to Iran. Later, the Iranian
leadership stimulated a new movement it could better control: the
Supreme Council of the Islamic Revolution in Iraq (SCIRI). (Both
Da`wa and SCIRI are now predominant in post-Saddam Iraqi politics,
about which more later). War with Iran put Iraqi Shiites in a delicate
position. Although Khomeini organized groups of Da`wa saboteurs to
work behind Iraqi lines, most Shiites did not revolt, nor did Shiite soldiers desert: common Arab nationalism apparently still transcended
divisive religious loyalties. But the Islamists' passivity came to an end
after the 1988 armistice. The end of the Cold War opened a window of
détente in the Middle East, which in turn allowed internal tensions to
express themselves more forcefully—a dangerous conjuncture, in particular for minority-based dictatorships such as Iraq's. Iraq, therefore,
becomes the *trait d'union* connecting our analysis of the second fundamentalist wave with the third and most recent one.

1991–2001: THE THIRD ISLAMIST WAVE

8

The Seven Marks of Current Islamism

In the early 1990s, French specialist Olivier Roy divided Islamic fundamentalism into three periods.[1] A first generation in the 1960s and 1970s, running parallel to Third World decolonization, was elitist. Its ideologues Abu al-Ala al-Mawdudi and Sayyid Qutb were still little read; most followers were university students. This first wave culminated in the assassination of Sadat. The second generation, in the 1980s, was more visible, especially in Iran. It based its militancy on an alliance among Islamist intellectuals, the conservative religious middle class, and the recently urbanized but traditionalist masses. However, its plan to conquer state power and found the Islamic utopia miscarried nearly everywhere else.

Looking forward to the 1990s, Roy foresaw in his *Failure of Political Islam* a weaker third generation, demoralized by repression, its terrorism fragmenting, and its movements diverging. Instead, Roy observed the growth of an alternative, less politicized, and more individual Islam—neofundamentalism, a new religiosity that he read as a sign of Islam's globalization, or even Westernization. Gilles Kepel, another well-known French expert, predicted that Islamism, without disappearing, would become but one among many competing ideological commodities on the Islamic world's political marketplace.[2]

What we have witnessed in the past years, on the contrary, is a never-ending escalation of Islamist incidents, of which 9/11 was only the most dramatic. How to explain this reemergence, though? Others made opposite predictions. One year after Roy, Samuel Huntington published his famous "Clash of Civilizations?" article, in which he predicted that in the post-Cold War era, international conflicts would no longer be so much ideological (e.g., capitalism against communism) as civilizational.[3] Huntington divided humanity into seven or eight civilizations, characterized by religions of questionable compatibility. He argued that the new era would be marked by the revolt of "the rest" against the West, as other civilizations would no longer accept Western patterns (democracy, individualism, human rights, etc.) as universally valid. Of these civilizations in revolt, Islam (either alone or in a marriage of convenience with China) would be the most threatening to Western predominance. Huntington observed that "Islam has bloody borders": wherever the Islamic world collides with other civilizations, conflicts arise.

Huntington's article was an instantaneous public hit but his provocative thesis has been harshly criticized—by, among others, many Middle East specialists—as reductionist, overly culturalist, and alarmist. Thirteen years later, while some of his prophecies (notably Western-Islamic confrontation) have come true, this crisis has not, in contrast to his prediction, expressed itself primarily in interstate conflict. Nonstate actors are ever more present—among them, terrorist fundamentalist groups. Nor are most Muslims worldwide as solidly anti-West and anti-modern as he would have it. Islamism seems to grow, and attracts ever more followers; and its activity appears increasingly predicated on an anti-Western stance that has echoes outside the Islamic world. Superficially, cultural confrontation seems each year more credible. In reality, *the confrontation is between two incompatible ideologies whose battlefield does not follow the "bloody borders" of any civilization but* traverses *heterogeneous cultural terrains.*

Huntingtonian fatalism accords well with the ideology of both certain rightist milieus in the United States and Europe, and of Islamists themselves, who adhere to the thesis of a long-term inevitable clash with the West: not Huntington or the Middle East scholar Bernard Lewis, but Mawdudi and Qutb were the inventors of the clash of civilizations. Theirs is, however, the fanatical belief of a minority; many more Muslims see their faith as a source of inspiration for pluralistic coexistence, and for dialogue between civilizations. In recent years, fundamentalists have undeniably conquered terrain in a range of Islamic countries; the more progressive "other Islams" are on the defensive. However, this is not an irreversible shift, although, if current trends continue, the future of Western-Muslim relations looks bleak.

The Seven Marks

It is easy enough to criticize Roy's and Kepel's predictions today, but their assessment makes more sense if we contextualize it in the period when it was made, fifteen years ago. After the Iranian project of exporting the Islamic Revolution had reached its limits, whatever succeeded lacked the second Islamist wave's spectacular events. No new conquests, no new revolutions: Islamism seemed to have spent itself—at least until September 11, 2001, and its trail of subsequent terror acts and explosions of ethnic-religious hatred all over the Islamic world, from Nigeria to Indonesia. Today's terrorism and savagery are, however, unintelligible unless we decipher them as the outcome of a long series of half-hidden preparations. The following paragraphs attempt to analyze these dynamics.

Afghanistan, Israel-Palestine, Algeria, Kashmir, New York, London, and Baghdad have been the "highlights" of recent Islamist violence. Violence against non-Muslims and "apostates" has supplanted the earlier, more limited, struggle against "corrupt" leadership in Muslim countries. Meanwhile, Egypt, Tunisia, Pakistan, and a host of other Muslim societies have been undergoing a quiet Islamization of their social and cultural life—gradual but profound shifts that rarely make headlines. What we are witnessing in these countries is the broadening of Islamism's social base. The first wave, which petered out around 1980, had limited appeal; Qutb enthusiasts were engineering students, with a few marginal `ulama` lending theological support. The second wave had higher volume, but even more limited span: only Iran combined all the necessary preconditions for an authentic revolution. Shiism's "Karbala paradigm" provided the spark, but limited the expansion: the only groups susceptible to the ayatollahs' message were other Shiites. For Sunnis, in contrast, the second wave was mainly a threat, hence their support of Iraq's war, which eventually succeeded in putting the brakes on Iran's advance.

The latest wave, however, was an iceberg, at least until 9/11. Roy may be right that some Islamists have shifted strategy, and are now trying to conquer society first. He is, however, mistaken in not seeing that this is just a preliminary stage to conquering state power. And many Islamist movements remain as focused on attaining political power as were their predecessors. Today's Islamism constitutes a new, third generation—more pluriform, encompassing a wider area, but, in its more radical wings, even more ambitious and confrontational than the two earlier Islamist waves. This current third Islamist wave is the subject of this chapter. Far from being weaker than its predecessors, post-1990 Islamists operate simultaneously on seven fronts: (1) Islamization of politics; (2) of civil society; and (3) of culture; (4) construction

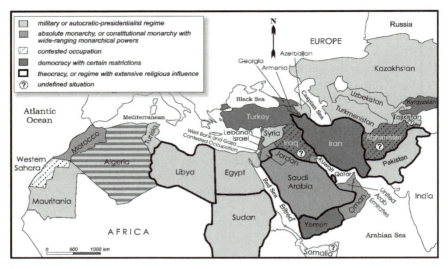

Figure 8.1
Political regimes in the Middle East today

of a global Islam; (5) violent struggle over a range of regional fronts reaching far beyond the boundaries of the Middle East; (6) (re-)Islamization of Western diasporas; and (7) waging a sporadic international war against the West, launched by al-Qaeda. This last front was in 2003 the trigger of a new war against Iraq.

The Islamization of Politics

The Gulf War as a Hinge

Except for the terrible five-year Taliban interlude in Afghanistan, not one government has decisively turned Islamic in the last fifteen years. Yet everywhere, Islam has turned into a more potent political and polemical force. From Nigeria to Malaysia, over Iraq and India, and even in France and the United States, Islam's public presence is much more pronounced now than it was a generation ago. In a paradoxical manner, the trend to "empower God" reflects an equally strong trend of "power to the people." Despite great opposition, democracy is growing, in spurts, throughout the Islamic world. But wherever Muslim populations achieve self-determination, political Islam raises its head. For better or for worse, the nexus between democratization and Islamization is undeniable. It also represents the greatest political and moral challenge to the Western democratic model. The mechanisms by which this nexus has been growing are complex and imperfectly understood.

But its roots are in the Middle East, and have certainly to do with the end of the Cold War and, immediately subsequent to it, the Gulf War. The events of 1988–91 unleashed a chain of consequences that have not yet played themselves out.

The three stages of Islamism in the Middle East are separated by rapid transition periods—hinges—of which the first was 1979–82. After years of relative (and deceptive) calm in the mid-1970s, the Middle East entered a storm zone: the Iranian Revolution, war with Iraq, the Soviet invasion of Afghanistan, and then the rise of Islamic resistance. Egypt was excluded from the "Arab concert," Sadat was assassinated, and then came Israel's expulsion of the Palestinians from Lebanon, which in turn led to the emergence of Shiite resistance. These changes interacted with momentous shifts in the international scene. As Reagan confronted the communist "evil empire," a second Cold War froze détente. In the USSR, the Brezhnev gerontocracy gave way to attempts to revolutionize the Soviet regime from within.

After this transitional phase followed a period of relative continuity and, for the Arab world, stagnation. Lebanon decayed into civil war. Saddam Hussein's army staunched Iran's revolutionary expansionism. Israeli occupation in Palestine continued. Not until the 1988 Iran-Iraq armistice and the first Palestinian *intifada* did we enter a new phase of seismic transitions. By 1989 the Russian adventure in Afghanistan was over; the collapse of communism in Eastern Europe and the end of the Cold War soon followed. Two years later, the Soviet Union had itself imploded into fifteen independent states, six of them Muslim. In the first international war after the Cold War, an international coalition confronted Iraq over its occupation and annexation of Kuwait.

The 1991 Gulf War is key to understanding Islamism during the last fifteen years. For the dominant view in the Arab-Islamic world was not that international legitimacy had been violated by one of their own. For most Arabs, Kuwait signified an illegitimate U.S. intervention blocking an attempt of the Arab nation to regain its freedom of action. As such, it marked a shift for the worse in the (already unfriendly) relations between the Islamic and the First World, and deepened the cognitive dissonance between the two sides. Immanuel Wallerstein was not alone in analyzing the 1991 Gulf War as the first war of the Global South against the North,[4] a perception that may explain the rather widespread sympathy for Islamism among Third World Muslims *and* non-Muslims. For the same 1989–91 convulsion was also the hinge between the second and third Islamist waves. We must therefore pay attention to the Islamic ramifications of the Gulf War.

Saddam Hussein's war had surprising Islamic connotations indeed. By 1988, Iraq had succeeded in destroying Iran's potential to threaten existing Arab regimes with its Islamist revolution. Saddam had smartly played the nationalist card of historical Arab-Persian antagonism, and with Arab and international aid and at a terrible price, he eliminated the prospect of Iranian regional hegemony. To finance his war, Iraq borrowed heavily from its neighbors, in particular from its minuscule neighbor Kuwait. From Saddam's point of view, these sums represented but a tiny part of what the Arabs owed Iraq, which protected their flank at the cost of heavy sacrifice. The end of one war was inevitably the harbinger of another. Iraq's army was materially at the top of its strength, but its one million soldiers (from a population of twenty-five million) could hardly be reabsorbed in a civil economy in shambles. Iraqis were also brainwashed to expect new acts of grandeur from their leader, who now had the wherewithal to threaten his neighbors. The Arab system had restrained Iran, but had in the process raised a monster in its own backyard. It did not take long for this pressure cooker to blow up in the neighbors' face.

Saddam's August 1990 annexation of Kuwait wiped out Iraq's war debt. It also was an immediate menace to Saudi Arabia and the Gulf principalities. Iraq was now a regional superpower that could have redrawn the Arab map, but it let the moment slip. While the United Nations denounced the violation of Kuwait's sovereignty, demanded instant Iraqi withdrawal, and imposed sanctions, the United States sent thousands of soldiers as a barrier to protect the Saudis; soon it was Saddam who found himself encircled.

Most Arab governments (not much more democratic or legitimate than Saddam's own) lined up behind the West. Arab populations from Rabat to Amman, however, adored Saddam as a hero. His popularity soared when he linked his withdrawal from Kuwait to Israel's from the occupied Palestinian territories; Arab regimes had for twenty-five years been unable to budge that occupation.

Saddam's challenge to the West allowed him to present himself as not just an Arab hero but as a Muslim conqueror. He reminded the Arabs that the borders that partitioned the Arab nation had been drawn by foreigners. Hence, he argued, Iraq, as vanguard of the Arabs, was in its right to demand rectification of the injustice. Beyond Arab support of the annexation (and in its prolongation, Arab unity), one discerned the hope for a more equitable division of oil wealth, and for a more assertive attitude toward the ex-colonizers. Saddam's posturing was wildly popular—soon he was compared to Salah al-Din (Saladin), who had liberated the lands of Islam from the Crusader yoke.

Thus started the surprising religious Islamic identification with an expressly secularist regime that had just concluded a war against Islamist Iran. Saddam's blatant defiance of a world order drawn up by the West won him the applause of numerous Islamic authorities, who met in January 1991 in Baghdad. For those present, the promise that Saddam would defeat the West sufficed to turn him into "the good Muslim." Some called for crowning him caliph.[5] The Ba`th regime at once changed its colors, put God's name in Iraq's flag, and evoked Him in every discourse. Even Iran now had no choice but to proclaim its support for its erstwhile foe.

None of these maneuvers saved Saddam, of course. In 1991, the Western-led alliance expelled Iraq from Kuwait, and nearly cost Saddam his regime. However, the specter of regional destabilization led the United States to call off deep invasion of Iraq itself. Preferring Iraqi territorial integrity, the allies let Saddam smash the Kurdish and Shiite revolts that they themselves had called for. Iraq's army was cut down and its illegal WMD and missile programs were submitted to United Nations-controlled dismantlement. A rigid system of economic sanctions, designed to weaken Saddam's regime, soon turned Iraq's population into one of the world's most destitute. But the regime remained in power.

Democratization or Islamization?

How does all this relate to the growth of Islamism in the wider Arab world? Iraq's defeat was a bitter disappointment for Saddam Hussein's legions of admirers. Under Western patronage, the 1991 war succeeded, once more, in bolstering the Middle Eastern system of separate states against a challenger. At the same time, it also evidenced how loathed this system was by its own people; the collusion of Arab regimes with the West was not forgotten. In years to come, the legitimacy of these regimes was not restored. Into the breach leapt the Islamists with their proposal, immune to earthly defeats because it was inscribed in God's own plan.

In the following years, practically all the Arab regimes found themselves called into question, and *political Islam was nearly always their strongest rival*. After the Cold War, there was no longer a progressive block of states: most regimes turned pro-Western, though neoliberal prescriptions failed to deliver the promised prosperity. Except for Lebanon and, to lesser degree, Palestine, all regimes were authoritarian. Efficient controls relegated coups and palace revolutions to the past. But the apparent stability of the Arab state masked a deeper crisis.

Arab elites felt the pressure and reacted with policies ranging from limited democratization to outright physical repression. Here was the paradox: democratization was fatally accompanied by legitimization of the Islamist current. Liberal, progressive, and secularist oppositions continued to exist; however, the principal challenger now came from the resurgent religious Right. Egypt's combination of repression and accommodation preserved Mubarak's rule. The price paid, as discussed earlier, was a gradual giving in to Islamist cultural demands. Guided democracy became guided Islamization. Similar processes occurred in Jordan and Kuwait; the democratic opening went furthest in Morocco. Everywhere, elections helped Islamist movements to become the main parliamentary opposition.

Even in Saudi Arabia, whose monarchy derives its legitimacy from strict Wahhabism, and where opposition has hardly any room, underground critiques grew strong enough to alarm the regime. Most opposition did not call for secularization, but came from groups that considered the rulers insufficiently religious. It is true that Saudi Arabia is something of an exception—a backward society compared to the Fertile Crescent, its still partially tribal structure and absolutist dynasty surviving thanks only to oil wealth and outside support. Even in this atypical case, though, opposition is primarily an Islamist affair.

Complete opening risks complete loss of control, but its opposite, total repression, may trigger a popular explosion, as in the shah's Iran. Most Middle Eastern regimes try to avoid either extreme. Civil war looms wherever an unfree and unconstitutional regime government and opposition forces balance each other. Such was the tragic case of **Algeria**, which exemplifies the delicate tradeoff between democratization and Islamization. Algeria provides a stark warning: democratization without liberalization may derail popular emancipation.[6] After its bloody independence war, and with a socialist pan-Arab orientation under the National Liberation Front (FLN) regime, the country had become, in the 1960s and 1970s, an icon of the international Left. Few cared that the postrevolutionary regime was becoming corrupt, or that incipient Islam was already making a comeback as mainstay of national identity. A popular revolt in 1988 promised democratization, but the Islamist Islamic Salvation Front (FIS) was poised to decisively defeat the secular parties. In 1992 an army coup, meant to forestall a "second Iran," put democracy on hold and plunged the country into an interminable civil war. The military persecuted Islamists; the latter responded with massive terrorist campaigns against civilians. Soon, the relatively moderate FIS had been overtaken by Armed Islamic Group (GIA) extremists with Afghan battle experience, who specialized in butchering whole villages. The carnage continued unabated for years. By the time the FLN stalwart Ahmad Bouteflika was elected as "reconciliation president" in 1999, 100,000 had died in Algeria.

Democratic openings in the Middle East, then, do not necessarily create a pluralist society, but risk creeping Islamization, and hence antidemocratic, or at least antiliberal, evolution. The more society Islamizes, the less successful a non-Islamic government will be in retaining its legitimacy. This makes it increasingly vulnerable to violence or coups. Where the political elite prohibits even controlled democratization, and military and police repression already exist, tensions simmer and there, too, Islamism tends to dominate the opposition. Such is also the case in states too fragmented to risk opening up, as in Syria and, until 2003, in Iraq. The current democratization of Iraq is empowering strong Islamist parties. The question is whether or not democracy can survive Islam's coming to power. Turkey demonstrates that this is possible, to the extent that Islamist movements themselves embrace democratic values—an arduous but not impossible ideological metamorphosis.

Turkey: A Counter-example?

Turkey is the great exception in the Middle East. It is the only Muslim-majority country that for decades was without significant fundamentalist threat, and is the Islamic world's major functioning democracy. (Indonesia is larger but its democracy younger and more fragile.) Turkey's democratic transition was not easy. Anatolia and a little European foothold in East Thrace were the only regions where Turks constituted solid majorities—elsewhere they were a thin ruling stratum. While the victors of World War I were cutting up the Ottoman Empire, ethnic concentration allowed the Turks to throw the occupiers out of their own country. It will be recalled how in 1920–22, Kemal Atatürk salvaged the Turkish independence; he also persuaded his compatriots to make a clean break with the Empire's past and its religious setup. Atatürk's Turkish Republic was a classic case of a development dictatorship. He built a secularized, one-party state based on Western law; among other reforms, he abolished polygamy.

Atatürk's Kemalism launched Turkey on a path that parted company with the Arab world in three ways. First, war and population exchanges created ethnic homogeneity: the Balkans had already been lost; European powers conquered the Ottomans' Arab portions; Armenians were largely exterminated; Greeks were expelled; and Turks dispersed throughout the former Empire returned home. Thus Turkey merged *qawmiyya* and *wataniyya*. Only the Kurds remained, but Turkey simply denied their existence.[7] Religious homogeneity was the second factor: with non-Muslims gone, Muslims were encouraged to forget their religion. The bond between state and mosque was broken, religious educated restricted, and politically active Sufi orders driven underground. Alphabetization in Latin letters completed the breach with the past. Third, Turkey used its independence to lay the bases of industrialization and a national bourgeoisie, and escaped the neocolonial predicament of Jordan, Morocco, and other Arab nations. Terms for joining the club of advanced nations were easier in Atatürk's days than in Nasser's. Turkey did not become a second Japan, but neither did it stay in the league of an Egypt or a Pakistan. Devoid of oil, it also avoided its corrosive effects.

After World War II, Turkey became a reliable U.S. ally. American pressure combined with that of local entrepreneurs pushed for multipartyism. With liberalization, the field opened again for Islam. Reemerging Sufi orders spearpointed the combat against official secularism. Democratization also created a dangerous Left–Right polarization. Proletarianization produced a strong labor movement, but rural zones returned to religion: the result was chronic ungovernability. Thrice the army, guardian of Kemalist legality, intervened—the last time, in 1980. Partial redemocratization was soon permitted, though, and the country embarked on its current neoliberal course.

To complete its secularization and modern development, Turkey's elites ardently desire to join the European Union. However, the bid for rapprochement has been repeatedly snubbed, formally because of Turkey's human rights violations and because its economy is regarded as too state-controlled. Europe's rejection is really more civilizational than economic, and humiliates the Turks who ask: Does a Muslim country have a place at Europe's table? It remains to be seen whether the recent opening of formal entry negotiations—late in 2005, and against the wishes of many Europeans who deny their "Oriental" neighbor's Europeanness—will prevent a reorientation of Turkey toward the Islamic world.

Islamism has become a dominant force in Turkish politics. The 1980s saw the beginning of religious revival, with a new generation of intellectuals, of the "Hearth of Intellectuals" current, which criticized the country's pro-Western and materialist course and attempted to redeem Islam as part of its culture. In the interests of its own battle against Leftist "subversion," the military regime tolerated these attacks. By the 1990s, Islamists were taking control of schools and media. In 1994 religious candidates won muncipal elections in Istanbul and Ankara. Islamization indeed dovetailed with democratization. Once internal violence was contained, the military withdrew. Democracy is today more strongly institutionalized than in Turkey's earlier experiments. Behind the scenes, though, the army continues to act as guarantor of secularism, a subtle power-sharing system that seems to be welcomed by many Turks who still harbor frightening memories of 1970s' street violence. Still, Turkey's more mature civil society and the greater legitimacy of its political process compare favorably with most Arab states, where opposition can express itself only through violence, and where a hard-to-quantify but significant portion of public opinion hopes for destabilization.

Secular Turkey's limits appeared in 1996, when the Islamist *Refah* Party of Necmettin Erbakan came to power: army pressure soon overthrew it, and Labor's Bülent Ecevit took over. But this was not the end of its legal Islamism. Turkey's external debt led in late 2000 to a financial crisis that put it at the mercy of IMF austerity packages. The reaction came in November 2002, when elections brought another, formerly prohibited, moderate Islamist party to power: *Adalet ve Kalkinma* (AK, Justice and Development), led by Tayyip Erdogan, who had himself been banned earlier for "attempting to undermine secularism." Yet AK belied Western fears: Turkey has stayed on its pro-Western course. Thus Turkey is a strategic bridge between the West and the Islamic world, and has a unique experience that is a potentially important precedent for pluralist democracy, combined with a collective identity that reaffirms its Islamic roots.

Although Islamic identification is on the rise, it is of a different type than the one emerging in other parts of the Islamic world. Kemalism produced an "Islamic church" not unlike Christian churches in the West; and for the moment at least, the Islamists' demands are more cultural than political: more mosques, more religious education, more respect for religious norms ("family values"); privatization of religion is not contested. The AK is closer to conservative Western political parties like the German Christian Democrats and the U.S. Republican Party than to Qutb's *Jihad*. Parallel to low-intensity Islamization, Westernization and pluralism are also progressing, in such critical areas as cultural rights for Turkish Kurds, women's emancipation, abolition of the death penalty, and Western tourism. It is a mixed situation, and the jury is still out.

Islamization of the Social Sphere

The growing influence of Islamist parties in domestic politics in many Muslim countries follows their increasing social presence. The struggle for civil society, possibly the most decisive battlefield, is being fought in two arenas: in social services and in public debate over society's cultural identity.

In the Islamic world, no less than in the West, the modern state has been colonizing a gamut of responsibilities that far surpasses that of its premodern predecessor. In the Ottoman Empire, the sultanate's prime function was the provision of external and internal military security; its second, to keep the economy running by controlling provisions and honest market practices. Both functions depended on taxes, soldiers, and a corps of civil servants. As a third task, the state maintained Islam's supremacy, which demanded yet another group of functionaries. Legislation, however, was not within the purview of the sultan: God is the only lawgiver, and the `ulama interpreted His word. Theoretically, government was there to keep a political framework within which subjects would fulfill their religious and social obligations.

Many of the social responsibilities of the modern state were formerly under private or communal control (e.g., feeding and educating the poor and orphans, paid for by *zakat* and the income generated by *waqfs*). There is no need to idealize these premodern mechanisms, doubtlessly replete with petty social controls, tensions, and humiliations of the weak by the strong. Yet *grosso modo* they functioned. Islam includes an awareness of mutual obligation that favorably compares with other civilizations. Modernization eroded its mutual aid system. Introduction of private property stimulated egoism; secular education undermined communal identification; urbanization weakened traditional bonds. According to the modernization vision *en vogue* until the 1960s, the Middle Eastern state would compensate for these losses by taking over erstwhile communal responsibilities. This expectation has lately run aground.

"Interventionist" states such as Egypt, Syria, Iraq, and Algeria operated hospitals, schools, and social security networks, while their political parties penetrated social life; in "conservative" states such as Jordan or Morocco, traditional bonds remained intact longer. Everywhere, however, pervasive webs of patronage linked power centers, received clients' loyalty, and in turn dispensed favors: a visit to the doctor, a sinecure job in some office, a permit to travel. This system, too, has largely decayed over the past decades. Development never kept up with population growth. Except in oil-exporting states, public incomes have declined, and with them, the means to provide benefits to the population. Liberalization brought in cheap foreign products and threatened local producers; privatization destroyed more jobs than it created; while red tape, political instability, and war kept foreign investors away. The socioeconomic crisis has deepened from year to year.

The incapacitation of the Middle Eastern state, however, offered Islamists a point of entry. In the slums of Cairo, Gaza, Karachi, and elsewhere Islamist movements provide daycare centers, schools, clinics, social clubs, sports, homework assistance for the youth, and financial support for the indigent. These services are organized around the mosque; or more correctly, around mosques linked to Islamist groups. Often, welfare is handled by idealistic volunteers whose disinterest stands in stark contrast to the corruption of the officials. The difference between the social services provided by the Palestinian Authority and Hamas is a case in point; Hamas's pensions to relatives of suicide-bomber "martyrs" are an extra propaganda point for the Islam-is-the-solution thesis. The critical point here is that these services come with a bonus of religious worship, exegesis, and brainwashing. Thus Islamist movements construct a countercultural space that is progressively immune to state control, and constitutes a recruitment ground. Penetration of civil society leads to a growth of popular support for Islamism. Starting with intellectuals, Islamic parties have successfully reached out to sectors of the petty bourgeoisie frustrated in their upward mobility or threatened with social decline; and from there, to the recently urbanized poor. In many corners of the Arab world, copies are growing of the Islamist triangle (i.e., intellectuals + conservative middle class + traditionalist masses) that was so lethal to Iran's shah.[8]

Islamization of Culture: The "Discursive Field"

Another dimension of Islamist conquest of civil society lies in the realm of ideas. What is at stake is hegemony over the hearts and minds. Egypt provides, again, the clearest example. The country once prided itself on its liberal traditions. Yet Islamism has over the past twenty years significantly increased its scope, to the detriment not only of secular nationalism but also of modernist Islam. More Egyptians today opt for the *shari`a*-based Islamic state than twenty years ago. Secularist voices have been violently silenced. Fundamentalists were behind the outlawing and exile of progressive thinkers. They applauded the execution for heresy of liberal Sudanese theologian Muhammad Mahmud Taha in 1985. In 1992, Farag Foda, Egypt's foremost liberal Muslim critic of fundamentalism, was assassinated. In 1994, Naguib Mahfouz, a Nobel laureate defending liberal positions and peace with Israel, narrowly escaped a similar attempt on his life. Intimidation narrows the field of what can safely be expressed in public, whereas religious propaganda receives official sanction. TV sermons, Qur'an exegesis, and religious talk shows are far more numerous today than one generation ago. If Egypt is diverging more and more from the Habermasian model of a communicative sphere, it is not hard to imagine the lack of freedom of expression in countries

that never had a liberal past to begin with—in Algeria, Jordan, the
Gulf, or in dictatorships like Syria.

The problem is not the paucity of pluralistic and anti-fundamen-
talist Islamic thinkers. It is in the difficulties they face to make their
voice heard. Modernists are on the defensive; some of the freest spirits have found a more congenial atmosphere in the West than in
their Islamic homelands. Control of the media is comprehensive.
Some of the best and most courageous Muslim journalists are in
London and New York rather than in the Middle East. And *al-
Jazeera*, editorially independent if not exactly a paragon of liberalism, exists only by the grace of Qatar's enlightened prince. The brain
drain of the most daring intellectuals creates of course a reciprocal
alienation. One should not impute this to Islamist influence alone.
The absence of freedom of expression predated Islamists, whose own
publications were also often banned. (Qutb's *Milestones* is only sold
under the table in Egypt.) Thought control has long since been part
and parcel of civil society's weakness. But in the current constellation, Islamists benefit more from and strengthen the climate of
intellectual closure. In the battle between Islam and Islamism, the
latter appears to be winning.[9]

Islamism's International Integration

The constitution of an informal "Islamist International" is another
expression of the Islamic awakening. Since the 740s' `Abbasid revolu-
tion, Islam has viewed itself as a belief system for humanity as a
whole. True, expansion reduced the concept of the *umma* to a symbolical aspiration. Yet Islam always implied inter-Muslim encounter and
solidarity in spite of its numerous internecine conflicts. Since the
nineteenth century in particular, the *hajj*, occasion for direct contact,
has been a unifier of ritual and dogma. Communication with the great
Middle Eastern centers helped disseminate normative Islam in
regions hitherto more permeated by popular Islam. The Muslim
world, it can be said, invented globalization *avant la lettre*.[10]

Today's globalization is resuscitating and intensifying this process of
isolated societies entering into close connection, and is having profound
influence on the Islamic world. Using electronic communications technology, Muslims are becoming the kind of global community that was
inconceivable just a generation ago. Television, satellite telephony, and
the Internet cut both ways. These channels of Western cultural invasion
facilitate Islamic propaganda and messages between terrorists with the
same ease that they transmit Hollywood movies, democratic campaign-
ing, or pornography. Nasser's pan-Arabism was carried on radio waves;

the first Palestinian *intifada* snowballed from town to town through TV reportage and fax; the Iranian revolution would have been unthinkable without its taped sermons; and suicide bombers multiply their impact with videotaped farewell messages. International Islamic nongovernmental organizations (NGOs) discuss and transplant themselves from locale to locale through Web sites that force dictators into rearguard battle for control of the Internet. Centralized regimes view any expression of self-organization as challenge, and electronic media present civil society with a powerful weapon indeed. Cybercafés were the preferred contact point of Iranian reformers until theocracy shut them down. Saudi Arabia tries to block access to some 15,000 sites. How long will such measures succeed? For all (or perhaps because of) its physical insecurity, Baghdad is fast becoming a Weblogger's paradise. The "network society" already exists in most Islamic cities, coexisting tensely with the surrounding traditional-authoritarian society. Public opinion, once tightly controlled, is growing in the Arab world as well as among Muslim Diasporas in the West. Globalization, however, is a game that Islamists, no less than democrats, are adept at playing. For the first time, a virtual *umma* is emerging, proselytizing among Muslims and others outside the Middle East. Islam is internationalizing, thanks to the West's new technologies. Less benignly, terrorist groups are among the electronic media's most avid users.[11]

Proliferation of *Jihad* Fronts: Islam's Frontiers Outside the Arab Core

In the social sphere, Islamist expansion proceeds gradually and generally in peace. However, it is the recrudescence of violent confrontation between Islamic and non-Muslim communities sharing the same territory that has become the hallmark of the recent "rise of Islam." Islamist movements have in fact participated in bloody conflicts that have spread far beyond the original Middle East perimeter. Open war is now waged along all of Islam's frontiers, and Islamists play a crucial role in turning them into unforgiving civilizational clashes. Five such frontiers may be distinguished; some have become clashes of competing fundamentalisms:

1. Islam's frontier with the Orthodox Christian and communist (or formerly communist) worlds—expressed in conflicts in Russia, western China, the Balkans, and the Eastern Mediterranean
2. Islam's frontier with Judaism in Palestine, where Islam faces not only the state of Israel but also a homegrown Jewish fundamentalism

3. Islam's frontier with Hinduism: in India, the Muslim minority confronts Hindu fundamentalism
4. Islam's frontier with Christianity, Buddhism, Chinese traditions, and ethnic and religious minorities in Southeast Asia
5. Islam's frontier with Christianity along the broad African front encompassing Nigeria and Sudan

In part, these are regional conflicts, with Islam simply one weapon against some nearby, non-Muslim group. More commonly, though, historical and often colonial vicissitudes that planted non-Muslims among Muslim populations (or vice versa) are the cause of today's political and cultural conflicts; although this does not explain why so many have turned so vicious. Some of these flashpoints are analyzed below. First, however, attention must be paid to one case that combines the struggle against communism in Russia with the struggle against "lapsed" Muslims: Afghanistan.

The Christian Orthodox and (Ex-)Communist Frontier

Afghanistan

The Soviet Union occupied Afghanistan in 1980. Islamist resistance became in the following years one of the factors that critically weakened communism, internally and against its geopolitical rival. Mikhail Gorbachev, who wanted to modernize and humanize communism at home, decided to cut Soviet losses, and in 1987 the USSR began a humiliating withdrawal that would be completed two years later. The pro-communist regime of Muhammad Najibullah was unable to hold out on its own. In 1992, the capital city of Kabul was overrun by Islamist *mujahidin*, who started at once to quarrel among themselves. A cruel civil war ensued. Slowly the tide turned in favor of the most radical Islamist wing, the Taliban—Afghan refugees who had become conservative extremists in Pakistan's fundamentalist *madrasas*. The Taliban conquered Kabul in 1996, and established an Islamist regime based on the strictest interpretation of *shari`a*. Apart from many other acts that shocked Western observers, they became infamous for their brutal repression of women's rights. Rigorously excluded from social life, Afghan women were forced to abandon all work outside home, prohibited from going to school, and obliged to wear *burqas* that covered body and face. Music, sports, and other entertainment were banned; transgressions severely punished by the Islamic police. Public executions in the Kabul football stadium horrified the world, but no one intervened. The *mujahidin* leadership isolated Afghanistan from the rest of the world; only three countries, one of which was Pakistan, recognized the new regime. The United States had initially helped the fundamentalist guerrillas, but now kept quiet, especially after the Taliban banned opium production.

Civil war dragged on, with obvious ethnic overtones. Afghan society is very heterogeneous, the result of a history of protracted foreign interventions. First Persia and the Indian Mughals dueled to control it, then Britain and Czarist Russia, and finally the United States and the Soviet Union. After the Cold War, Russian power was gone, and the United States was occupied with other worries. Few outsiders cared about the interminable bloodletting. So Afghanistan was for a while left to its own devices, but the price of isolation was as high as that of intervention. Millions fled to Pakistan, creating what was then the world's largest refugee crisis. Many Afghan displaced persons became the easy prey of mafias and fundamentalist recruiters.

In Afghanistan itself, the Taliban were connected to the largest ethnic group, the Sunni Pashtos. Both Shiite minorities and non-Pashto Sunni minorities in the north (Uzbeks, Turcomans, and others) found themselves on the wrong side of the divide. Attempts at securing a ceasefire between the warring groups failed. By 1998, the Taliban controlled 90 percent of Afghanistan, and started to massacre Shiite Hazaras. *The Economist* granted the country the dubious title of "Planet's Worst Place."[12] By early 2001, international criticism, coupled with what the Taliban considered belated humanitarian relief, had irritated the Afghan regime enough that it destroyed two giant medieval statues of the Buddha. In happier times, these had been symbols of the country's rich cultural inheritance; now they epitomized idolatry. Relations with the United States deteriorated when the Taliban offered asylum to Saudi Islamist leader Osama bin Laden, accused of killing 300 civilians in terrorist attacks against U.S. embassies in Kenya and Tanzania. Their hospitality was to cost Afghanistan's rulers dearly after 9/11.

Central Asia, Russia, and Chechnya

Afghanistan was only one part of the Soviets' troubles with Muslims. A giant territorial band connected the USSR to its Muslim subjects, most of them Central Asians who in earlier centuries had been converted by Sufi brotherhoods. Islamic states had ruled this territory until the tsars absorbed it in the nineteenth century. Islam had been a strong source of resistance against Russification and Sovietization. Despite its brutality, Stalinism never succeeded in imposing full secularization. By the 1970s and 1980s, the nationalisms of Muslim populations had become one of the forces tearing communism apart. Some adopted religion to emphasize their claims for greater autonomy. In

1991, implosion of the Soviet Union led to independence for six Muslim-majority former Socialist Soviet Republics: **Azerbaijan, Kazakhstan, Turkmenistan, Uzbekistan,** and **Kyrgyzstan** (all of Turkic stock), plus **Tajikistan** (culturally Persian). All are weak states lacking traditions of self-government, and their identity is complicated by the presence of numerous ethnic minorities, some of whom are descendants of Russians and other Europeans who were sent to colonize Central Asia under tsars and Soviets. The harsh climate limits agricultural production, but huge gas reserves are attracting international interest.

Islamist movements are active in all these new states, though their strength varies. Immediately after independence, civil war broke out in Tajikistan between a power-hungry post-communist elite, and Islamists aided by sympathizers across the Afghan border. Before the former restored order (with Russian help), 20,000 civilians had died. More recently, tensions have risen in Kyrgyzstan, Uzbekistan, and Azerbaijan.

Within the Russian Federation proper, Sunni **Chechnya** declared independence from Russia in 1991. Moscow feared that recognizing the secession would signal weakness and serve as a precedent for further atomization. However, a war to retake the rebellious republic failed, and after two years (with 100,000 dead), Russia conceded a fragile autonomy. When Wahhabite Chechens invaded neighboring Daghestan and proclaimed an Islamic state in 1999, they gave Vladimir Putin (then Boris Yeltsin's prime minister) the pretext to profile himself as a nationalist candidate for suppressing the Islamist attempt. The clampdown was followed by terrorist attacks in Moscow that killed hundreds. Putin blamed Chechen separatists, and launched a second war against the breakaway republic. In the 1999–2000 winter, Russian troops occupied the capital Grozny and crushed Chechen independence. Putin won the presidential election. However, Russia's occupation provoked a fierce guerrilla war. Chechens also took to terror. In November 2002, rebels hijacked a Moscow theater and its audience of 700; Russian forces "liberated" them, but only at the cost of more than one hundred lives. Other attacks followed. One of the worst, in 2004, was the hijacking and crashing of two civilian airplanes by female Chechen terrorists. This was followed by the occupation of a school in Beslan, North Ossetia; most of the 340 dead were schoolchildren. Russian pacification has demonstrably failed.

Former Yugoslavia

Fundamentalism was only marginal in the wars of Yugoslav succession—and then mostly on the Christian, Serb Orthodox side.

Muslims, however, were the majority of victims in the Bosnian and Kosovar conflicts, and the images of their victimization have had implications for Islamists. **Bosnian** Muslims descend from Slav Bogomiles, a medieval Manichean sect related to the Cathars; persecuted by the Orthodox Church, they may have adopted Islam after the Ottomans conquered their territory in 1463. In spite of some tensions, relations with the two other Bosnian communities, the Orthodox Serbs and the Catholic Croats, were reasonably peaceable under Marshal Josip Broz Tito's federative communist rule. Mixed marriages were common in Sarajevo. War broke out in 1993 as a result of the post-Cold War radicalization of the Bosnian Serbs demanding reunification with neighboring Serbia. With the connivance of Slobodan Milosevic's nationalist government in Belgrade, the latter conquered parts of Bosnia. Mass murder, ethnic cleansing, concentration camps, and mass rape made Bosnia the worst killing field in Europe since World War II. Not unlike in Lebanon's civil war, in Bosnia's triangular communal war, religion functioned as a badge of group identity more than as expression of personal faith. However, Middle Eastern Islamists saw in the Bosnian conflict a perfect fit with their ideology of Muslim-Christian incompatibility; international passivity seemed to prove Western indifference to the Muslims' lot. Hence, they argued, the necessity of international Islamic solidarity. Saudi money indeed funded small battalions of fundamentalist "Afghans" to help Bosnians. The carnage continued so long because foreign powers could not agree whether or how to intervene. The United Nations could do no more than protect a couple of Muslim and Croat enclaves, and even this incompletely. In 1995, a Dutch United Nations contingent failed in its mission in Muslim Srebrenica, where 7000 Muslims were slaughtered by the Serb paramilitary. Serb military supremacy bore diplomatic and territorial fruit. Bosnia was partitioned as per the Dayton Accords. From the truncated independent Muslim-Croat Bosnia that emerged, the Islamist volunteers were quietly expelled.

Four years later another war involving Muslims broke out. **Kosovo**, an autonomous region within Serbia, was historically Serb: the Field of the Blackbirds, where Turks crushed Serb resistance in 1389, created a Serb "Wailing Wall." Ottoman pressure in the seventeenth century caused Serb migration to more northern regions, and Kosovo lost its demographically Christian character. In recent decades **Albanian** Muslim Yugoslavs, who had long been present in the area, increased their settlement until they constituted 90 percent of the population. Albanians—spread out over Kosovo, the Former Yugoslav Republic of Macedonia, Greece, and Albania proper—are one of the few other Balkan peoples to have embraced Islam in Ottoman times.

Milosevic used the Albanian "invasion" for his own nationalistic ends, abolished the province's autonomy, and started to discriminate against the Albanian Kosovars. This climaxed in 1999, when Serbia, fearing international intervention, started preventive ethnic cleansing: one million Kosovars fled to neighboring countries, raising fears of a chain reaction that might detonate the Balkan powder keg. NATO intervened, defeated Serbia, and brought home the refugees (who promptly expelled their Serbian neighbors). Meanwhile the influx of Muslim refugees provoked civil war in Macedonia; in Serbia, military defeat led the way to democratic revolution, and Milosevic was handed over to the International Criminal Tribunal in The Hague.[13]

The Yugoslav wars were among the few recent conflicts involving Muslims where Islamists were little more than onlookers. However, this did not prevent propagandistic exploitation of these wars by Islamic fundamentalists in the Middle East—as well as by Muslim-haters in Europe.

Palestine and Hamas

When it was still no more than a limited territorial dispute between two nations, the Israeli-Palestinian conflict was already the most globalized of conflicts, with each victim paraded as televised trophy by its own side. In 1972, three Japanese militants of the anarchist Red Army opened fire on Guatemalan Catholic pilgrims in the Tel Aviv airport, killing twenty-six. Neither perpetrators nor victims belonged to any of the groups directly involved in the conflict, yet everyone understood the rationale behind this grotesque act of terror. Jerusalem is not only a place, but also a concept, with meaning for millions of people around the world who have nothing to do with its conflicts. Such universality simply does not pertain to Kosovo or Kandahar. Thirty dead in Tel Aviv or Bethlehem cause more political fallout than 3000 in Algeria or Chechnya—no equality in death here. It was inevitable that Islamists would try to exploit the presence of hundreds of foreign journalists in the Holy Land; the nearly professional expertise Israelis and Palestinian have developed in capturing headlines would have inevitably attracted religious extremists. Yet fundamentalism also has its endogenous causes. The last fifteen years have witnessed the "religiosization" of an essentially national conflict. How did fundamentalism become central to the Palestine conflict? How did Palestine become central to fundamentalists?

Islam occupies in Palestine the cradle of both Judaism and Christianity, the two religions Muhammad came to supplant. Palestine has the world's oldest Christian community, subdivided into many competing churches, and now in decline. At least 85 percent of present

Palestinians are Sunni Muslims. Before undergoing Islamist influence, twentieth-century Palestinians were rather secularized; Western influence goes back to the Crusades, and intensified during the 1920–48 British mandate. The period of Zionist immigration ended with the mandate's partition into two states. However, the establishment of the state of Israel, and failure to establish the projected Palestinian Arab state, made the area one of Islam's most controversial. Israel's very existence is, for many Muslims, an affront to Islam. Its occupation of additional Arab territory since 1967 has added fuel to the flames.

Islam was significant in interwar anti-British and anti-Zionist resistance; but it was a defensive, conservative Islam. In order to appease opposition, Britain granted ample authority to the Supreme Muslim Council (SMC). In the interwar years, Hajj Amin al-Husseini, its leader, used the SMC as platform for his anti-Zionist campaign. He gravitated to racist anti-Semitic and pro-Nazi positions. The SMC, in the hands of the Palestinian elite however, was eclipsed by the 1936–39 popular revolt. `Izz al-Din al-Qassam, a puritan *shaikh*, incited landless peasants to wage guerrilla war against the British and the Jews; it was only with difficulty put down. (Hailed as father of Islamic resistance in Palestine, Qassam would lend his name to the Hamas brigade responsible for most post-1993 terrorism.)

After the failure of anticolonial revolt, the next battles occurred in 1948. Catastrophe could not be avoided; Palestinian society broke down. The 1948 defeat led to prolonged demoralization; not until the mid-1950s would a new generation of Palestinians jumpstart nationalism. However, the new national movement that emerged in the refugee camps where most Palestinians lived was not Islamic. The Palestine Liberation Organization (PLO), established in 1964, defined its aim as a secular multiconfessional state; more recently, Palestinian *wataniyya* has emphasized its Canaanite (i.e., pre-Islamic) roots. Eventually, secular Palestinian nationalism had to define itself in relation to a strong competitor: Palestinian Islamism. However, such differentiation into nonreligious and Islamist wings occurred only in the 1980s, in the Israeli-occupied territories—nearly one generation after the 1967 Six Day War. It will be recalled that that crucial defeat of secularist Arab states opened the door to Islamism in the Arab world. In the short run, though, it helped secular Palestinian nationalism, which now took the torch. As Fatah and other commandos were militarily insignificant against Israel, Palestinians were forced to rethink their strategy. By the late 1970s, the aim of destroying Israel and replacing it by a unitary Arab state was giving way to the more modest and realistic goal of two states: an independent Palestinian

state on the West Bank and Gaza Strip, which would coexist alongside the Jewish state. Armed struggle was de-emphasized in favor
of diplomacy. Islamists, however, rejected this out of hand, and a
fundamentalist political movement emerged to challenge the PLO,
which had enjoyed a monopoly on nationalist legitimacy. In the
1980s, the universities of the West Bank and Gaza—one of the few
Palestinian institutions left alone by the Israeli occupation—were
the battleground between Fatah and the Left against Islamists. In
the Islamic world as in the West, academia is a barometer of ideological change. Islamists were already in control of the campuses, formerly the bulwark of secular nationalism, before they showed up in
other places. From here, the trend to Islamize politics and lifestyles
spread to the rest of society. Initially the Islamists were even
encouraged by Israel, which mistook them for an innocuous alternative to the PLO's nationalists.

The period since the late 1980s has seen a paradoxical Islamization
of the Israeli-Palestinian conflict—paradoxical because the same
period also inaugurated steps toward a peaceful solution. The first
intifada (1987–93) enshrined the dominance of the internal front (Palestinians of the occupied territories) over the external (i.e., Palestinian refugees dispersed over the Arab world). Yasser Arafat was only in
partial control, while, through its confrontations with Israel, the
Islamist wing became sufficiently powerful to constitute an alternative to the PLO. By the late 1980s, *Jihad Islami* (Islamic Jihad) had
become the most active fundamentalist movement in the territories.
Then it was overtaken by Hamas,[14] a radical offshoot of the Muslim
Brotherhood. Its leader, *shaikh* Ahmad Yassin, criticized the Brotherhood's gradualism. Hamas overtook the secular nationalist factions in
extremism; its 1988 charter expresses its ideology.

Hamas rejects the PLO view that the conflict pits the Palestinian
Arab *nation* against Zionism, an extension of Western imperialism. It
understands the conflict as a war of *religions* and sees Zionism as a
crime that not only despoils the Palestinians, but also corrupts
Islamic morality in a battle of Good Islam against Evil Judaism. The
influence of European anti-Semitism is much clearer than in secular
Palestinian nationalism.[15] The latter tries to differentiate Zionists
(who bear the brunt of the blame) from Israelis and Jews. For Hamas,
the Jews are the root of the problem. They are accused of wanting to
rule the world, manipulating both communism and American capitalism,
and of planning to rebuild their temple in Jerusalem (*al-Quds*), Islam's
third Sacred City. For Hamas, World Jewry is a cancer that is smothering
Islam—a complete inversion of Islam's traditional, rather favorable view
of Jews. Palestine may have been relatively unimportant in Islam, but

Jerusalem's sanctity made up for it. Palestine belongs to *Dar al-Islam*, hence in principle to all Muslims. Therefore the Palestinians have no right to cede any of its territory.

There are obvious parallels with the Zionist Right, which considers the Land of Israel as belonging to all Jews, and with Jewish fundamentalists, who view it as God's real estate, making any partition with His "enemies" illegitimate. For Palestinian Islamists, the eradication of the "Zionist entity" and the establishment of an Islamic state in its place call for universal *jihad*: Israel's annihilation will fructify Islam's rebirth. A certain inconsistency reigns as to the lot that should befall the Jews: either Jewish survivors will be welcome as *dhimmis*, or all will be expelled, or the struggle will go on until it achieves the world-wide liquidation of all Jews. In Hamas's ideology, it follows logically that any political process is tantamount to treason—hence its hostility to Arafat's nationalist leadership. Tactically, however, neither of the major currents could risk being seen by Palestinian opinion as a schismatic threat to national unity. As a result, their relations remain ambiguous, shifting from occasional open violence to operational moderation. In practice, however, Hamas and the smaller Islamist outfits have endeavored to delegitimize the PLO and build a "virtuous" counter-society. Already the first *intifada* showed traits of a cultural counterrevolution with the killing of collaborators, drug dealers, and prostitutes; the veiling of women; and other coercive measures.

Between 1991 and 1999, the peace process injected a dose of hope in Israeli-Palestinian relations. It started inauspiciously. The PLO was weakened by its solidarity with Iraq in the Gulf crisis; popular enthusiasm for Saddam had left Arafat no other option. After the Gulf War, the United States forced Israel and its Arab neighbors into peace negotiations that implied indirect recognition. But the PLO had enough residual power left and eventually Israel had to negotiate directly with Arafat. The resulting 1993 Oslo Accords included mutual Israel-PLO recognition, and set a framework for staggered Israeli withdrawal to make room for a Palestinian state.

By 2000, this peace process was dying: both sides had been less than wholehearted in living up to their commitments. Israel's withdrawal was slower and less than Palestinians had expected, and Israel continued building settlements that could not but make future withdrawals even more difficult. Arafat's Palestinian Authority (PA) took over wherever Israel left, but failed to suppress Palestinian terrorists out to sabotage Israel and the peace process. Although it is hard to disentangle each side's responsibility, extremist violence on both sides was certainly the single greatest stumbling block to the political process. Although some radical Zionist settlers tried their level worst, fundamentalist Muslims easily outdid their Jewish counterparts in cruelty. Islamists attacked the peace process at its Achilles heel, physical security. Israeli Jews, heirs to a long history of persecution, distrusted Palestinians' intentions a priori. For Hamas, continuing military (more properly, terrorist) operations against the enemy was the surest strategy to weaken Arafat. From 1994 on, Hamas and related groups perpetrated a chain of kidnappings and suicide attacks against mostly civilian targets. This created the desired shock effect, breaking the dynamism of Israeli-Palestinian rapprochement. Israeli punitive raids unavoidably hurt more Palestinian civilians than perpetrators, or their handlers. Arafat now sat between two fires— in Israeli eyes, he had failed to curb Palestinian terror; to his own people, he appeared incapable of shielding them against Israel's ire. Political Islam was the beneficiary of this quandary, with Hamas gaining additional popular support thanks to its network of social services. Eventually, one-third of Palestinians came to identify with the Islamists.

In 1996, a numbed Israeli electorate brought to power a right-wing government that broke off negotiations with the Palestinians. Closure of the territories impoverished the Palestinians, further limiting the scope of Arafat's patronage. He responded to his people's rising frustration just as Mubarak in Egypt had: with preventive Islamization. He also called for national dialogue with Hamas, although the latter maintained a polite distance and continued anti-Israeli terrorism. By the time the Zionist Left returned to power in Israel, it was too late; amid growing mutual impatience and intransigence, the failure of the July 2000 Camp David summit between Arafat and Israel's new Left-leaning leader Ehud Barak was not surprising. The consequences, however, were tragic. A second *intifada* broke out, provoking Israeli retaliation. The ensuing cycle of violence precluded all meaningful negotiation, and strengthened the extremist wings even more. While insecurity deepened among both Jews and Arabs, the rest of the world helplessly watched the ghastly deterioration. Compelled to resort to ever more extreme rhetoric, Arafat "lost relevance": by mid-2002, Israeli counterterrorist incursions had reduced him to a pathetic prisoner in his bombed-out palace.

As prospects for a political way out receded, terrorism, initially rejected by most Palestinians, came to be seen as the ultimate weapon to demoralize and destroy the Zionist enemy. Israeli-Palestinian dialogue became a victim, too. In Israel the violence shattered the morale of, and politically emasculated, the peace camp, its champions now painted as traitors to the national cause. This brought Ariel Sharon, hard-line leader of the Greater Israel wing, to power. Under his leadership, Israeli countermeasures scored successes against the Palestinian terrorist resistance (mainly but not exclusively Islamist). In 2004, the assassination of Yassin, and of his successor, decapitated Hamas leadership. However, this has hardly affected the Islamists' popularity, which is based more on rejection of PA impotence than on ideological extremism. Arafat's death appeared to remove an obstacle to Israeli-Palestinian rapprochement; but the power it brought to his more moderate successor, Fatah's Mahmoud Abbas (Abu Mazen) is very circumscribed. Abbas appears no more able to streamline Palestinian administration, keep the lid on Palestinian terror, and overcome Islamist opposition than was his predecessor—a weakness that condemns the post-Arafat leadership to continued "irrelevancy." Thus, as long as the international community remains unwilling to intervene, and Arab governments are unable to, Israel enjoys an unlikely interregnum during which it can steer developments. A conjuncture Sharon used in 2005 to unilaterally withdraw Israeli forces from the Gaza Strip—in the process, breaking the resistance of Israeli settlers and a political taboo against giving up "national" territory. This may open a Pandora's box that Israel will be unable to control. Already, non-negotiated separation from the Palestinians is producing significant political realignment. Israel's retreat, however, was driven more by opportunism than by any hope of conciliating the Palestinians. In Gaza, withdrawal did little to pacify the Islamists, who succeeded in convincing their followers that Palestinian armed resistance was what had made Israel turn tail. Lack of perspective for a negotiated solution and popular rage against Fatah's corrupt practices swept Hamas into power in parliamentary elections in January 2006. The new Hamas administration refused to accede to Western pressures to recognize Israel, renounce violence, and accept earlier agreements. Its insistence (at least rhetorically) on calling for destruction of the Jewish state—echoing similar calls from Iran's Islamist leadership—has earned it international opprobrium, isolation, and a financial boycott that is further impoverishing the Palestinians. In Israel, meanwhile, new Prime Minister Ehud Olmert (successor to the suddenly incapacitated Sharon) threatens to unilaterally define Israel's definitive border by further selective retreats—unless negotiations with the Palestinians can be brought back from their current state of suspended animation. By mid-2006, little hope for peace on the part of either nation had survived a decade of disappointments and five years of relentless violence.

Although for now Israel has kept its military superiority by a wide margin, in the long run, Islamists may yet be the winners, for the "military option" they impose on Israel mires the Jewish state in an endless series of battles in which it must defeat the Palestinians one by one, without ever winning the war. Each new round only brings more publicity to the Palestinian cause as a symbol of Islam's struggle. The more relevant Islamism becomes for the Palestine conflict, the more moral ground Israel loses—a development all the more worrisome for the Jewish state as popular mood in the Arab world becomes ever more grimly set against coexistence, and more susceptible to anti-Semitic reinterpretation. The eventual outcome of the Zionist-Islamist duel may well be determined by the wider Western-Islam confrontation.

Finally, what about Palestine's relevance for Islamism? Blaming the Israeli-Palestinian conflict and "automatic" U.S. support for the Israeli side (for Muslim anger) is overly simplistic. Palestine has become a very useful Islamic symbol; however, no (hypothetical) resolution of this conflict will eliminate the fundamentalist challenge. Palestine packages Islamist demands in a visible and easily marketable way. Israel, from an Islamist point of view, has been a gift: if Zionism did not exist, they would have invented it! But Islamism has multiple roots, and these may continue to bear fruit, with or without Palestine.

The Hindu Frontier

After the Middle East, the India-Pakistan couple is at the center of the second most dangerous confrontation of the Islamic world with another civilization. Things have not gone well over the past fifteen years. In a paradoxical turn, the Congress Party, former standard-bearer of pan-Indian secularism, had become the protector of tens of millions of Muslims remaining in India after the 1947 partition. Over the next decades, however, the long conflict with its Islamic neighbor, Pakistan, as well as internal developments, brought forth a Hindu nationalism, or fundamentalism, which has been pushing for India's desecularization. But if *Mother Bharat* were to become a Hindu-first community, Muslims would become second-class citizens. Congress was not immune to the communalist virus; yet it still acted as a defensive wall of the religiously neutral state. However, Congress declined as the Hindu fundamentalist *Bharatiya Janata Party* (BJP) grew.

The BJP came to power in India in 1998 under Atal Behar Vajpayee, riding the crest of right-wing agitation. At its worst, in 1992, thousands of Hindus destroyed in Ayodhya the Babri mosque erected in the sixteenth century on the birthplace of the Hindu god Rama, triggering the worst outburst of Hindu-Muslim violence since 1947. The fascistoid *Shiv Sena* (Shiva's Army) attacked Muslims in Delhi, Mumbai, and other mixed cities. The violence cost 10,000 lives, a toll that deepened Pakistani hostility. Shockwaves of indignation tempered BJP radicalism, so that when the Vajpayee government eventually took over in 1998, it turned out to be less radical than initially feared. Congress' return to power in 2004 confirmed India's democratic practice, and may herald a further mitigation of anti-Muslimist trends.

Although atrocities on the 1992 scale have not recurred, community tensions have not abated. Hindu extremists continue clamoring for "saffronization," (saffron being the color of the extremist Hindu movement, *Rashtriya Swayamsevak Sangh*, National Self-Reliant Union). There are two tension points: Kashmir and Gujarat. In the former, a two-thirds Muslim state claimed by Pakistan, *Hizb al-Mujaheddin*, an Islamist movement close to the Afghan Taliban (and purportedly to Pakistan's Mawdudist *Jami`at-i Islami*), has been waging a separatist guerrilla war since the late 1980s. This low-intensity conflict brought in the Indian army and has already claimed 30,000–60,000 lives, many by terrorism. India accused Pakistan of supporting the separatists; Islamabad answered that its support is only moral. Tensions along the demarcation line were inflamed in 1999, after both India and Pakistan tested nuclear arms and missiles. Kashmir has at least twice brought the two countries to the brink of total war, and in Pakistan brought Pervez Musharraf to power in a military coup. In 2000, a ceasefire with the insurgents fell through when India vetoed Pakistani participation in the talks.

Here too Islamists have taken a regional conflict into the center of the enemy's civilization. When in 2001 pro-Pakistani Kashmiri Islamists attacked parliament in New Delhi, an immediate international crisis erupted; India suspended diplomatic relations. Musharraf was now in the middle of a triple crossfire: (1) he had a conflict with India, and his own trigger-happy military elite was intent on a revenge war against the hereditary foe; (2) 9/11 put Pakistan in the center of U.S. attention as key sponsor of the Taliban regime; and (3) growing sectors of his own population identified with the Islamist cause.

In 2002, after the massacre of thirty-five Indian troops in Kashmir, one million soldiers were dispatched to the border; nuclear war was in the air. Only after U.S. pressure did Pakistan withdraw, and stop its guerrillas from infiltrating Indian Kashmir. State elections took place, in spite of a threatened separatist boycott; but the momentum toward regional détente was interrupted when Islamist attacks recommenced. Although civil war has not ceased, Indian-Pakistani diplomacy has recently intensified efforts to defuse the conflict. Even a terrorist attack on a Delhi market in 2005, claimed by a possible alias of *Lashkar-e-Toiba* (Army of the Pure), a Pakistan-based Islamist group aspiring to reimpose Islamic rule over all of India, has not derailed the process.[16] Although respective political positions on the Kashmir dispute have not softened, both sides agree to some confidence-building measures. The calamitous October 2005 earthquake may yet have an unintended positive effect here, similar to the impact of the December 2004 tsunami on the Acehnese conflict in Indonesia.

Gujarat became a second focus of tensions. In 2002, Hindu activists in a train returning from Ayodhya were burned alive, triggering a new wave of slaughter. At least one thousand people perished; by Indian yardsticks, it "could have been worse." Analysts see local institutions where Hindus and Muslims cooperate as the strongest dam against communal violence and although such bonds do indeed exist in many places,[17] mutual fanaticism puts them under pressure. The Hindu-Muslim clash of civilizations seems even more inflamed than the clash of Islam against the West. Community tensions also worsened in **Pakistan** itself, where attacks against *muhajirin* immigrants, Western targets, Christian churches, Shiite mosques, and Ahmadi Muslims (seen by orthodox Islam as apostates) have multiplied, although Sunni worshippers have also been victimized. Indeed, official Islamization has created a situation in which Islam is no longer the common denominator but has become the banner of a political struggle to define who in Pakistan holds identity-related rights. Pro-Taliban parties strengthened their position, conquering power in Peshawar, an Islamist stronghold not far from the Afghan border. Civil war remains a possibility—in fact it is already occurring in Waziristan, an anarchic tribal frontier with Afghanistan, which since 9/11 has become a haven for Taliban and al-Qaeda fugitives.

Islam's Southeast Asian Frontier

Indonesia

The world's largest Muslim nation sends contradictory signals— some pointing to a viable democracy, others symptomatic of fragmentation and Islamist-inspired violence. Disgust with existing power and financial crisis fueled a democracy movement that ended Suharto's long rule in 1998. However, the first free elections in forty-four years did not bring any single winner because nationalistic and liberal Islamic currents canceled each other out. Democracy survived, albeit amid economic and environmental difficulties. In 2001, parliament impeached the Islamist president Abdulrahman Wahid (linked to the conservative *Nahdatul Ulama*, NU), accusing him of corruption. His nationalist competitor took over peacefully; and the 2004 elections further strengthened the young democracy.

Yet regime change also stirred up grave community tensions. As in Russia and the Balkans, implosion of an authoritarian *ancien régime* let the decentralizing genie out of the bottle. Tendencies, whose gain in strength might theoretically cement more equitable power sharing among the archipelago's heterogeneous populations, triggered religious and ethnic pogroms. Ethnic and religious factors are often aggravated by immigration of newcomers from overpopulated (Muslim) Java, brought to the peripheral islands (that were often Christianized by the Dutch) by official *transmigrasi* policy aiming at a more balanced population distribution. The bloodiest clashes occurred in the Moluccas, where a longtime Christian majority was being undermined by recent Muslim immigration. In 1999 and 2000, thousands were killed by *Lashkar al-Jihad* militias; many more fled to other islands, until a fragile ceasefire was signed in 2002. Similar atrocities hit Sulawesi (Celebes) where the equilibrium between the Christianized north and Islamized south was disturbed by mostly Muslim newcomers. Meanwhile in energy-rich North Sumatra, the Aceh independence movement, struggling for an Islamic sultanate, displaced hundreds of thousands of peasants and locked thousands of Indonesian troops in place. In 2003, an accord collapsed that would have stopped the rebellion by granting Aceh regional autonomy (and a good slice of its gas wealth). However, when a devastating tsunami hit Aceh, killing more than 200,000 in December 2004, it facilitated a new accord with Jakarta. Disarmament of the Free Aceh Movement (*Gerakan Aceh Merdeka*, GAM) was completed by the end of 2005.

Indonesia's traditionally tolerant Islam (even in Aceh, *shari`a* courts are often more lenient than elsewhere) has recently become polarized, with the most extreme wings even cooperating with al-Qaeda. In October 2002, a bomb in a nightclub on the Hindu island of Bali killed 180 (mostly Australian tourists); it was the worst terrorist attack since 9/11. Abu Bakar Bashir of the Jemaah Islamiyah (JI), a sect devoted to the cause of an Islamic state, was incriminated, but authorities had difficulty pressing charges. Since then, other terrorist attacks have hit Jakarta and Bali. Entrenched in a minority of the network of Javanese *pesantren* (Islamic schools), JI and similar organizations reject *pancasila* and secularism as Western-Jewish "cultural terrorism." One must, however, balance such extremism against a much larger modernist population that interprets Islam as personal faith. Although many Indonesians view the Qur'an as source of inspiration, relatively few accept it as a *Diktat*. Moderate *Nahdatul Ulama* and the modernist, mentality-wise, nearly Calvinist *Muhamadiya* are two movements of millions controlling an empire of universities, hospitals, and similar institutions. Indonesia's moderate Muslim majority prefers coexistence with its 20 million non-Muslims. However, Indonesia is in the same race as other Islamic societies: will democracy grow faster than its alienated and radicalizing Islamist minorities?

Malaysia

Encompassing the Malaya Peninsula (without Singapore) and Northern Borneo (except for Brunei), Malaysia is a rather artificial conglomerate, composed of colonial parts of the East Indies that Britain did not restitute to Holland in 1824 but kept under its own control. Today's twenty-two million Malaysians provide an interesting contrast with neighboring Indonesia. Although 60 percent of them are, like the Indonesians, (mostly rural) Muslim Malays, another 30 percent are Confucianist or Buddhist Chinese, descendants of immigrant workers in tin mines and on rubber plantations who, as elsewhere in Indochina, drive their adoptive country's economic growth. The remaining 10 percent are Hindu Tamils. Racial and religious polarization have marked Malaysia since its independence in 1957, when poor Malay *bumiputra* (children of the earth) began demanding "affirmative action." They got their way in 1969, when national Islamization imposed Malay language and anti-Chinese measures. This has created a new Malay elite, albeit one from which most Malays remain excluded. Against a background of rapid urbanization and dislocation, an early Islamist project got wind in its sails. Student leader Anwar Ibrahim propagandized among Malay youth for not just cleansing their popular Islam of accretions, but also for an Islamic state according to the Mawdudi blueprint. Pressures built up on conservative leader Mahathir bin Mohamad to Islamize public life. He responded by building Wahhabite mosques and schools, policing morals, and enforcing Islamic banking rules. In 1982 he co-opted Ibrahim and his Islamist young guard into his government.

For the next fifteen years, Malaysia enjoyed strong economic growth. It joined the league of Asian Tigers, and fostered its own Islamic version of the ideology (also popular in Singapore and Indonesia) of anti-individualism, order, and discipline, supposedly inherent in the Oriental mind. Mahathir combined these "Asian values" with a global capitalism-friendly Islam. Meanwhile, Malaysia's dependence on international finance grew. The 1997 crisis had severe consequences. It also unleashed a storm of criticism from the more extreme Islamists. Soon afterward, the Islamizing state disciplined its own "ultras." Ibrahim, convicted of sodomy in a show trial, became the scapegoat as an increasingly dictatorial state showcased his private behavior as an "affront to public morals" to shore up its Islamic credentials. (Ibrahim was released in 2004.) When Mahathir stepped down in 2003, Malaysia appeared to have found some stability in a middle way between Islamism and modernization. In spite of being loathed in the West for his anti-Western and anti-Semitic utterances, Mahathir remains popular in the Islamic world.

By no means do these cases exhaust the panorama of Southeast Asian Islam, which includes restive Malay Muslims in southern Thailand and minority populations in Cambodia and Myanmar (Burma). In the **Philippines**, *Moros* ("Moors") in the south of Mindanao and some other islands constitute 5 percent of Filipinos. They have a tradition of resistance—in the early twentieth century they kept up a rebellion long after the United States had pacified Luzon and the rest of the archipelago. Returnee *hajjis* and foreign teachers have, here as elsewhere, criticized lax religious practices and stimulated a return to orthodoxy. Filipino Islamic activism bears a strong regionalist mark, although it has recently also linked with Islamist internationalism. After independence in 1946, official policies meant to assimilate the *Moros* to Catholic- and Tagalog-dominated Filipino culture, and the opening of Muslim tribal provinces to colonization by Christian settlers from other islands, led to resentment and land disputes with ethnic and religious overtones. From the 1960s on, radicalized Muslim youth of the Moro National Liberation Front (MNLF) started a guerrilla war that eventually degenerated into mutual terrorization of Christian and Muslim gangs. Sending in the army did not improve matters. By the time the central government finally relented in the late 1980s and accepted *Moro* regional autonomy, the effects of industrialization, women's emancipation, and other developments were creating their own upheavals. Most *Moro* nationalists accepted the power-sharing deal, but radicals did not. They allied themselves with the *jihadist Abu Sayaf* group, which has engaged in kidnapping and bombing campaigns, and is suspected of cooperating with al-Qaeda.

Islamism's African Front

Islamism became a major challenge in some African nations in the 1990s. Islam's expansion in Africa takes place across a north-south front, slowly advancing over the Sahel steppes between the desert and the jungle. Behind this huge belt are predominantly Muslim societies; in front of it are mostly Christian or animistic ones that include, however, substantial Muslim minorities. The worst conflicts hit divided countries astride this line. Coexistence has become a particularly explosive issue in **Nigeria**, where 132 million inhabitants are concentrated, one-seventh of all Africa. As a state, Nigeria is the product of British colonial pressures that joined a massively Muslim North (interspersed with Christian minorities) to a more mixed South where some nations, like the Yoruba, converted in part to Islam while other nations remained Christian or animistic. Southern Nigeria has remained predominantly non-Islamic, although today a majority of Nigerians are Muslim.

With its myriad contending ethnic groups, Nigeria has been turning to federalism for pacification, although federalism also creates new problems. In northern Nigeria, where Islamic identity is solidly entrenched in Sufi brotherhoods, schools, parties, and sundry clientelistic relations, memories of Islamic sultanates are feeding fundamentalist tendencies. Zamfara and some other northern Muslim states have introduced *shari`a,* including Qur'anic punishments (although these are contested at the federal level where the constitution's liberal provisions still prevail). The conflict between state and federation over *shari`a* threatens national cohesion. No supraregional religion-based identity exists in southern Nigeria, where tribal antagonisms are stronger. Centrifugal sub-identities rival pan-Nigerianism: Southerners fear the North's ascendancy, resulting in political instability. Religious radicalization is also stirring up anti-Christian sentiment. In 2000, Christian–Muslim massacres in northern Kaduna left 2000 dead. A supposedly immoral beauty contest two years later provoked renewed pogroms.

With thirty million inhabitants, **Sudan** is less populous than Nigeria but its tensions seem even more intractable. Torn between a ruling Arab-Muslim north and the subaltern Christian Black south, Sudan illustrates another face of the incompatibility between pluralism and fundamentalism. When it reached independence in 1956, Sudan was still split between proponents and adversaries of union with Egypt, the country that had ruled it in the nineteenth century. Proponents, the *khatmiyya*, were relatively tolerant conservatives who hoped Egypt's weight would counterbalance that of the *Ansar*, descendants of the nineteenth-century Mahdists who strove to turn Sudan into an Islamic state. Political identification is reinforced by tribal lineage, even among sedentary Arabs. When the Mahdist tendency won out, independent Sudan started to forcibly Islamize its south. Black nations like the Dinka rose in revolt, beginning one of the longest, cruelest, and most overlooked of civil wars. Parliamentary politics did not appease spirits. By 1981 through 1983 the military ruler Ja`far al-Nimeiri had grown close to the *Ansar* and initiated Islamization. Under `Umar Hassan Ahmad al-Bashir in the 1990s, the process was accelerated, egged on by the fundamentalist *shaikh* Hassan al-Turabi, the power behind the throne. (Turabi eventually fell out of favor in 1999 when Bashir further centralized control.) Sudan became the world's second Islamist state, after Iran. Discrimination and harassment by the ruling Islamist current against non-Muslims, non-Arabs, and dissident Arab Muslims made continuation of civil war a certainty. For Islamists indeed, federalizing Sudan in a power–sharing pact with "God's enemies" would be apostasy. After millions had been victimized, peace was concluded in 2005 on the basis of southern autonomy and the sharing of power and resources. Controversially, *shari`a* will officially be valid for the whole country, but may be regionally amended for non-Muslim populations: the latter will ratify or reject the arrangement in 2011.[18]

Islamist Expansion in the Diasporas of the Muslim West

From an Islamic perspective, Muslims in the West appear as just one more front. However, there is every reason to believe that Western Muslims' unique position has put them in a strategic vanguard position, either as spearhead of Islamist extremism or as bridgehead between two civilizations. Rejection and alienation have made these Muslim Diasporas especially vulnerable to fundamentalism. The second generation, born in Europe or America, is less tolerant of discrimination than the previous one. A healthy political and social self-organization has surfaced, but this inevitably also includes extremist fringes. Islamist circles have become active among Moroccan, Pakistani, and Turkish youth, proposing a way out, a social "roof," and a spiritual solution.

Radicalization, which long seemed to be limited to minute groups, is now making rapid inroads, and there have been a number of shocking episodes. European Muslims' radicalization has advanced very fast, with voluntary segregation and political demands for self-determination escalating into physical pressure on less strict coreligionists, anti-Semitic and homophobic incidents, and culminating in complicity in terrorist activities. In May 2004, the assassination in Holland of Theo van Gogh, who had made a film critical of Muslim treatment of women, sparked a wave of incidents—Islamist as well as Islamophobic. In July 2005, British-born suicide bombers killed tens of people in London; the following November, France was plagued by widespread arson and rioting undertaken by mostly North African Muslim youth from poor neighborhoods. Although no Islamist instigation was proven, this was the most serious challenge to public order since May 1968; it spilled over to neighboring countries before petering out. Meanwhile, a Danish newspaper published a series of cartoons of the Prophet Muhammad, in an attempt to highlight what it saw as a misguided new European self-censorship in the name of political correctness. However, the experiment misfired, provoking in the first months of 2006 violent uproar throughout the Muslim world—and in the West, a difficult debate on the limits of freedom of expression.

Extremist groups have become a concern because of the high motivation of their members, and their perfect knowledge of and proximity to the "enemy" in whose midst they operate. If the problems of Muslim marginalization are not tackled, these currents will only grow in spite of stringent controls by the authorities. Muslim radicalization easily plays into the xenophobic tendencies of the autochthonous populations.

International War: Osama bin Laden's al-Qaeda _____

With the September 11, 2001, attacks, the third Islamist wave became a declared war against the West, waged in Western lands by Islamists using terrorism. The lasting consequences of this confrontation of unprecedented proportions have yet to be gauged. Islamist attacks against Western interests were of course not unknown before, but most of their targets had been in the Middle East. In 1981, France's ambassador in Lebanon was assassinated. In 1983, French and U.S. interventions in Lebanon were met by trucks full of explosives, killing hundreds of Western soldiers; the West withdrew. Earlier and on Western territory, planes had been hijacked and terrorist attacks perpetrated by Palestinian commandos against Israeli, Jewish, or even neutral targets—all designed to put Israel under pressure. Such bloody (and sometimes clearly racist) incidents started shortly after the 1967 war. However, their scope remained limited. They stoked fear in Jewish communities but hit few Gentiles; and they did not have an obvious Islamic content.

This started to change in the 1980s. In 1985 and 1986, bombs exploded in Paris and in trains throughout France; suspicion fell on Islamic fundamentalist groups, possibly linked to Lebanon. In the same period, Westerners were kidnapped in Beirut. In 1988, an attack against a Berlin discotheque popular with American soldiers left three dead and 230 wounded. In 1988, a civilian PanAm airliner exploded above Lockerbie in Scotland, killing more than 200 passengers, the crew, and a dozen civilians on the ground. (Libyan agents have recently been convicted, but doubts about unidentified accomplices linger.)

Perhaps these isolated incidents were not even Islamist. But with the 1991 Gulf War, a new page was turned: the United States now "occupied" Arabia, its support for Israel and the peace process—execrated by Islamists—intensified, and it enforced U.N. sanctions that victimized innocent Iraqis. All these grievances were Islamized. Fundamentalist terrorists started to commit—at an increasingly steeper curve—acts against primarily American targets, both within the Islamic world, where U.S. soldiers and civilians were hit, and outside. The first attempt to blow up the New York World Trade Center in 1993 failed, although there were casualties and material damage. The attack had been masterminded by the Egyptian `Umar `Abdul Rahman, residing in the United States, who had earlier been associated with the

Jama`at al-Jihad group that assassinated Egyptian President Sadat. In 1995, France was hit by a series of lethal terrorist attacks. Algerian Islamists angered by France's aid to Algeria's military regime were suspected. That same year, a car bomb hit Americans in Riyadh. Scope and rhythm of the attacks increased toward the end of the decade. In 1996, nineteen Americans were killed in an attack on a military base in Dhahran, again in Saudi Arabia. Then in 1998, *al-Qaeda (al-Qa`ida,* the base), a hitherto little-known fundamentalist organization, simultaneously blew up U.S. embassies in Tanzania and Kenya, killing 300. This was one the most daring terrorist operations ever; technically speaking, it was a huge success for its organizer, a billionaire Saudi engineer of Yemeni origin: Osama bin Laden.

With bin Laden, a new and fanatically anti-Western phase began. The recruits were now not just poor and alienated youth but solidly middle-class citizens. Anti-Westernism was, of course, nothing new. However, more than any earlier group, al-Qaeda emphasized the global and profoundly intransigent aspect of Islam's war against the West. Most other groups of the third wave still aimed primarily at "apostates," "lapsed" Muslims, and "infidels." In contrast, Osama bin Laden took the struggle into the enemy's heartland.

Bin Laden's ideology is well known through his public declarations. A son of a wealthy family linked to American oil interests, he broke with his country, viewing the Saudi regime as impious, corrupt, and controlled by Western interests. In a *fatwa* published in 1998, he accused the Americans collectively of three crimes against God: occupation of Arabia's sacred soil, support for the Jewish occupation of Jerusalem, and imposing suffering on the Iraqi people. These crimes, which his document views as a continuation of the Christian Crusades, deserve the death penalty and obligate all Muslims in all countries to engage in an individual *jihad* to kill all Americans, military and civilian. The *fatwa* alludes to suicide actions. Bin Laden has proven to be as good as his word, and his attacks, in Africa and elsewhere, bespeak a technical sophistication.[19]

In retaliation for the embassy attacks, the United States bombed a pharmaceutical plant in Sudan that was alleged to be hiding a chemical arms factory financed by Osama bin Laden—a completely useless riposte. Osama bin Laden simply moved to Afghanistan, where he was welcomed by the Taliban. While he opened training camps for his *mujahidin*, his money propped up the Kabul regime. In 2000, a new Islamist attack in Yemen, linked to al-Qaeda, damaged a U.S. battleship and killed seventeen sailors, probably in protest against the continuing American presence on the peninsula.

Finally came the master coup. On September 11, 2001, nineteen al-Qaeda members, most of them Saudis living in Germany, hijacked four U.S. passenger planes and launched them against bastions of U.S. economic, political, and military power. In New York City, two planes destroyed the World Trade Center, symbol of financial power and, supposedly, of world Jewry. In Washington another plane crashed into the Pentagon. The last plane, possibly headed for the Capitol, was taken over by its passengers and crashed into a field in Pennsylvania. These acts of suicide terrorists cost more than 3000 lives, nearly all civilian—the single largest sudden mass killing since Hiroshima in 1945, and unprecedented in peacetime.

The effects of September 11 were incalculable. The first foreign attack on the U.S. mainland in nearly two centuries brought Islamism into every American household and destroyed the nation's sense of security. Apart from the magnitude of human suffering, the attacks caused heavy material losses, although less than initially feared. There is no doubt that 9/11 has entered the annals of history as a key date, rivaling 1914, 1945, and 1989. Like a latter-day Herostratos, Osama bin Laden became the planet's best-known face overnight. Reactions varied. U.S. President George W. Bush was doubtlessly right to define the attacks as a declaration of war—but the enemy remained for the time being unclear, hiding under the umbrella of "Terror." The American public was shocked; hate crimes against Arabs and Muslims escalated. All over the Western world, Americans suddenly basked in widespread and spontaneous sympathy. The Bush administration managed to squander this capital in less than a year.

Reactions also differed among Muslims. Most shared the West's shock and immediately condemned terrorist acts as antithetical to Islam. Some were scandalized by their coreligionists' acts, and expressed remorse or shame. Others firmly rejected terror yet linked its expressions, however terrible, to the West's deplorable record in the Islamic world. They recalled the West's long history of colonization, exploitation, political imposition, and support for Israel against the Palestinian people. Finally, some Muslims recalled the "cultural invasion," the Islamists' own shibboleth. There were also those who denied al-Qaeda's guilt and insisted that obscure forces—the CIA and the Israeli Mossad being the preferred *bêtes noires*—had engineered the hecatomb in order to impugn Arabs or Islam. One even heard, in the Palestinian territories and elsewhere, sporadic expressions of Schadenfreude of the Yankees-had-it-coming type. Soon indeed Muslim sentiment turned more clearly anti-American. Bin Laden's struggle of one Islamist "NGO" against the world's only *hyperpower* enjoyed diffuse but unequivocal sympathy among wide strata of the Islamic world.

Bin Laden hinted at authorship of the September 11 attacks in videotaped declarations and interviews. The United States bombed suspected al-Qaeda bases in Afghanistan but the Afghan regime refused
to hand over the terrorist. Thus the suicide pact was consummated
between the impoverished and backward country and the high-tech
millionaire terrorist. Commitment to extreme fundamentalism bound
them together, and anti-American demonstrations in Pakistan,
Malaysia, and Indonesia appeared to applaud this weird alliance. In
October 2001, and with U.S.-led international support, the Northern
Coalition—an opposition coalition of more moderate *mujahidin* ethnically different from the Taliban—toppled the Taliban regime. In the
following months, U.S. forces hunted al-Qaeda throughout Afghanistan and destroyed many of its camps. But the survivors scattered,
and bin Laden escaped. Under international auspices, a moderate
multiparty regime was installed under President Hamid Karzai's
Pashto leadership. Civil liberties were restored, and the martyred
country began the slow, insecure process of reconstruction and reconciliation, trying a middle way between political modernization and
social-religious traditionalism. More or less successful elections legiti-
mized a rudimentary democratic regime. From that point on, however,
avoidable mishaps have been accumulating against the backdrop of
an emasculated civil society and destroyed infrastructure: badly
understaffed foreign security forces (diverted to Iraq), warlordism, far
too little international aid (forcing destitute peasants back into poppy
production and in turn stimulating trade in narcotics), mishandled
endeavors to conciliate former Taliban, rampant corruption, and popular disappointment with the failures of the nation-building project.
The Taliban fighters have regrouped in a de facto no-man's-land
across the border with Pakistan. Their occasional residual terrorism
has expanded into full-blown insurgency, and they appear to have
retaken at least partial control of their former Pashto heartland.
Although it is too early to evaluate the results of Western intervention, Afghanistan seems at risk of falling back into the sort of failed
state that the American "export of democracy" project sought to supplant in the first place. This bodes ill for the "war against terror."
Whatever the eventual outcome, Islam is certain to play a dominant
role in the future of Afghanistan.

2003: The War Against Terror Reaches Iraq

In order to piece together the puzzle that forms today's worldwide
battlefront between radical Islamism and the Western democracies,
we must now back up a little in time, and focus on what has become of

its most central arena: Iraq. For the war against terror did not end with al-Qaeda's dispersion; it just changed the target. In 2002, President Bush accused an "Axis of Evil"—Iraq, Iran, and North Korea—of menacing U.S. security. U.S. suspicions pointed ever more ominously at Iraq, and the Bush Administration began planning for a preemptive attack against the regime of Saddam Hussein. However, U.S. attempts to garner for this undertaking the same international approval that it won for its Afghan war foundered: they evoked on the contrary worldwide protest.

The choir of voices against the new war was not *unisono*: pacifists were singing in it, but so were multilateralists, financiers interested in the survival of the Ba`th regime, and others (including many Americans) convinced of an oil-motivated capitalist conspiracy. Islamists added their voices, holding mass antiwar demonstrations throughout the Muslim world while shouting slogans in favor of international *jihad*. Meanwhile, neither Bush nor terrorist groups deviated from their paths.

The years 2002 and 2003 were bumper years for violent fundamentalists. In April 2002, Islamists killed German tourists visiting a Tunisian synagogue. October saw in Indonesia the first Bali outrage. Around the same time, car bombs,possibly planted by separatist fundamentalists of the Abu Sayyaf group, killed scores in the Philippines. In November, Israeli tourists died in a terrorist attack in Mombasa, Kenya. Chechen Islamists held 700 Russians hostage in a Moscow theater. Such was the constellation when, in November 2002, a unanimous resolution of the U.N. Security Council demanded the disarmament of Iraq, which had been accused of developing WMD. One of the main motives was fear that the Baghdad ruler would transfer biological or chemical weapons, or even a primitive nuclear bomb, to some al-Qaeda-like group. Nonstate actors were already changing the very concept of war. International arms inspectors searched, returning with ambiguous conclusions. Diplomatic crisis ruptured the international consensus in February 2003. On one hand, there was no proof of prohibited weapons, but on the other hand, Iraq did not come clean. Accusing it of collusion with Islamist terrorists, Bush now insisted on regime change in Baghdad. While France and Russia led the international opposition against war, Britain sided with the United States. In March, a U.S.-led invasion overthrew, with Kurdish support, the Ba`th regime, and occupied Iraq. Saddam Hussein disappeared—and with him, the elusive WMD that had triggered the war. The fallen tyrant was captured by U.S. forces in December 2003, but his WMD (apparently phantoms of faulty intelligence) were never found.

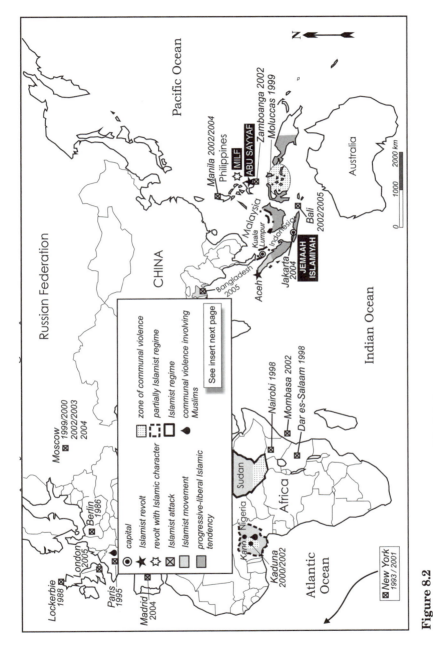

Figure 8.2
Islamism in the contemporary world: global panorama

Legend:
- ⊙ capital
- ★ Islamist revolt
- ☆ revolt with Islamic character
- ⊠ Islamist attack
- ▨ Islamist movement
- ▨ progressive-liberal Islamic tendency
- ▨ zone of communal violence
- ⬚ partially Islamist regime
- ▢ Islamist regime
- ◆ communal violence involving Muslims

See insert next page

Lockerbie 1988
London 2005
Paris 1995
Berlin 1986
Madrid 2004
New York 1993 / 2001
Moscow 1999/2000 2002/2003 2004
Russian Federation
CHINA
Pacific Ocean
Manila 2002/2004
Philippines
MILF
ABU SAYYAF
Zamboanga 2002
Moluccas 1999
Malaysia
Kuala Lumpur
Bali 2002/2005
Indonesia
Jakarta 2004
JEMAAH ISLAMIYAH
Aceh
Bangladesh 2005
Australia
Indian Ocean
Nairobi 1998
Mombasa 2002
Dar es-Salaam 1998
Sudan
Africa
Nigeria
Kano
Kaduna 2000/2002
Atlantic Ocean
0   1000   2000 km

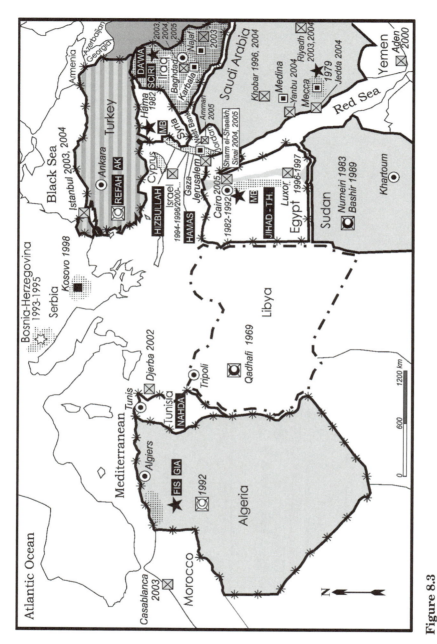

Figure 8.3
Islamism in the contemporary world: the arc of crisis (West)

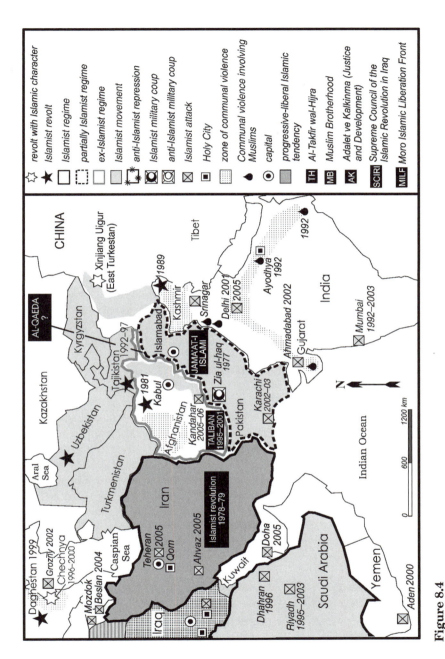

Figure 8.4
Islamism in the contemporary world: the arc of crisis (East)

Once in Iraq, however, the United States could not easily extricate itself. Its military presence evoked contradictory reactions. The Kurds, who had suffered genocidal persecution at Saddam's hands, were overwhelmingly in favor. For Shiites, the presence of U.S. forces meant release from the nightmare of Saddam's dictatorship but also a humiliating foreign presence. Gratitude, nationalist revulsion, and suspicion of American motives formed an ambivalent mixture. Shiites could freely celebrate the `Ashura for the first time in twenty years. Civil liberties were re-established all over the country, and political organization permitted.

This renewed struggles for leadership among the "mujtahidar-chy," and reopened discussion over quietism versus political engagement. Despite Iranian propaganda and Western fears, most Iraqi Shiites had never accepted the theocratic patterns that since 1979 had prevailed next door in Iran; nor do they opt for them now. Iraqis do not relish the prospect of becoming a satellite of Persian nationalism. Two opposite trends stand out. The old guard of moderate clerics temporarily made their peace with Western occupation. Their gambit has been tacit cooperation with the United States, as a means of reconstructing a democratic Iraq in which, by their demographic weight, Shiites would automatically win control. This line of thought was espoused by the charismatic SCIRI leader, Muhammad Baqr al-Hakim of Najaf and—after the latter's assassination in 2003—by ayatollah `Ali al-Sistani, who became the Shiite *éminence grise*. This group was, however, contested by more radical young *mullas* who called for *jihad* against the Americans, finding the conditions ripe for an Iranian-type Islamic government. Their best-known politician is the young scion of a prestigious family—Muqtada al-Sadr—who is popular among excluded youth from poor Baghdad suburbs, where his "Mahdi's Army" acts as the morality police. In reality, all political factions (reflecting class, regional, and tribal antagonisms no less than theological fissures) have their own military wings. Some build patronage networks through provision of food, medical care, or education.

Iraq Occupied: Democratization, Islamization, or Civil War?

Many valuable arguments pro and con have been raised over the "export of democracy" (more correctly, the facilitation of democratization) promoted by U.S. neoconservatives, and its feasibility and/or wisdom remain controversial. There can be no doubt, however, that the attempt to implement this project has been marred by disastrous mistakes, in spite of efforts (some of them quite effective) to emancipate segments of Iraq's population and "teach democracy." By staking his military campaign on Iraq's possession of WMD, Bush morally weakened the whole endeavor to transform Iraq when these weapons proved unfindable. As time passed, another justification took its place: that of bringing democracy and liberty to the peoples of the Middle East as a precondition for winning their support in the war against terror. However, hinging the intervention only in second instance on its democratic significance rang false.

Moreover, serious doubts arose as to the feasibility of erecting a Western-type democracy by force of arms. The United States had not prepared well for a prolonged occupation. Its military resources were stretched too thin, and economic aid was too slow in coming. As a result, severe infrastructure problems were allowed to fester; the insurgency was allowed to grow. Provision of public security was from the onset the chink in the occupier's armor, but it is security that will determine Iraq's future. The United States and its allies were spread thin over a vast country. The result was often near-anarchy. Insecurity of the Iraqis in turn tempered their approval of the U.S.-led intervention.

In August 2003, an unclaimed terrorist act killed one hundred Shiites in Najaf: it was the beginning of an endless series of atrocities, whose frequency and lethality only increased over time. The massacres, suicide bombs, car bombs, and summary executions signaled destabilization, and the near-genocidal potential for communal conflagration. Sunnis are the most active in a nameless and programless insurgency that includes former Ba`thists and local and foreign Islamists, as well as common criminals, which has gradually degenerated from anti-American resistance to wholesale massacres of Shiites. Erstwhile masters of Iraq, Sunnis were the greatest losers of regime change. They have been consistently anti-Western, snubbed invitations to participate in the political process, and have dominated the insurgency. The resulting chaos seemed to broadcast the message that the United States wanted to achieve its objectives "on the cheap," whereas a project of this scope demands a substantial, long-term commitment. Forcing upon a torn country an (ever delicate) democratic transition without adequate means, stamina, and consensus has left the impression that the United States was either not as strong as it appeared, or not completely serious: either conclusion could not but strengthen the hand of Islamist radicals.

Although their overall direction is not at all clear, the last three years have been decisive for the future course of Iraq and the Islamic world. The year 2004 saw a resurgence of anti-Western resistance in Iraq in a series of disparate popular revolts. These centered on the "Sunni Triangle"; Fallujah and some other cities were temporarily under insurgent control. Even more alarming were the simultaneous attacks of Shiite "Sadrists" in Najaf, Karbala, and parts of Baghdad. Eventually the latter proved to have limited support and collapsed. A Sunni-Shiite anti-American united front never materialized: most Shiites kept to Sistani's more cautious line. Aware that their newly-won freedom and empowerment rest with Western protection, many Shiites want the Americans to go home—but just not yet!

It is precisely this ambivalence that may yet give the edge to Bush's democratic project. Even worse violence occurred in 2006, particularly in the center and west of Iraq, with massive terror campaigns of suicide bombs and other atrocities, yet violence and intimidation failed to win over significant parcels of either the Shiite or Kurdish population. The insurgency's support base has remained quasi-exclusively Sunni. Winning this disaffected and estranged minority over to a nonviolent political process has become the main challenge, not just because no viable effective government and peaceful outcome are possible without a majority of all three main populations on board, but also in order to avoid civil war.

The direct result of the 2004 revolt was to accelerate transference of sovereignty to Iraqis themselves, first to an appointed provisional government led by the secular pro-Western Shiite politician, Iyad Allawi, and then to elected leaders. Three times in 2005, Iraqis went to cast ballots in ever-greater numbers, thereby indirectly legitimizing the U.S.-instigated process. First Shiites and Kurds elected a constitutional assembly, where religious Shiite parties led by *Da`wa's* Ibrahim al-Ja`afari held most of the power. The Sunnis had excluded themselves with a massive boycott. The resulting constitution bore the hallmark of Shiite and Kurdish frustration with Saddam's centralized and secular pan-Arabist regime: it excluded Ba`th members and promised ample power to separate ethnic regions. Detractors warned that excluding Sunnis from access to Iraq's oil wealth would spell the end of Iraq as a state. The constitution also affirmed the principle of "Islam as a basic source" of legislation, but left its thorny application (e.g., regarding women's rights) for future parliments to decide. The project was accepted in a constitutional referendum; this time the Sunnis participated in a futile bid to block its passage. A third election, at the end of 2005, saw even wider participation by all communities. It confirmed the Islamist Shiite alliance's predominance, although not that of the Iranian model.

Democratic elections, however, have not so far brought about democratic reconstruction of the tortured Iraqi nation. On the contrary, deepening sectarian identification resulting from pervasive insecurity and lack of power-sharing traditions, along with the failure of political forces to transcend inter-community fault lines, may now be Iraq's gravest risk factors. While a precious half-year was lost in politicking to build a Shiite-Sunni-Kurdish coalition government led by Nouri Maliki, insurgents have redoubled their effort to scuttle whatever efforts at pacification and conciliation are underway. The gambit of the Sunni Islamist "al-Qaeda in Mesopotamia," (led until his liquidation in June 2006 by the Jordanian-born Mus`ab al-Zarqawi) beholden to Osama bin Laden, is to unleash communal war by incessant terror attacks against Shiite civilians, and thus to defeat the U.S.-initiated project. The insurgents have more than once come perilously close to achieving their strategic objective—closest perhaps in the aftermath of their attack on the al-`Askari shrine (with the tombs of the Tenth and Eleventh Imams of Twelver Shiism) in Samarra in February 2006. This led to an outburst of anti-Sunni revenge killings, imputed to Shiite militias, which in turn have fueled the beginning of "ethnic cleansing"—Iraqis fleeing mixed-community quarters. Although the cycle of reciprocal intimidation and revenge has not (as of this writing) degenerated into irreversible civil war, a Pandora's box of immediate dangers is looming over Iraq—none worse, perhaps, than the anarchy of competing militias. There are also more hopeful developments. Underreported, popular empowerment, emancipation, and reconstruction are growing in the shadows. It is impossible to predict whether and to what extent they will counterbalance sectarian incitement, or the unending bloodshed. (From the 2003 war through 2006, at least 30,000 Iraqis died as a result of anticivilian violence.)

With terrorism unabated, a host of constitutional issues unresolved, continued U.S. military presence uncertain, and the economy still critical, it is far too early to say whether Iraq has turned the page. As long as it remains in the danger zone, so will the "war against terror"—and the wider U.S. project "to make the world safe for democracy."

International Effects

No less important than the vicissitudes of nation building within Iraq, and the role of Islam in it, are the international consequences of the responses to 9/11. Here, too, the balance sheet of the U.S.-led war against terror is mixed. Although Osama bin Laden remains at large, al-Qaeda as an organization has been weakened. Not so its ideology, though: the U.S. attempt to decapitate it spawned local al-Qaeda clones. Increased vigilance has prevented major new Islamist attacks on U.S. territory, although at the price of significant pressure on civil rights. Other countries have been less lucky: al-Qaeda struck in Karachi, Casablanca, Istanbul, Morocco, and multiple times in Saudi Arabia, which for a while tottered on the edge of destabilization. Indonesia

was hit by massive suicide attacks against Australians and aggression against local Christians in 2002, 2003, and 2005; Islamists hit
Catholic Filipinos and Buddhist Thais; Chechens slaughtered Russians and Ossetian schoolchildren. In March 2004, 200 were killed in
subway attacks in Madrid—enough to tilt Spanish elections and force
withdrawal of Spanish troops from Iraq. More than fifty died in similar strikes in London in July 2005. Islamist attacks against Westerners (or their supposed local followers) have also occurred in Tunisia,
Jordan, Egypt, Pakistan, Yemen, Kenya, and elsewhere—without
counting Islamist victimization of Israeli citizens. Many of these
attacks have been attributed to al-Qaeda and its galaxy of associated
organizations. Although it would be rash to affirm that these outrages
would not have happened without the U.S. interventions in Afghanistan and Iraq, there can be no doubt that the post-9/11 turn in U.S.
foreign policy exacerbated anti-Western sentiment in the Islamic
world. Weakened or not, *universalistic Islamism remains at present as
the only significant coherent ideological challenge to the "Western" (but
really universal) model of modernity.* Whatever its shortcomings, for
four years after 9/11, the U.S. government's was the only coherent
answer of any consequence.

The price of Bush's war against terror has been high. Geopolitically,
the Iraq War created an unprecedented breach between, on one hand,
the Unites States and its allies (Britain, Italy, Australia, Japan, and
South Korea), and on the other, nearly all other Western powers, led by
France. Whether justified or not, preventive war is at odds with international legality, has been widely suspected of less noble ulterior motives,
and was everywhere opposed by very considerable parts of the population, even where governments sympathized with the United States. The
Iraq war has undeniably affected the moral stature of the world's only
superpower, seriously constraining its future latitude (as well as that of
the United Nations), should fresh international emergencies arise.

Strategically, while U.S. intervention may have frightened some
potential proliferators such as Libya into abandoning their WMD
plans, others have dug in their heels. North Korea and Iran may be
cases of "preventive proliferation." Whether spurred to go nuclear by
defensive or offensive considerations, an Iran armed with WMD cannot but signify a major boost for radical Islamism globally—and
would be a critical clamp on Western possibilities to interfere in the
Islamic world. Nor has the occupation's messy outcome made Iraq
more attractive as a democratic role model for Muslim autocracies in
the Middle East and beyond. Of the three other Sunni linchpins,
changes in Saudi Arabia and Egypt (under evident U.S. pressure)
have so far been mainly cosmetic, and nonexistent in Pakistan. Cau-

tious democratization is continuing in Morocco and in some Gulf principalities, but has been shelved in Jordan.

Popular emancipation has arguably progressed in Lebanon. However, Syria's retreat from Lebanon in 2005 is an atypical case. Since the end of its civil war in 1990, Syria's overbearing influence on tiny Lebanon, through the presence of Syrian soldiers, spies, and up to a million guest workers, was always unpopular. The February, 2005, assassination of former Prime Minister Rafiq Hariri, a billionaire politician who dared stand up to Damascus, and suspicions (later corroborated by independent U.N. investigations) of Syrian foul play triggered unprecedented mass demonstrations in Beirut. Maronites, Sunnis, and Druze demanded Syria's retreat. In spite of pro-Syrian Shiite Hizbullah counterpressures, Asad saw no alternative but to withdraw. However important in themselves, though, the connection of these events to the American intervention is not evident.

Iraq has meanwhile become a magnet for foreign jihadists. Although probably fewer joined the Iraqi insurgents than observers initially believed, the growing radicalization of sizeable Muslim sectors in the Middle East, Asia, and the West cannot be denied. The "democratic panacea" continues to suffer from selective application. Where the United States is required to choose between its strategic interests against terrorist or rogue-state threats, and pressing friendly dictators to empower their peoples, as in Pakistan and Uzbekistan, the former prevails. And everywhere the risk remains that democratic elections could bring antidemocratic Islamists to power.

Coda: Modernist Islamic Thinkers

The Islamist vision points to a head-on collision with Western modernity. It is no surprise that the ensuing scenario is pessimistic. It would, however, be erroneous to conclude our panorama of the current Islamic world without mentioning the existence of a more progressive opposition within Islam—reformers who do not look forward to a clash of civilizations but hope to harmonize faith with modernity. Reformism tries to develop an Islamic foundation for such integration. It thus brings the battle to the Islamists' own terrain. Reformism means hope for coexistence between peoples and religions: hope for a third way, between totalitarian Islamism and unchecked Westernization.[20] However, in waging an unequal struggle for Muslim opinion, reformism has remained a minority option, both in absolute numbers and in its public projection.

Interestingly, reformism and fundamentalism have identical roots: both trace their origin to Afghani and `Abduh, the two thinkers who in the late nineteenth century opposed traditionalism and attempted to renew Islam by a return to the sources, claiming the right to *ijtihad*, or innovative personal interpretation. Both thinkers rejected the "superstitions" of popular Islam and opted for a more normative (and increasingly standardized) sort of High Islam. They privileged written sources over live oral tradition. Today, both fundamentalists and modernists want to revitalize an Islam seemingly impotent to repel the West's onslaught.

Here the similarities end, though. Impelled by the traumas of their confrontation with modernity, Islamists developed a project of nostalgia for a lost Islamic paradise. Hence, Islamism's holistic vision of a restored Islam that would combine the three "D's"—*din* (belief), *dawla* (government), and *dunya* (customs)—into one totalizing lifestyle. Reformists, in contrast, try to reconcile Islam and modernity, taking something from each. Their analyses and recipes vary. Some, like Tariq Ramadan, are not far from Islamism; the most radical may be close to secularism. However, all reformists reject assimilation of *din* = *dawla*, or the concept that religion and politics are one, which is so characteristic of political Islam.

Modernist theorization has a long history in the Islamic world. The year 1924 is a good starting date, with Turkey's abolition of the caliphate unleashing heated polemics. For years afterward, Cairo would be the capital of modernists and Islamists alike. Conservative thinkers, Ridda in particular, created their first Islamist formulations, but another student of `Abduh's, `Ali `Abd al-Raziq, argued that the caliphate was not indispensable for an Islamic polity. He thus made short shrift of the aspirations of some other candidates to the vacant position—the king of Egypt in the first place! For Raziq, Islam was solely a religion and must keep out of politics, a historically questionable position that won him instant condemnation by the religious authorities of Cairo's al-Azhar religious academy, the traditionalists' bastion. Both Islamists and modernists criticize the traditionalists, but the modernists' liberalism puts them on a collision course with the `ulama, while Islamists and traditionalists share a vaster terrain, permitting certain accommodations.

`Abd al-Raziq became a reference for generations of modernist thinkers, including Khalid Muhammad Khalid who, in contrast to his coeval Banna, founder of the Muslim Brotherhood, embraced liberal rationalism and defended democracy as an offshoot of the Islamic concept of consultation (*shura*). But in the conservative 1980s, Khalid came under Islamist influence and recanted his earlier liberal positions. His case is far from unique: in the last quarter-century, Islamism has made huge steps toward conquering cultural hegemony, leaving little leeway for competing ideologies.

No less heterogeneous than Islamists, modernists grapple with the same questions that bedevil their counterparts. But being more open-minded and using other philosophical tools, they move in a different mental universe. In this as yet poorly mapped terrain, four tendencies stand out. Among current Islamic reformers, a first group of thinkers is primarily concerned with the political question, using juridical or historical precedents to argue for separation of state and religion: "God has wanted Islam a religion; but [some] people want it to be politics."[21] Muhammad `Imara claims that Islam never granted a religious character to the state, but that the two were apart from the start. In short, government should be Islamic in culture but not necessarily in its policies. Farag Foda turned to secular nationalism as a solution: justice, he believed, would result from limited government, not from the idealism of religious rulers. In Iran, today's most significant Islamist regime, Abdolkarim Soroush of Teheran University defends severing the link between clergy and political power. He argues that contaminating politics with religion destroys not just civil liberties, but also Islam's own creativity.

A second approach historicizes Islam's sacred sources. Sayyed Mahmud al-Qumni's comparative history of religions is breaking taboos. Others try to prove that Islam never knew a total rupture with *jahiliyya*, the period of ignorance that preceded Muhammad's prophesy, but that it incorporated some pre-Islamic peninsular Arab ritual and cultural patrimony. Implied in such continuity is a certain secularization of the Islamists' sacred cow: Muhammad's Medina polity. If true, it also legitimizes the secularization of today's Islamic society. Indeed, for Muhammad Sa`id al-`Ashmawi, many *shari`a* laws reflect contingent conditions of past epochs, and hence lack eternal value. The punishments dispensed in the Qur'an reflect for him a concept of justice that was elaborated by `ulama who collaborated with historical Muslim despots, and does not commit our generation. All this opens room for new legislation—including the constitutional sphere.

Reinterpreting *shari`a* logically leads to a third line of thought: restoring Islam as a religion of compassion. In other words, Islam would inspire, not impose, ethical behavior in the private and public sphere. The amputation of a limb, certain authors reason, might have been an appropriate punishment in a pastoral society, where a cattle thief would cause the death of the people from whom he had stolen, but this crime does not have the same lethal consequences today, hence the sanctions have lost their logic. One should, then, reconstruct Islamic law from its spirit and not its letter. Hussein Ahmad Amin proposes such a reconstructed compassionate Islam, but retrieving Islam's lost self-confidence may be a precondition no less than hoped-for result of such an endeavor.

The critique of literalism and fundamentalist "verbolatry" leads to the fourth project: postmodern reformism, which proposes a new reading of Qur'an and *hadiths* based on contemporary linguistics and semiology. If the meaning of Arabic words shifts over time, then the whole *shari`a,* which is, after all, based on an assumed immutability of meanings, loses its stability. The consequence is that Muslims will have to differentiate their divine and eternal message from the humanly received and historically dated Book. The revolutionary implications are obvious—and they go in a direction diametrically opposed to that advocated by the Islamists. The Egyptian Nasser Hamed Abu Zeid, the Syrian Muhammad Shahrur, and in particular the Algerian Mohammad Arkoun are some of the best-known exponents of this approach.[22]

Influenced by Derrida's and Foucault's philosophies, Arkoun introduces an Islamic poststructuralism. His project is to retrieve a libertarian, more imaginative Islam. Critical of the traditional logocentric interpretation of the sources, Arkoun distinguishes the "writing" of the Qur'an—which he views as a spontaneous and transcendent irruption—from its "reading." The correspondence between text (signifier) and signified, which is automatic from the fundamentalist point of view, collapses. This procedure allows Arkoun to demolish the literalist version of Islam. If such a correspondence does not exist, there cannot be one correct interpretation, nor any authority in whom is vested the privileged reading that would commit all believers.

For Arkoun, Islamist indoctrination and interpretative rigidity are outcomes of the failure of the ninth-century progressive philosophical movement and of the later suppression of creative and libertarian popular Islams. The aim, then, cannot be the establishment of an Islamic state but implies a democracy that would permit the retrieval of authentic popular cultural traditions and intellectual freedom. Only thus may one transcend the gap between Islamic reason and philosophical thought. Arkoun's books have predictably been banned in several Arab states; he has long since established himself in Paris. Abdullahi Ahmed an-Na`im from Sudan, the late Fazlur Rahman from Pakistan, and the Egyptian Tariq Ramadan are other Muslim Islamologists who can work only in the West. Will their ideas penetrate the Islamic world? The future of Islam will to a significant degree depend on the reception given to innovative alternatives to the impasse that Osama bin Laden and his ilk have created.

WHAT DO THE
ISLAMISTS WANT?

9

Islamism as Politicization of Religion_____

Islamism is at once an ideology and a social movement. Behind the
slogan "Islam is the solution" lies a theocratic model of society that
posits itself as an alternative to the West's, and rejects its central values and symbols: secularism and individualism. Idolatry of the modern is seen as the root of Western permissiveness and decadence
which express themselves in alcohol, drugs, licentiousness, and con-
sumerism. However, for Islamism the West's "badness" expresses
itself also in racism, colonization, and exploitation of the non-West.
Thus, Islamism combines the antimodernism one sees in all stripes of
fundamentalism with a critique of imperialism, which sounds like a
Marxism without class analysis.

Rejection of Western modernity, however, is only the negative side
of Islamic fundamentalism. It has also an original political and social
program. Restoration of *shari`a* as law of the land is reductionist, for
the formula is too vague (although Islamists and many other Muslims
recognize themselves in it). *Shari`a* is not a complete system but a
method to "apply" and "deduct from" sacred sources rules that guide a
wide array of ritual, social, economic, and juridical questions. No consensus on the sources exists and the applications evolve with society,

which presents ever-new challenges. Therefore, there is a permanent debate over the exact content.[1] This is reflected in the differences among Islamist currents. Thus in Iran, women participate (adequately covered) in public and professional life; in Afghanistan under the Taliban, they were imprisoned in their homes, without rights to education or to work. In Saudi Arabia, Islamism goes together with a lavish lifestyle (God favoring private property) whereas Iran's equally Islamist *Mujaheddin-e khalq* preach socialization of means of production. Besides, some subjects were historically neglected in Islamic law. For their critics, the Islamists' political solutions are little better than farfetched a-historical readings of a couple of poly-interpretable verses. All Islamists aspire to transform society, and would emulate Muhammad's original virtuous society. Even here, there is a rather deep chasm between political Islam and the more private-life oriented neofundamentalists.[2] However, in spite of all divergences, it is possible to point to the following principles as shared by all Islamists:

1. Human beings are not their own masters but owe obedience and worship to their Creator Who is sovereign and Who communicated His will through the prophets, of whom Muhammad was the last.

2. The ideal polity is the Islamic state, although there is more concensus among Islamists about its government than about its scope. For some Islamists, any state will do as long as it is Islamized; for others, devout Muslims may or should establish a new Islamic state wherever they have the opportunity; for the most radical, all existing states and borders are illegitimate, and the Islamic state should therefore include the totality of *Dar al-Islam,* and eventually the whole world.

3. Government must be by an Islamic instance that will have Islam's absolute truth and axiomatic supremacy as its starting point and will, in the name of the *umma*, enjoin respect of the rules of Islam. Differences exist as to modalities: many Sunni fundamentalists want government by (or guided by) `*ulama*, others an emirate or new caliphate; Shiite Islamists are also divided, not all accepting the rule of *mullas* or the *faqih*. Although the Islamic state does not have the Western concepts of citizenship or democracy, some currents identify *shura* with democracy and have in practice if not in theory come to accept pluralistic democratic rules.

4. Separation of the public (social) from the private (family) sphere, the first being the terrain of men and the second that of women, who are subordinated to men. The intention is to keep each sex in his or her natural sphere where each can best contribute to Islamic society.

There is more separation between the sexes than in Western society, often with specific dress and behavior codes, in addition to prohibitions on alcohol and other forms of "corruption."

5. The aim of the Islamic state is to stimulate and facilitate a religious lifestyle for all Muslims and thus optimize their chances for salvation. Hence the state will maintain a framework of Islamic ritual and public prayers and guarantee religious education.

6. Islamic economy remains controversial but, at a minimum, includes an interest-free banking system. For most Muslims, Islam recognizes the right to private property but enjoins (e.g., through *zakat*) solidarity with the weak: widows, orphans, the sick and disabled, the poor. The gap between theory and practice is large here.

7. *Taghallub*, the superiority of Muslims over other subjects, must be maintained. Although the position of non-Muslims must be inferior to that of believers, there are disagreements, both as regards Christians and Jews (the most extreme demand a return to *dhimmi* status) and in relation to polytheists.

8. Application of Qur'anic penalties (*hadd*) for specific transgressions.

9. Because Islam is universally valid, an Islamic international order under God's government must be promoted.[3] This order is based on a perpetual antagonism between the territory of Islam (*Dar al-Islam*) and the rest of the world (i.e., the territory of war, *Dar al-Harb*), until Islam's final victory. Consequently, Islamists at least in theory deny the legitimacy of nation-states and the current international order based on them. Most Islamists consider the struggle to Islamize the whole world as a *jihad* that, under specific conditions, may include the use of violence. Significant disagreements exist as to the application of this general concept. The most radical envisage a life-and-death struggle against the existing order.

Although many non-fundamentalist Muslims would accept some of these points, it is their combination that defines Islamism—an ambitious politicization of religion. Islam lends itself to multiple interpretations: the traditional religiosity of popular Islam in the close-knit ritualistic village community, the mysticism of Sufi brotherhoods, the reformism of Islamic modernists who understand Islam as an ethical inspiration, not a political project. It is the political factor that distinguishes Islamists from other Muslims even if some would, once in power, abolish the political sphere as such.

Islamism as Ideology

Islamism takes Islam from religion to ideology. Ideology is of course among the social sciences' most controversial concepts; we will apply it here simply in its original rationalist-Enlightenment meaning of "the *logos* of the ideas"—the endeavor to improve society starting from universal abstract principles. Although Islam's points of departure— belief in God and His prophet, the truth of Qur'an, and so on—are non-rational (or at least unprovable), this is no different from many other ideologies that have presented themselves as panaceas. Once one accepts the principle, the rest follows logically: a near-scientific and coherent *Weltanschauung,* a program to remedy defects through real-world changes, and an insistence that those who accept the ideology commit personally to its realization. Islamism, like other ideologies, demands total and irrevocable engagement that turns the believer into a militant. Because this struggle precludes the demands and pleasures of daily life, the real idealist must abandon everything. Enthusiasm may lead to death, the ultimate sacrifice for a transcendent ideal, realization of which is already certain for, like other ideologies, Islamism entails a deterministic view of history as combat between good and evil. The individual is called upon to enlist in an army whose victory is certain; one's role is to hasten a (meta)historically unavoidable outcome. Submitting to an automated process (or one, at least, independent of individual will) has its psychological quid pro quo—that of joining an elite with a privileged historical task: the elected people, the intellectuals, the proletariat, or the party of God. Islamist militants form a vanguard bringing closer God's enjoined order, thus escaping the uncertainty of an indeterminate future and with it, the burden of choice and responsibility. The follower surrenders his or her doubts to God All-knowing and All-powerful. Suicide bombers do not necessarily sacrifice their own and their victims' lives for political gain: results are less important than the sacrifice to God. The outcome is in God's hands and He will take care of the rest.[4] Modern ideologies typically aspire to state power, understood as the lever to realize paradise on earth. Crisis and perhaps war may be indispensable; great suffering will precede final salvation. Terror against internal and external enemies may be needed to protect the revolution. The prototype of this type of thinking is in Jewish messianism; similar traits are seen in Islamic revolutions. As in other ideologies, thus also in Islamism, a revolutionary minority that despairs of gradual reform and opts for the path of violence differentiates itself from the pragmatic and relatively moderate majority preferring persuasion, dialogue, and political education (e.g., the current Muslim Brotherhood). Fatalism ("Death is certain, but the hour of death is in God's hands") and voluntarism ("If one must die, then let it be for God") combine in an explosive mix: We will win because *"these youths* (i.e., Muslim jihadists) *love death as you love life."*[5]

Obsession with transformation of immanent reality separates fundamentalism from traditional religion, which is more concerned with the transcendent and preserving a premodern social order supposedly reflecting the cosmic one. Yet it would be an error to label Islamists as politicians who consciously manipulate religion for political ends. Although their (sincere) religious experience leads to political action, it cannot be reduced to it. Subjectively, Islamists do not see themselves at all as revolutionaries out to establish a new order, but as believers who will restore an older and better order that existed before the calamities of modernity. Without such authenticity, Islamists would soon be unmasked, and would not be the international peril they are. However, contrary to their self-understanding, the Islamist way of thinking is expressly modern. Islamism, like other fundamentalisms, is a *reaction against modernity produced by modernity, during modern times, using modern means, and irreversibly partaking of modernity.* Its authentic character shows also in its attempts to introduce an ideal order. The "transvaluation of all values" that will occur after the fall of the West and Islam's global victory, is already foreshadowed in small cells, Islamist communes closed to the outer world's corrupting influence. The "pure" society-to-be, even if imposed by force, will exist in order to produce the virtuous New Man, devoted to his transhistorical mission. Such a program can—and in order to make progress, must—create fanaticism; if it succeeds, it may lead to totalitarian social engineering.

Islamism as a Movement

While Islamism is an ideology with a specific psychological makeup, it is first and foremost a social movement. Who is attracted to its program? An analysis of its social basis sheds light on both Islamism's success and its limitations. In the 1960s and 1970s, when it did not yet transcend the Arab world's borders, it was essentially restricted to students (mainly in medicine, engineering, and the hard sciences), with the occasional support of some `ulama. Followers were superficially Westernized, yet hardly educated in the type of critical thought required in the social sciences or humanities. Overcrowded Arab universities were still steeped in rote learning. Islamists were recruited among the best students; but they had never been really prepared for modern life.

The second wave, the Islamism of the 1980s, cast a wider net, including massively Shiite Iran, where its social reach was wide enough to topple the shah. Three social strata joined forces: (1) the traditionalist-conservative block of premodern merchants (*bazaris*) and *mullas*; (2) the *mustadh`afun*, or newly urbanized, unemployed, or informally employed groups (equivalent to the *Lumpenproletariat* that had been the backbone of the Far Right in interwar Europe), who became the revolution's foot soldiers; and (3) the *"Lumpen-intelligentsia,"* who were its officers: radicalized, half-modernized, and frustrated youth, still close enough to their ancestral religion to allow for a return to their roots, yet too educated to return to their parents' traditionalism, and too smart not to see through the failure of Westernization in their countries.[6]

The current, third, wave of Islamism seems to be based on the same coalition as the second, but with a much wider geographical scope. Most Muslims live in countries that suffer a double socioeconomic and cultural-identity crisis. This is one of the paradoxes of globalization: it intensfies communication between formerly distant groups, yet sharpening their awareness of differences. Today this crisis is much deeper than it was ten years ago, and old strategies for dealing with it have lost traction. Although the Islamic world is not the only civilization to suffer increased ethnic and religious conflict, Muslims are particularly hard hit by it, as their religion particularly insists upon worldly supremacy. Globalization has facilitated inter-Muslim contacts. It also spreads information about the Islamist alternative. Coming from the Arab world, Islam's world center, the Islamist example is today inspiring an international Islamist domino effect.[7]

Islamism as Tribalism

The recent phase of Islamism, unlike its predecessors, also recruits among marginal and tribal populations who use it for their own interests. The cradle of Islam was in the tribal Arab Peninsula where there existed a kinship-based social structure characteristic of prestate nomads. Transitioning to state level would normally have implied sacrificing primordial bonds in favor of a territorial organization. Here Islam's emergence in a prestate context, distinct from the birth of other universalistic religions such as Buddhism and Christianity, would have grave consequences. As it spread beyond Arabia's confines, Islam tried but ultimately failed to supplant divisive local and ethnic loyalties through commitment to a common universal faith. Although the religious legitimacy of political leadership was at stake in conflicts over caliphal succession, family and tribal loyalties determined their course. Arab military conquest and colonization spread such pre-

Islamic divisions and transplanted them over today's Middle East, if not over the whole Islamic world. As a result, universal pretensions notwithstanding, the Islamic empire never succeeded in bringing forth an integrated state; it forever functioned politically on the basis of fissiparous tribal and ethnic lineages. The never-ending factional war of all against all impeded integration on the basis of impersonal rules, neutral bureaucratic functions, and merit-based distribution of resources. In Weberian terms, Arab-Muslim society never overcame its traditional monarchical or charismatic leadership style, however much Islamists emphasize objective, law-supported leadership. Until today, many Middle Eastern societies struggle to construct a modern state. Neither a pan-Arab or pan-Islamic state nor (with a few significant exceptions such ⋯ ⋯ ⋯ ⋯ ial nation-states have come into being ⋯ es to be an important attribute of pc ⋯ Syria, Iraq (at least until 2003), Sauc ⋯ es, and Morocco. Colonial privi-legir ⋯ es and tribes deepened internal fissu ⋯ e been able to manipulate them to su ⋯ tered deep preexisting divisions. The: ⋯ nium of Ottoman rule, but were acti⋅ ⋯ stem was more tolerant than the nati ⋯ osed by European monarchs, but it ir ⋯ flicts that plague today's Middle Eas ⋯ gligible proportion of the popula-tion ⋯ e that gave birth to its original trib ⋯ onds have survived sedentariza-tion ⋯ bligations continue to mold rela-tion ⋯ neage.

T ⋯ fundamentalism is not immediately ⋯ lly emphasize universalism, not particularism. There are, however, exceptions: the Taliban recruited among specific Afghan ethnicities, and in Algeria, Islamist violence was unmistakably anti-Berber. Islamism has been a prop of group or ethnic demands of the Chechens against Russians, of Arabs against Sudanese Blacks, among competing nations in Nigeria, and elsewhere. In Lebanon, Hizbullah acts as the vehicle of sectarian Shiite claims; in Pakistan, Islamist movements mask Pashto and other ethnic demands. Basically universalistic Islamism can, under circumstances, mutate into (sub)national particularism; where this happens, it deepens its social base, but at the cost of its breadth. It remains a question, whether these exceptions show the malleability of social mechanisms in utilizing disparate ideologies, or the instrumentalization of ethnic strife by universalistic Islamism.

Islamism as Answer to Urban, Generational, and Class Crises _____

Phenomenal population growth is part of the Middle East's and South Asia's uneven modernization. Iran had twenty-five million inhabitants in 1965, forty million at the time of the Islamic revolution, and sixty-five million today. Egypt counted fewer than thirty-five million in 1965, but has more than double that number today. Algeria's population, fewer than ten million at independence in 1962, has more than tripled. No economy can absorb such population explosions. Even with scarce mechanization, agriculture does not provide enough jobs; the human surplus flows into the cities. Today's Middle East is heavily urbanized, and so are its Islamist movements. Its youth pass through understaffed, overburdened schools and colleges, many of them deplorable. Once the diplomaed "doctor" enjoyed prestige, but today's education is of little use; jobs are scarce and the state no longer provides sinecures. Without employment, though, prospects for marrying and establishing a family dwindle. Meanwhile, the new generation is also permanently exposed to modern temptations. Boys and girls imbued with traditional norms from home and ill-prepared to cope with the other sex find themselves suddenly in confusingly close contact. Television, movies, and lyrics exalt the luxuries of a well-paid career, sexual choice, travel abroad, and individual liberty. The West dangles in front of young urban Muslims a disconcerting vision, at once attractive and scandalous, and most often well beyond their reach.

The ambiguous mix of attraction and repulsion pushes many into the arms of Islamism. Islamism explains their situation, attributes guilt (to imperialists, Jews, or Christians. . .), and teaches return to faith as a first step to mitigating frustration. It also opens vistas to a worthier future, when the unjust, powerful, and decadent foreigners will be punished, along with their imitators at home. The return to religion thus gives meaning to disjointed lives and provides a defense against temptation. The moral and social crisis of the half-modernized is key to Islamist growth. Until the Islamic world's socioeconomic situation improves, or another ideology emerges that helps it better to confront reality, Islamists will continue to thrive and recruit among these groups.

Islamist Strategies between Charismatic Leadership and Institutionalization _____

Islamism is an antimodern reaction that belongs to modernity; this paradox is also seen in its organization, operation, and propaganda. Islamist movements are modern social movements that are completely different from traditional Muslim communities. Islamists aspire to political power as the means of societal change. In order to reach their goals, they need to organize. But the complications of their modus operandi, and the perseverance of personalistic leadership habits, betray their ambivalence to modernity. Still, modernity enters. Proto-fundamentalist movements such as the Indian *deobandi* school network hit already in the 1860s upon a key modern principle—an institution independent of its founder, headmaster, or chief theologian.[9] Political parties would be the next logical step in Islamist institutionalization, were it not that in most cases, authoritarian and repressive states deny them legitimate access to the political sphere. Most Islamist movements are borderline clandestine (or in a kind of legal limbo, such as the Egyptian Muslim Brotherhood). The absence of representative politics does not automatically lead to revolutionary strategies, yet the scarcity of legal opportunities has pushed many over the brink of violence.

Significant strategic differences exist among Islamist movements. Some "conquer" a mosque that will serve as their base of operations (e.g., Hamas in the Palestinian territories); others organize in *madrasas* around prestigious teachers (e.g., in Pakistan). Algerian mass movements differ from communes, such as the oppositional *groupuscules* in Fayyum in Egypt. In Shiism, where the clergy enjoys wider autonomy, *mullas* are often in the center of politics; their Sunni counterparts, the `*ulama,* are paid functionaries, and are viewed as corrupted by their proximity to power. In Sunnism, Islamist movements rally in opposition to these "Sultan's advocates."

In Sunni movements, leadership is often self-proclaimed and charismatic, as in the case of the *amir al-muminin* (Commander of the Faithful, traditional title of caliphs), who is not selected through any formal process but knows himself to be God's elect and agglutinates around himself, through preaching or by personal example, a core of followers. Whereas Islamist leaders sometimes obtain more traditional religious legitimization through one or the other `*alim,*[10] more commonly the leader becomes a sort of guru, ruling his followers' behavior and establishing a hierarchy of lieutenants through whom he maintains contact with his rank and file. From the moment they believe their leader has God's sanction, the latter will obey his authority. At this point, a counterpower (as yet, microscopic) arises, no longer subject to state authority. If this evolves, it may eventually spawn a revolutionary situation. The new Emir or Imam arrogates to himself the authority to promulgate religious edicts. In contrast to most Christian churches, Islam knows no circumscribed and permanent authority, institutionalized through specific selection and recognition procedures, so any Muslim can in principle claim this mantle, a claim that will grow stronger by his efficiency in attracting a following, defeating his competitors and enemies, and implementing his program. Such "natural selection" and "survival of the fittest" have occurred more than once in Islamic history. Although institutionalization would improve an Islamist movement's chance to survive its founder, most never reach this point.

Between Withdrawal and Activism _____

Islamism tends toward decentralization. Owing to newcomers and splits, the number of movements is forever growing and, although each aspires to strict organization, on the contrary, clandestine conditions foment a non-hierarchical network structure. Fragmentation, however, hinders the struggle against terrorism. Typically, opposition Islamist cells are numerous, small, dispersed, zealous, and suspicious of infiltration. Competition over purity and leadership claims generate further radicalization and schisms. If one group is eliminated, others take its place. If one leader moderates his stance, stricter fundamentalists will brand him a traitor and try to silence or liquidate him in order to save the pure, unadulterated course. What we see happening in political Islam is therefore akin to the proliferation of ever more, and ever more radical, sects that characterized early Christianity and, more recently, Marxism. The dynamics of radicalization also explain some structural constraints on reconciling ethnic and religious differences and resolving protracted conflicts. However many factors are sucked into the political process in places like Northern Ireland, Israel/Palestine, Cyprus, and Sri Lanka, there is always one splinter or another that, in the name of the ideal, rejects accommodation with the sinful or guilty other side and believes in its right to impose its view and block *rapprochement* by terrorizing the majority. From this angle, Islamists have more in common with fundamentalists of other religions and with secular political extremists than with their more liberal Muslim coreligionists.

According to the Israeli historian Emmanuel Sivan, realizing the Islamic state is really a triangular path, with consecutive isolationist, educational, and violent steps.[11] First comes withdrawal from corrupt, neo-*jahili*, society. Believers start over by establishing their own small, puritan communities, typically near the desert or far from the city's (or the West's) corrupting influence. In this stage of meditation and self-purification, the reborn Muslim is in *hijra*, internal exile that may prepare him or her for the second stage: reentry. Peaceful educational and political work (*da`wa*, "call," or mission) will, it is now believed, bring one's co-Muslims to the correct view. This practice emphasizes individual transformation as prelude to that of society. Patient construction of local institutions and social support of underprivileged Muslims combine local empowerment with Islamization. However, if this activism does not bring forth the expected fruits, disappointment may set in. Then comes the third, revolutionary, stage, which may be an Iranian-type mass uprising, Lebanese-style guerrilla warfare, autonomous small-cell terrorism, or still other forms of violence. *Jihad* and acts of self-sacrifice are supposed to shake the condemned regime and awaken the faithful masses. If this violence does not succeed and repression is effective, a group of the survivors may again take the path of exile and cloister themselves far from the corrupt world, closing the cycle—or starting a new one.

Half-Modernity: Using Technology but Rejecting Its Reason[12]

Islamists' use of modern technology proves that, reactionary ideologies notwithstanding, they are part of modernity. While Islamists reject Westernization, they have no qualms about Western technology based on rationalism. The anti-technological bias of authentic traditionalists illustrates this difference well. When Ibn Sa`ud established his ultrapuritan state in the Arabian desert in the 1920s, the `ulama were opposed to use of the radio and other inventions of the devil, at least until the Saudi king showed that wireless waves could just as well transmit verses of the Qur'an, God's word.[13] Invention and science were proven to be neutral. In a certain sense, Ibn Sa`ud was thus the first Islamist, and current Islamism would be unthinkable without modern technology: the muezzin's call to prayer is prerecorded and electronically amplified; cassettes spread sermons; demonstrations are coordinated by telephone, fax, and e-mail; videos perpetuate the image of the suicide martyr; and Islamism's most terrible organization is named after the supercomputer that is purportedly collecting the names of international militants: *al-Qaeda* means "base" or "database." Islamists cannot succeed without a science and technology that are rationality's fruit, but they reject as idolatrous the values and thought processes that produce them. Embracing technological modernity while rejecting sociocultural modernity is a contradiction that may become Islamism's Achilles' heel.

Results

Can Islamism solve the crisis of the Middle East? Assessing Islamism's achievements is arduous. First, it may be premature. Without Calvinist Reform, would there have been a Puritan movement that, a century later, established on North America's east coast the nucleus of a pluralist democratic society that eventually evolved into the United States? Calvin's contemporaries could not have known this. What they saw was the drama of the Wars of Religion with their persecutions and burning of heretics; and Calvinism was initially as fanatical as the Catholic Church it criticized. Likewise, the French Revolution initiated a process that ended serfdom in Europe and launched the principles of citizenship, equality before the law, and individual liberties that permeate the modern world. Many eyewitnesses, however, were more impressed with the guillotine. Through an as yet unknown and paradoxical dialectic, may Islamism unwittingly be the harbinger of long-term emancipation in the Islamic world? How can we, who witnessed 9/11, profess enough distance to judge it objectively?

Second, where are consensual criteria to evaluate a fundamentalism that precisely rejects Western criteria? While most TV spectators in America and Europe (and not a few Muslims around the world) are upset by Islam's radicals' repeated use of terrorist violence against civilians, our judgment is based on widespread, but hard-to-prove principles. Violent Islamists reject these values; for Osama bin Laden, there are no innocent Americans, just as for Hamas's Yassin, there were no innocent Jews. Because both the United States and Israel, two of the most popular targets, are strong and rich nations and not averse to using massive violence against Muslims, one hears (still cautious) voices starting to reinterpret terrorist violence as a more or less legitimate response to Judeo-Christian interventions, invasions, and occupation. Such logic ends up decoding violent Islamism as a disconcerting but ultimately legitimate revolt against Western supremacy: either the local expression of traditional socioeconomic demands of the Third World's oppressed, or (more postmodernly) the legitimate search for cultural authenticity against the imperialist colonization of subjectivity.[14] But not even such readings can hide a certain apologetic tenor. Except for a minority of Islamists themselves, nobody really likes their violence. Few go so far as to equate the dead buried at Ground Zero with the victims of the guillotine—a deplorable loss, but indispensable to realize a new order: "manure of history." All the same, whichever the ethical perspective one uses to judge Islamism (prerational), value choices are unavoidable.

Leaving moral judgment aside, what can be said of Islamism's results in practice? We must limit ourselves to Iran, Afghanistan, and Sudan, where Islamists have come to power. And we must discard the latter two, for the Taliban no longer rule, and Sudan is mired in interminable wars. Iran is the only case then, and judging it is made easier by the fact that its power transition and terrorist revolutionary phase lie already a third of a century in the past. Teheran's half-despotic and half-democratic clerical regime may not be as totalitarian as its detractors claim, but it has certainly rejected most Western-style liberties. Media and education are controlled, women's freedom curtailed, juridical mutilations common.

Stalin's and Mao's fellow travelers used to argue that civil liberties are bourgeois luxuries compared to the indigent masses' immediate and more basic needs for food, housing, heating, and medicine. What if we apply this yardstick to Iran's socioeconomic development? Agrarian reform has not been implemented; unemployment is high; absolute poverty has diminished, but not the gap between rich and poor; and corruption has returned. The population crisis has worsened due to Islamist opposition to birth control. The country is still as dependent as it was on world markets, and survives by exploiting a single nonrenewable resource: oil. While the Islamist regime may not have worsened development, neither has it improved it. One must add to this balance sheet the hundreds of thousands of mostly young killed and disabled, voluntarily sacrificed in a useless war that could have been stopped much earlier. The clearest indicator of regime failure is, however, in the massive mobilization of major parts of the population—the less conservative young, the educated, and women—in favor of democratization. Iranian civil society projects neither a re-Westernization nor the elimination of religion from public life; but it does demand political pluralism and individual freedoms. At least half of all Iranians want to loosen the clergy's stranglehold on political life and reopen Iran to communication with other civilizations. After three decades of "God-government," they want something else (the 2005 electoral victory of the extreme Islamists was the result of the reformers' boycott). The records of the Afghan Taliban and Sudan's Bashir regime are even worse. In conclusion, "Islam is the solution" has (so far) not been true in the Islamic world—at least it has not been the solution to its development crisis.

The Islamist rebuttal is simple and effective. Islam is not a Western-type economic system designed to maximize material growth: that would keep it within the materialist, individualist and atheist logic it came to replace. Unlike capitalism or communism, Islam cannot be judged by economic but spiritual achievements. Islam provides a context within which to worship God as He instructed, which is humanity's aim in life. For Islamists (and for many non-Islamist Muslims), success is not measured by worldly progress but by religiosity. Islamists are the first to admit that even in the spiritual sphere a good deal is left to be desired. However, any failure is attributed not to Islam but to the Muslims—like the rest of us, fallible human beings. Islam itself is per definition inerrant: what is needed is a more assiduous application. Islamism has thus immunized itself against any defeat, and no criterion is left by which human beings can judge Islamist society's failure or success. One may only remark that most of humanity does not seem to like its proposal. But taste cannot be discussed.

CAUSES OF ISLAMISM 10

Modernity's Myth

Why have fundamentalisms emerged now, and with such virulence, in the Islamic world? In order to understand its success (and possible limitation), Islamism's hate-love relationship to the modern world is a useful starting point. When we describe Islamic fundamentalism as an *antimodern product of modernity,* what defines this "modernity" that Islamism opposes so vehemently? As an ideal type, modernity divides society into a public and a private sphere: in the first, members are equal citizens, free to express and organize themselves politically; in the second, each is free to pursue his own interests and religious, ideological, or lifestyle preferences. In economic terms, modernity appears to lead to industrial capitalism; in political terms, to impersonal law and bureaucracy, access to functions based on competence, and democratic participation in decision making. Modernity is based on reason: modern society does not presuppose the primacy of any specific idea, religion, or ideology—except that of nonprimacy itself. The free and peaceful competition among ideas leads logically and historically to tolerance and pluralism. Therefore, modern society knows freedom of religion, yet religion belongs to the private sphere. Often modernity goes together with urbanization, weakening of traditional

bonds, individualism, women's emancipation, and the universaliza-
tion of education. The modern state is sovereign within its borders,
and is part of an international society with its own consensual values
and rules.

While this package does not wholly correspond to any known society, it does describe the ideal of most Western societies. Societies we
call modern are the outcome of a long and convoluted evolution, in the
course of which earlier, traditional social forms were absorbed or eliminated. Starting from Western Europe and North America, these modern forms have proven more efficient than any other (owing to their
superior values, according to its proponents) in terms of invention,
productivity, and military supremacy. As a result, modernity has in
the past few centuries spread over the whole world, defeating and
transforming practically every other society. Colonization, however,
partially modernized the colonies. Westerners, with their modern
techniques and methods, were in general not interested in exporting
to their colonies the values of rationalism and liberalism that under-
lay their efficient methods; but in the long term, they could not do one
without the other. Colonial elites were educated in Western schools,
where they appropriated these principles, applied them to their own
situation, and eventually used them against their colonizers. Most
decolonizing societies thus adopted the ideas of self-determination,
nation, and progress that had served the West so well. Once independent, they have constituted nation-states, and become new members
of the international community, starting their own development on
the basis of molds adopted from the West.

This is the myth of modernity: neither completely untrue nor the
full truth! Historical reality is vastly more complex. Our narrative
of modernization has primarily attributed to internal factors the
emergence of the West. We disregarded certain external factors: (1)
geographical location benefited certain regions more than others;
(2) the first societies to modernize had advantages over latecomers;
and (3) the world system now embraces all societies in a tight hug,
exerting *structural* constraints such that it is hard for any single society to escape from its systemic role. If we overlook these constraints,
the upshot would suggest that the non-West—including the Islamic
non-West—must have caused its own decline. If, on the contrary, we
are very politically correct, we may exaggerate the constraints and
fall in the opposite trap, completely exonerating the global South.
Completely emasculating *agency*, we turn three quarters of the world
into a mere object of the remaining one quarter. Neither one interpretation nor the other does justice to reality. Does a deterministic development teleology—a secularized version of God's plan for humanity in

an arc spanning from creation to last judgment—lurk behind modernization's manifold manifestations? The answer is unknown. Yet *something* like a modernization process undeniably exists, penetrates Muslim societies, and provokes responses. These responses are obviously reacting to how modernization is perceived. And while such perception will be strongly marked by one's immediate experience at the hands of the penetrating outsider, it cannot but be colored as well through the prism of the responding civilization's psychological habits, values, and earlier experiences with the invader. This mechanism also applies to the Islamic world in its confrontation with the West, and may help us understand Islamism. For after attempts at imitation and adaptation failed, the confrontation now evokes rejection. Among the rejectionists, Islamism has pride of place.

Islamism: Reaction Against Modernity

Islamism is at the contemporary end of a long line of revivalist movements in Islamic history. Movements to purify faith and recreate an idealized past are as old as Islam itself, and have parallels in other religions. However, such "pre-modern fundamentalisms" (a contradiction in terms, if the foregoing analysis is correct) never had the means, as are available today, to exhaustively remodel and control society. Nor did early Islam have to confront today's secularist and democratic challenges. These differences represent a qualitative leap, and the ensuing discontinuity explains some of the virulence of Islamism's antimodern reaction.

An event like the creation of Saudi Arabia in the 1920s as a rigid Islamic state was, in spite of superficial analogies, not Islamism, but one of the last of Islam's recurrent premodern nomad revolutions. Indeed, Ibn Sa`ud's *Ikhwan* were not reacting against the penetration of modern life in Najd, but against what they saw as the superstitions of popular Islam: worship of saints' tombs, magic, ecstatic ceremonies. The attempt of a small Saudi band to occupy Mecca's Great Mosque in 1979, however, is definitely Islamist; it did not combat popular Islam (long since exterminated by the Saudi monarchy), but the monarchy itself and its `ulama, viewed as corrupt and in the pay of Western interests.

Islamism is marked off from earlier puritanisms by both a different object (namely, a Muslim society already partially affected by modernity coming from outside), and by a new and earlier nonexistent subject: the alienated Muslim who reconstructs (by nontraditional *bricolage*) his or her own Islam. Therefore, Islamism grows in the most advanced Muslim countries—Egypt, Lebanon, Iraq, Iran, and

Pakistan—where the dilemma of overlapping but incompatible collective identities is strongest, and where the impossibility of achieving a balance among them has been most painful. As we have seen, the failure of competing ideologies such as local patriotism, pan-Arabism, communism, and Western liberalism opened the door to radical religious alternatives.[1]

The Failure of Modernizing Development: How Islamism Was Born

Evidently, one first needs Islam to allow later for a flourishing of Islamism. In the Middle East, secularist ideologies introduced by the West were limited to intellectual and professional strata, and failed to erode traditional popular religiosity. From the 1970s on, globalization has been transforming Middle Eastern societies; rapid social change intensifies cultural alienation. Islamism grows where socioeconomic and cultural pressures converge. Among Islam's half-modernized youth, some respond by reasserting their "authentic" cultural identity through a return to personal religiosity; some, by political engagement in the first truly Islamist cadres. However, effective political action also demands masses supportive of such a self-appointed Islamist elite—ideally, conservative, recently urbanized, not yet secularized masses. Conflicts such as the Gulf War or the Palestine crisis weld these two groups: their alliance produces pressures to further Islamize society. Once a critical mass of sympathizers begins to act as an extremist lever challenging Westernizing elites, repression may plunge Muslim society into a vicious cycle of radicalization and counter-radicalization.

What about Islamist tendencies that, at a subsequent stage, manifest themselves in Muslim societies outside the Middle Eastern core? In Africa, Central Asia, and Southeast Asia they grow: (1) as copies inspired by the Middle Eastern original; (2) because Muslim societies affected by the same forces of globalization (but later than in the Middle East) produce similar effects; and (3) because in some cases, peripheral Islamisms are reactions to idiosyncratic local conditions.

How Islamism Grows: Social and Psychological Factors

Psychological mechanisms facilitate the transition to Islamism. People look for an ideological compass, but not in isolation. The defeat of rival ideologies raises the psychological and social price for those who would embrace such discarded alternatives as Marxism or liberalism. Modernity lives by dialogue: however, communication without pre-established verities demands greater maturity than surrender to a group of like-minded others. Islamism, with its closed and logically unassailable system (i.e., unassailable once one accepts on belief the first step), offers a facile solution: obeying authority and fleeing the burden of costs less mental energy than exerting personal responsibility. By glorifying victimhood, propagating conspiracy theories, and blaming outsiders for problems at least partly created by their own culture, Islamism uses and reproduces some deeply engrained Middle Eastern habits.[2]

Another psychological factor is linked to the Islamic world's current underdevelopment. Historically, Islam has not been a religion of the poor. In its golden age, it was the civilization of a sophisticated merchant class, perfectly adapted to a market economy. Today, however, in spite of the image of oil sheiks, most Muslims live in the world's more impoverished countries. Islamism dovetails with the poverty of most of its followers. Material riches are scorned in favor of dedication to God. Islamism returns to the nonmaterial, precapitalist values of honor, obedience, solidarity, and mutual aid. Islamic puritanism strengthens the ideological defenses against the permissive West's temptations. Moreover, it channels and sanctifies anger nourished by inequality, lack of opportunity, and humiliation in a faith-sanctioned struggle against the West. This does not mean one must be poor to be Islamist (most of the 9/11 assassins were not). There are really only two preconditions for joining political Islam: some contact with modernity, followed by disillusionment. Alienation is more important a factor than poverty. What counts is the feeling of exclusion.

Is Islam More Susceptible to Fundamentalization? _____

Although it may be hard to prove, impressionistic data suggest that fundamentalism is today more prevalent in Islam than in most other religions. If so, three predisposing factors may be responsible: (1) Islam's history of conflict with the Christian West; (2) the ideological and hence easily recuperable character of Islam's social utopia; and (3) Islam's universalism.

Anti-Westernism

Islamism's social program is too specific to appeal to more than a minority of Muslims. What makes it grow is its consistent exploitation of anti-Westernism, much more widespread in the Islamic world than the Islamist ideology itself. In their struggle for state power, Islamists brandish a secret weapon that fundamentalists of other religions lack. Christian fundamentalists have a problem: they are part and parcel of the Western secular civilization they ostensibly reject. Jewish fundamentalists, too, cannot for obvious political reasons afford the luxury of censuring the West; and Hindu fundamentalists operate in an environment less affected by Western cultural invasion (they are more anti-Muslimist than anti-Western). Only Islam can easily revive an identity based on historical antagonism with Christendom. All fundamentalisms make propaganda with their own theology, but Islamism alone can add ire against the West to its arsenal. The source of this anti-Western bias is historical and geographical. Islam came into being near Christianity's centers, erected itself against Christianity, and had throughout its history more intense (and more often than not, hostile) encounters with the West than the eastern civilizations in India, China, Japan, and elsewhere. Moreover, Islam has more in common with Judaism and Christianity: theological proximity produces fiercer competition. It is debatable whether Western powers are treating the Islamic world differently than they treat other civilizations; however, a long memory of antagonism has survived in Islamic consciousness. It continues to feed resentment.

Militancy of the Islamic Utopia

Islam sees religion and politics as inseparable—at least this is what the Orientalists tell us. Islamists themselves love to repeat the identity of *din wa-dawla,* or faith and state are one. However, Islamist insistence on this religion-state nexus (and the very term, political Islam) shows that their identity is not that self-understood. We have indeed encountered other Islams—more interiorized, a-political, ethical, or mystical. Still, Islam is undeniably communitarian and political. Not only is it impossible to be a good Muslim isolated from other Muslims, but the faith itself includes a vision of the good society. Islam's emphasis on social justice is, in contrast to the Christian *civitas Dei*, not a vague utopia. The effort (*jihad*) to realize it on earth corresponds to rather precise criteria, and is in principle incumbent on every Muslim. Literal reading of sacred sources gives ammunition to Islamist militants; other, more allegorical or subjective interpretations always risk distancing themselves too far from the text's immediate meaning. Political authority has often been in charge of introducing and maintaining the just social order. However, significant differences exist in this respect between civilizations. Some authors attribute the West's supposed superiority to the separation of state and church. However, the coexistence between these two spheres has been a good deal more complex than Jesus's simple instruction, "Give to Caesar what belongs to Caesar, and to God what belongs to God."[3] After the church's lording it over kings in the Middle Ages, and before Enlightenment thinkers came up with the notion of separation of powers, European caesars legislated, administered, and judged.

One encounters in the reality of Islam nothing comparable to either clerical power or the divine right of sovereigns. Caliphs and sultans impressed their Christian guests with an unlimited power that would be the envy of their counterparts in Versailles, Madrid, or Vienna. The myth of Oriental despotism—an integral part of Orientalism's dichotomous vision, according to its theorist, Palestinian-American literary scholar Edward Said—rested on a concrete base that was not mythical at all.[4] In this concrete sense, Muslim potentates knew how to extract the necessary justifications from their servile `ulama. Eighteenth-century Moroccan sultan Isma`il Moulay, it is said, arbitrarily tortured and cut off heads every day, to demonstrate his authority. Islam's caesars governed in the luxury of the Sunni adage, better a century of tyranny than one hour of anarchy.

However, if such was the Muslim reality, it was also a corruption of Islam, and Muslims knew this. In every generation, there were thinkers who compared reality to the example given by the Prophet, found it wanting, and said so aloud—not rarely at the risk of their lives. For Muhammad had shown ideal society as neither a golden age forever lost (as in China, the ancient Middle East, or classical antiquity), nor as utopia delayed until the hypothetical end of history (as in Judaism and Christianity), but as concrete prototype, to be emulated here and now. The king does not have the right to change the model, only to realize it. He cannot legislate, as God is the only Lawgiver; the task of the *umma*'s leader is to expand the reach of this immutable law over the whole world. In theory, his power is less than that of a Western president. He may only apply already existing rules, encourage obedience to given law, and punish transgression—and before doing so, he still must seek the consensus of those most versed in divine law (i.e., society's most pious members). The political leader of the Islamic state—whether caliph, imam, emir, or president—is essentially an administrator, limited to providing the social framework within which Muslims can pursue their religious and social duties.[5] He may build the house but has no jurisdiction over what happens within its walls: here *shari`a* rules.

Islamism proposes a concrete utopia: justice, stability, and security on earth, and paradise after the Day of Judgment. If utopian reality disappoints, the fault must lie with the Muslims who commit errors: Islam, the utopia, is perfect. Muslim society has always known tension between reality and the ideal, and its history is full of endeavors to restore original Islam and its just society. As often as not, an attempt would start with one Bedouin-type tribe or another enthused by the utopian vision of some preacher-saint. They would cleanse their religious practice of impure additions of the kind that easily proliferate in popular Islam. Next they would go to town to dethrone the sultan whose tyranny and debauchery had led believers into a life of injustice and apostasy. A new, more puritanical dynasty would take power and reconstruct society according to Islamic law. However, after a few generations, the new rulers would in turn succumb to the blandishments of power and luxury: absolutism and decadence would raise their head again—until the next incursion from the desert.

Grist for the mill of the Middle East's dynastic cycles, such puritanical revolutions were for the first time analyzed by fourteenth-century North African sociologist Ibn Khaldun, who identified the rise and fall of group solidarity (`asabiyya) as their driving force. British anthropologist Ernest Gellner updated the notion; all such protofundamentalist experiments were doomed to fail because premodern states lacked the machinery to create the polity prescribed by radicals. But although reality may fall short of expectation, the dream did not die. Islam is *a utopia that was never delegitimized, because it had never been really tested* (at least not by the radicals' lights). Thus the dream remained intact, forever inspiring new generations of reformers and revolutionaries. What distinguishes latter-day Islamism from its medieval precursors are the new technical and administrative possibilities; the state finally has the wherewithal to eradicate from Islam its "impurities" and impose the normative version—this time for good.[6]

In short, utopias appear in every religious and philosophical tradition, and may mutate into ideologies with the potential to revolutionize the world. Fundamentalism is one such political expression, and many religions thus harbor the seeds of fundamentalization. However, in Islam, the seeds are forever ready to be sown. Muslim society's crisis provides the fertile soil they need to sprout.

Islam's Universalism

Most fundamentalisms are linked to one national group (e.g., Jewish fundamentalism to Israeli Jews; *hinduttva* to India). This is even true of fundamentalist versions of the universalistic religions—American evangelicals are frequently also American patriots. Islamic expansion, however, is not thus limited; Islamists facilitate the export of their brand of the religion by shearing it of any cultural, local, or ethnic particularisms. For them, Islam is not some noncommittal proposal, but a profoundly obligating message—a global call that radically negates and condemns to disappearance all competing ideologies, including the nation-state and the international system "made in the West."

At the end of the day, the birth of any religion is something mysterious, beyond the ken of reason. Thus also with Islam. Islamism, in contrast, is amenable to rational understanding, and we can analyze its preconditions: (1) a religion with a strong political and social message, self-confidence, and with a background of resistance to outsiders; (2) a prolonged demographic, social, and cultural crisis, in a geopolitical context imposed by its chief outsider enemy; (3) successive defeats of rival emancipation projects; and (4) alienated social groups who find in the politicization of their religion a new dispensation. Wherever these four factors combine, Islamism is always a possibility. Because such a conjuncture occurs ever more frequently, new and possibly violent expressions of Islamism are probable. The ideological shift eventually produces a new Islam, as universal as globalization itself.

What to do? Although Islamism's emergence—vector of numerous nearly irresistible forces—seems to be inevitable, the outcome of its war against the West is far from certain. Many other factors make their weight felt: counterforces and alternatives within the Islamic world, in addition to Western actions and reactions. The choices to be made on both sides will determine humankind's course for decades.

PART III

Tomorrow

ISLAM AND THE WEST

11

Clash of Civilizations or Transcultural Dialogue?

Internalists and Externalists _____

"What went wrong?"[1]

Islamist violence is the most salient symptom of the malaise between Islam and the West, but not the only one. The Islamic world is in the midst of a grave and spreading crisis. In many Muslim countries, the economic situation is worse today than when they gained independence, and still deteriorating. Economic exploitation hurts many and benefits few. Fifty years ago, Egypt, Iran, and Algeria belonged to the same income group as Taiwan, Singapore, and Brazil. Nowadays, per capita income in the latter group is between three and fifteen times higher than in the first. Most Islamic countries have authoritarian or dictatorial regimes; in some, human rights are regularly and massively violated; Saddam Hussein's Iraq was just the most extreme case. In Latin America, Eastern Europe, Indonesia, parts of sub-Saharan Africa, and elsewhere, waves of democratization have swept autocracies out in favor of representative regimes. These waves have lapped at, but not flooded, the Arab world, Central Asia, or Pakistan. Few Muslim countries have crossed the threshold to pluralistic democracy. The human development index (HDI) of a good part of the

Islamic world falls in the lowest category. Of all the world's ancient centers of civilization, the Islamic world is today the most backward, fragmented, repressive, and anti-egalitarian, and—despite all verbal expressions of Islamic solidarity—anything but fraternal.

Of all regions once controlled by the West, nowhere are questions of cultural penetration and alienation higher on the agenda than in the Islamic world—the only civilization whose traditional religious culture has mutated into a fundamentalist ideology that is not only defensive, but also claims to lead the whole non-Western world against the West. Although fundamentalisms flourish in all religions, the sheer violence of Islamic fundamentalist movements sets them in a category of their own. *Today, Islamism constitutes the only universal, coherent, and assertive alternative to post-Cold War Western supremacy.* It is also the only one to challenge it militarily. In the vision of both Western culturalists such as Huntington, and of the Islamists themselves, we are facing a clash of incompatible civilizations: a life-and-death war of cultures. For Islamists, the outcome is not in doubt: the battle will end in Islam's global victory over God's enemies.

One does not have to accept either of these pessimistic and complementary worldviews to acknowledge that terrorist attacks and international tensions emanating from the Islamic world are escalating. A quarter-century ago, U.S. National Security Adviser Zbigniew Brzezinski coined the concept of the "Arc of Crisis" which designated as a zone of global turbulence the vast region spanning North Africa to South Asia, to the south of the former USSR. Twelve years after the dissolution of the former Soviet giant, it is impossible to blame communism for all the ailments and civil wars that afflict those living within this arc, which largely coincides with the Islamic world.

The long and bloody list of violent strife associated with Islamism casts doubt on the idea of the failure of radical Islam. News bulletins look made to order to convince us that the Islamic Middle East is the world's black hole. The Islamic world is exporting its crisis to the rest of the world and threatens to engulf it unless the international community comes up with a convincing answer. But what drives this crisis? As historian Bernard Lewis asks, "What went wrong?" Is Islam responsible for the evils that afflict Muslims, as critics accuse? If not Islam, then what? How to react? What to do?

Two Incompatible Visions?

The crisis of Islam and the threat of Islamism have been extensively discussed in both scholarly literature and popular media. Two opposing schools have arisen in the West: "internalism" and "externalism." Schematically, for the internalist school, Islam itself is the culprit. The long history of Western intervention in the Islamic world was not, internalists believe, as bad as often considered. It has brought both disadvantages and opportunities, although the Islamic world let all of the opportunities pass it by. As a result, it remains stuck in a vicious circle of rancor, self-pity, and violence. The main impediment to the Islamic world's development is Islam itself. Historically this theory has been associated with such famous Orientalists as Christiaan Snouck Hurgronje, Hamilton A. R. Gibb, perhaps Louis Massignon, and Gustave von Grunebaum. Nowadays Bernard Lewis, Daniel Pipes, and Martin Kramer are its best known proponents. Internalists, often labeled reactionaries and Orientalists by their critics, argue that Islam is something irreducible—the single most indispensable factor in understanding all societies touched by it, and the one that has driven Muslim society into its current *cul-de-sac*. After its epoch of glory in the Middle Ages, Islam failed to renew itself; hence its inability to provide solutions and modernize Islamic society. Islam is what prevents Muslims from fully adopting the principles of modernity.

The result, theorize members of the internalist school, has been a long series of historical failures. Locked in a thought structure that insists on the superiority of their own values but is unable to explain their repeated defeats, Muslim societies have in fact no choice but to blame the outer world, and especially the West, for their misfortunes. What is needed more than anything else is a reform within Islam itself, although the most radical essentialists consider the task nearly impossible. Until the needed internal reform occurs, the situation will only worsen, and ever-more young people will be attracted to deadlocked Islamism. This school of thought thus concludes that there will be more violence. The inescapable conclusion: the West will have to stand firm to protect its security.

The externalist school rejects the internalist vision as reductionist. Externalists minimize Islamic societies' responsibility for their own sorrows, and blame exogenous factors. They cite the West, not Islam, as the problem. For externalists, the Islamic world's endemic disunity and authoritarianism are the outcome of Western meddling. Current unrest is seen as a reaction to enforced integration in an unjust global structure with lopsided distribution of power and resources. The Middle East's and South Asia's geostrategic position attracts permanent Western attention to secure control of these regions. The West's need for oil leads to military action against whichever regime would challenge it.

For externalists, Islam is just one factor, and not necessarily the principal one, that determines Muslim reflexes and choices. Because

Muslim countries differ in terms of history, socioeconomic structure, ethnic makeup, type of religiosity, and economic options, one must distinguish many different Islams of varying compatibility with modern values. The real problem resides in the West's rejection of Islam. *Orientalism*, a Western structure of knowledge-as-power, has created a false, artificial, and hostile image of the Islamic world—an imaginary mental construction that sustains a domination project that the Islamic states' purely formal independence has only superficially eased. The West projects its own unrecognized and rejected aspects on an Orient that does not exist; this is what keeps the inequality in place.[2] Anouar Abdel Malek, Maxime Rodinson, Edward Said, and John Esposito are among the most notable representatives of the externalist school of thought, which views itself as progressive and anti-imperialist. Detractors like to debunk it as an Islamophile fifth column in academia.

As externalists see it, the reaction was inevitable. Although Islamism's expressions may not always please the Eurocentric observer, they boil down to a reappropriation of stolen cultural authenticity. Development and empowerment (although not necessarily Western-style democratization) will occur naturally in the Islamic world once global capitalism and the United States in particular finally leave it alone. The West would do better to confront its own racism; in fact, some externalists say, Islamic fundamentalism may well represent a salutary reaction to Western "epistemological colonization." Instead of prescribing what to do, externalists focus more on what *not* to do—namely, not to react violently against popular attempts of the Islamic world to determine its own course. The longer the West continues to meddle, the worse the situation will become. So externalists, too, reach the same pessimistic conclusion that more violence is inevitable. However, for them, it is the Islamic world that must strengthen itself—as safeguard against further Western encroachment!

These schools are more than just opinions: behind their respective positions lie paradigms that reflect two opposed worldviews. Although their representation here cannot but be overly schematic (with some of the best specialists of the Islamic world—e.g., Ernest Gellner, Olivier Roy, and Bassam Tibi—belonging to neither school), it is clear that both have strong arguments and that each is partially right. The struggle for the correct reaction to Islam is a microcosm of the *Kulturkampf*, the great ideological battle being fought in the West ever since the former colonizer was forced to double its efforts to understand the formerly colonized.

Winners and Losers in the Academic Debate

Before World War II, the internalist approach had flourished in the universities of colonial powers France and Britain, and functioned as intellectual cover of the colonial project itself. Some Orientalists justified colonialism in the name of a supposed superiority of Christian-Western civilization over Muslims and other "dark races." From the 1940s on, the United States became the center of Islamic studies. Throughout the 1950s and 1960s, the superiority of the Western model was still the axiomatic paradigm; but now success was believed to be within reach of the "underdeveloped" peoples, provided they adopted modernity. Externalist critiques contesting this vision—in particular, Marxist ones—were in the minority.

Decolonization, guilt over Western colonialism, frustration with development attempts, criticism of Western (especially U.S.) interventions against progressive Third World movements, growing acceptance of the Marxist anti-imperialist analysis, and the *dependencia* theory analyzing structural imbalance in First/Third World relations caused a shift in this conjuncture. Eventually, the Marxist alternative exhausted itself; then came the subjective and relativist turn in philosophy and social science. A gamut of new social movements— feminist, environmentalist, homosexual, African American, not to mention other ethnic, religious, and other minority causes—claims, each for itself, the right to difference, and has thus helped undermine the earlier evolutionary, hierarchical, and totalizing vision of human society.

Although quite a few of these movements have their own rather radical (at times separatist) aims, their collective consensus embraces an ideal of multiculturalism, namely, the coexistence of all differences in a generalized tolerance that refuses any value hierarchy. Newly hegemonic postmodernism and cultural relativism inform postcolonial studies. Generational struggle was another factor in this shift, as was the influx (most noticeable in American universities) of numerous Third World scholars. Among these, those of Middle Eastern and/or Muslim background naturally brought with them increased sensitivity to the Islamic world's subjectivity—as well as greater intellectual distance from the formerly predominant modes of Western thinking.

These trends in social science eventually reached the academic discussion on Islam. The 1980s and 1990s saw the gradual undermining of internalist hegemony in Western academia—in particular in the principal research and teaching centers in the United States, France, and Britain. By the same token, the externalist vision gained strength until it became the new politically correct orthodoxy.

The relevance of these debates transcends academia. We have already seen how Islam in its politicized form became a growing problem for the modern world (after the modern world itself became a problem for Islam!). Middle East and Islam "specialists" in the media, national and local bureaucracies, churches, and NGOs mold Western policies *vis-à-vis* Muslim minorities and the Middle East. These consultants wield considerable influence. Immigrant-friendly policies, an aversion to cultural protectionism, a growing openness to pro-Palestinian positions, and much more can be traced to them. On the eve of 9/11, survivors of the internalist school like Bernard Lewis had become rather marginalized in Islamologist circles.

Among the many transformations that Osama bin Laden's attacks have wrought, the impact on the discussion of how to deal with Islam is one of the most interesting. In turn, the Islamophile positions of the externalist school were radically challenged and delegitimized by the violence that a small bunch of Islamic marginals perpetrated against the West. After September 11, 2001, the vision of a global multiculturalism and a benevolent Islam—which only the West's own prejudices and deeply rooted Islamophobia prevented from peacefully coexisting with the rest of the world, to mutual benefit—suddenly seemed naïve.

Some made the farfetched accusation that the Islamophiles had ideologically prepared the ground for fundamentalist terrorism. It is, however, true that the tendency to look outside the Islamic world for the causes of problems impedes a proper understanding of Islamism as a twisted reaction to modernity coming from within Islam itself. Cultural and moral relativism preempt any in-depth assessment of the phenomenon; and the idea that all opinions have the same value hinders any serious dialogue between the West and modernist Muslims. Although much has been written since the attacks, externalist authors such as Said and Esposito did not publish really original new proposals on how to understand and react to the fundamentalist challenge. Dismissing the 9/11 criminals as mere isolated idiots, claiming that Americans had brought this punishment upon themselves, or insisting that a more peaceful Islam was still available, does not clarify the dilemma. The rhetoric hides conceptual poverty.[3]

Thus one observes a sudden new twist: while externalists stutter, their internalist competitors do not hesitate to accuse them of having psychologically disarmed the West. Appeals were voiced to expel the pro-Islamist Trojan horse from Western academia. These are signs of an incipient intellectual counterrevolution, which in itself contributes little to the necessary reflection on how to respond to an all-too-real challenge. Counterviolence may contain it, but cannot solve it.

Islam and Violence _____

Over the last decade Islam has been in the news every day, mostly in connection to some outbreak of violence. The conclusion that Islam is an inherently violent religion is nonetheless erroneous. Islam is neither more violent than other religions nor does it more predispose its followers to fanaticism. The Qur'an speaks of love for the neighbor, tolerance, and the sanctity of human life.[4] In part, the negative stereotype results from the journalistic tendency toward sensationalism. The opening of a modernist mosque is no news. When Muslim community leaders sign a declaration of peaceful coexistence with non-Muslim clerics, detailing preconditions for mutual understanding, it earns at best a footnote.[5] However, if the extremist preacher in a London mosque makes incendiary remarks after 9/11, his opinion is broadcast as if it represents that of most Muslims. Much violence is committed by Muslims indeed; meanwhile, misrepresentation is also rife.

Other religions have not been less cruel than Islam. Qur'anic sources are contradictory, with exhortations both to peace and to war, but the same ambiguity permeates the Bible, and it would not be too difficult to produce an anthology of biblical verses condemning to death (with punitions paralleling the Qur'an's) those who transgress ritual, ethical, and social commands. The New Testament has in general a softer tenor: Jesus was himself victim of persecution, and Christianity survived three centuries underground—until the Roman emperor Constantine legalized it. However, Jesus also warned "it is not peace I have come to bring, but a sword."[6] Though Christianity's founder was a man of peace, its history is hardly less violent than Islam's. Whereas Muhammad was "his own Constantine,"[7] with *jihad* corresponding to crusade, there is no Muslim parallel to the cruelties (often with Church benediction) of the conquest and exploitation of America, or the West's record in its colonies. Hinduism may thank Gandhi for pacifist prestige, but its holiest text, the *Bhagavad Gita*, contains a profound discussion of the warrior's caste duty to kill. Seventeen hundred years before Machiavelli, Chinese philosophers of the legal school disserted on the virtues of cruelty to instill obedience to the emperor. Japan's Buddhism resulted in the martial *samurai* cult. The French and Belgian killing fields of World War I struck in the heart of Western civilization. Nazism and Stalinism are two other references that may usefully put in perspective the so-called exceptionalism of Islamic violence. The Islamic world has yet to produce anything as monstrous as the Holocaust, or the more recent genocides in Cambodia and Rwanda (although Saddam Hussein came close). Terrorism had its origins in European anarchistic *milieux* of the nineteenth century, and as a systematic reprisal strategy was introduced in the Middle East in the 1930s by right-wing Zionists in the context of the struggle against the British and the Palestinians.[8] Suicide terrorism has been developed by Sri Lanka's Tamil Tigers. The facile association of Islam with violence rests at least in part on prejudice.

This does not mean one should be indulgent in the face of violence in the Islamic world. While Western interventions have sown some seeds of the current whirlwind, today's violence in the Muslim arc of crisis is largely self-inflicted; and most of its victims are Muslims. Consider Jihadists killing Coptic Christians and Western tourists in Egypt; the Islamic revolution in Iran; Hizbullah's and Hamas's anti-Israeli terror; persecution of Christians, Hindus, and Shiites in Afghanistan, Pakistan, and India; Muslim pogroms in Algeria; and communal violence and draconian Islamic laws in Sudan, Nigeria, and Indonesia. Earlier chapters illustrated *ad nauseam* the bloodletting in the Islamic world. So much hell on earth cannot be attributed to coincidence or to contingent, time- and locale-dependent factors. Nor can it be excused as merely a reaction to earlier structural violence brought by Western imperialism; China, Indochina, and Africa were no less victimized by the same imperialism, without showing comparable reactions. While Huntington's formula that "Islam has bloody borders" may be essentialist, we are facing a real problem. Whereas Christianity's past may have outshone Islam's in violence,[9] Christianity has for a considerable period now been losing political power, and has by and large accustomed itself to its new, more modest, societal niche. In contrast, Islam represents a "wounded civilization,"[10] an erstwhile superpower systematically defeated and humiliated over two centuries by its main antagonist—a "theological impossibility" that has set off a powder keg.

Motives for Violence

Violence in today's Islamic world occurs at the confluence of three forces: its open psychological wound; a worsening socioeconomic and political crisis; and ever more active Islamist groups riding the crest of mass dissatisfaction. The extremist wings of Islamists are responsible for most, and the most dangerous, violence in the Islamic world. While they represent only one option among many within Islam—and until now, that of an intolerant minority—they portray themselves as vanguard, and have often succeeded in silencing competing tendencies. Still, Islamism as a whole is just a container for a plethora of groups, only a minority of which adopts violence. It is the extremist minority within a minority that poses the imminent danger for Muslim society and, increasingly, the rest of the world.

Islamists see themselves as good (sometimes, as the only good) Muslims who are called to reform the rest. Although their interpretation may be uniquely strict, their arguments are drawn from sources many believers share. Like those of other religions, Islam's sources are susceptible to multiple interpretations: in all these respects, Muslims show no major difference from Christians or Jews: fundamentalists from all three monotheistic faiths use the same approach. What distinguishes Islam—and hence, Islamists—is the incomparably more *central position of the holy text* itself. The place of Qur'an in Islam is much more elevated than that of the Bible in Christianity and has no parallel in any religion (except possibly Orthodox Judaism's view of the Torah). Liberal Jews and Christians have been able to bracket a large number of "inconvenient" biblical injunctions (e.g., to stone homosexuals). For reasons that are not all clear, Islam's historical evolution was opposed, progressively restricting freedom of exegesis.

Since the text's eternity and immutability became dogma, the Qur'an cannot be studied as a product of its time; as a result, arguing the relativity of its most rigid commands becomes so much tougher. However, just as in the other faiths, such historicization is key to verifying what in the Qur'an reflects a nucleus of possibly extrahuman and supernatural inspiration—and what represents its humanly limited and conditioned reception—historical "noise" that impedes the message's true reception, and need not commit latter-day believers. Such a procedure, however, is still taboo in Islam. Islam, then, does not predispose more to violence than other religions, but contemporary Islam lacks, to a greater extent than other religions, the theological mechanisms to mitigate those factors that do allow or prescribe violence. Muslims who accept *shari`a* as basis for the social order are on average neither more nor less bloodthirsty than anyone else. They take upon themselves Islamic law's severity as the price to pay for the security they seek, often because the superficially more benevolent models of Western make have too often disappointed them.

Islam and the West

Old Contacts

Are we facing a war of civilizations? Before discussing the controversial clash-of-civilizations thesis, one must understand the term. Civilizations are not tangible entities, but fluid mental constructs that bind societies in webs of shared modes, norms, values, and epistemological, religious, or artistic sensibilities. Edward Said was right in unmasking how deeply the East-West polarization is imbued with ideological and interest-ridden constructions. However, this does not mean that civilizations as such do not exist, with their own sometimes overlapping, sometimes fuzzy borders. Modernization and globalization have brought formerly isolated civilizations into intense communication; but their contacts also create tensions, although civilization is far from being the only or most determining factor in relations between populations. Our world is a mixture of economic, political, and even cultural interdependences—but also includes defensive reactions on the part of religious, ethnic, and other groups threatened by the apparently irresistible progress of interpenetration. *Islam* and *the West* exist both as image and as more or less coherent civilizations; neither ever constituted a closed entity. Although important differences separate them, they have also a good deal in common. The similarities, at least until some 300 years ago, are striking when one compares Islam-plus-Christendom (as one complex based on revealed monotheism) with other civilizations farther east. Islamic-Western territorial and cultural overlaps illustrate how close their historical interaction was. Relations between them have swung between the poles of dialogue and conflict: neither conflict nor cooperation should surprise us. In fact, both Islam and Europe have to a significant degree defined themselves by their difference from the other.

Rival universalistic claims launched Islam and the West on a course of confrontations, marked by four key moments. The first moment (the seventh and eighth centuries), with Arab expansion to the detriment of the Byzantine Empire and various Christianized Germanic post-Roman realms, started in Muhammad's time and continued during the Umayyad and ʿAbbasid caliphates. Although Christendom permanently lost the Middle East and North Africa, it succeeded in a second moment (the eleventh through fifteenth centuries) in recapturing the Iberian Peninsula, Sicily, Muscovy (initially a Byzantine offshoot), and temporarily Palestine. In a third moment (the fourteenth through seventeenth centuries), Europe expanded overseas, but Muslims regained the initiative on land as the Ottoman Empire destroyed Byzantium, conquered the Balkans, and threatened Central Europe. In the fourth period (the nineteenth and twentieth centuries), European colonization broke the back of the Islamic gunpowder empires; retook the Balkans, Ukraine, and South Russia; went on to colonize densely Islamized zones in Central Asia, India, Southeast Asia, and Africa; and for a brief moment between the world wars, ruled the very heart of the Islamic world: the Middle East.

Western powers left untouched only regions that they considered too primitive to warrant the expense of colonization—among them, the Arabian Peninsula, with Islam's Holy Cities. Decolonization, essentially over by 1970, ended this fourth moment, although informal Western influence has not ceased in the Islamic world, and substantial Muslim minorities have now settled in the West. Thus we reach the present situation, where "Islam" means the Middle East, a good part of Africa, and South and Southeast Asia; whereas "the West" means a core of Western and Central Europe plus North America, but includes Latin America, Eastern Europe, and Oceania (not to speak of more limited Western influences in Japan, the Asian Tigers, South Africa, and India).

In light of these territorial vicissitudes, the relationship between Islam and the West indeed seems epitomized by *jihad* and crusade. Theology justified hostility: for Islam, Christianity was an outdated, contemptible version of the true faith. Christianity's view of Islam was more negative still: that of the false alternative *par excellence*. Dante Alighieri's *Divina Commedia* puts Muhammad in the ninth circle of hell. Yet antagonism was no more than a backdrop during long intervals of more positive interaction, when trade, cultural exchange, interfaith dialogue, and coexistence took center stage. Such encounters occurred more frequently under the more pluralistic auspices of Islam than in Christendom. In medieval Spain and Sicily, Muslims, Jews, and Christians took part in a common economy and culture; contact with Greek sources and philosophical and scientific interaction across religious lines was to prove vital for development of the West. Western economic interests also counteracted religious antipathy. Venice grew rich by transporting crusaders to the Holy Land, but was not averse to trading with the enemy. In the fifteenth century, a mutually profitable galley line connected Venice to Egypt's Mamluks, who traded Oriental luxury articles for European slaves. In sixteenth-century Christian Europe, political deals with the Ottoman Empire were not uncommon. *Raison d'État* brought French King Francis I of Valois into a pact with Suleiman the Magnificent, opening a second front against Charles V of Habsburg; later, the English East India Company cooperated with the Persian `Abbas I to weaken Portuguese maritime hold over the Indian Ocean. Over the next centuries, commerce trumped religion: the Turks were accepted into the incipient international system, albeit not on the same footing as Christian powers. In any case, after 1683 Islam did not represent a strategic threat to the West.

In the nineteenth century, imperialist rivalries tempted one power after the other to play the protector-of-Islam card. Napoleon Bonaparte in 1798, Napoleon III and Britain in the Crimean War, and Germany's William II at the turn of the twentieth century all showed off as "friend of the Muslims." In World War I, the British beat the Germans at their own game by successfully fomenting the Arab revolt against the Turks, Germany's ally. Post-1945 U.S. support for Saudi Arabia provides a more recent case in which ideological incompatibility and interest-based

cooperation are not mutually exclusive. Politics aside, Western intellectuals, too, tried to understand Islamic culture and thought. Renaissance thinkers were ardently interested in the Arab world. Leibniz and
Enlightenment *philosophes* from Montesquieu and Voltaire to Goethe
also showed a rather tolerant attitude. The eighteenth century witnessed Europe's first scientific research into the Islamic world, as well
as the spread of the first stereotypes about "the Orient." Not all were
disdainful; a certain admiration for the Orient periodically stimulated
exotic fashions, from "Turkish" furniture and musical motives to the
Thousand and One Nights. However superficial such exoticism, it usually reflected curiosity more than antipathy.

New Contacts

Nineteenth- and twentieth-century imperialist expansion complicated the relationship, although not all was negative then, either. Orientalist knowledge, developed to serve Western colonial control, included
attempts to understand Islam and its history on their own terms, and
not to serve Christian polemics. Anthropologists, philologists, visitors,
administrators, photographers, and journalists opened Islam's cultural
treasures to the outside world. Significantly, this corpus later proved
instrumental in the Muslims' rediscovery of their own civilization—
indispensable preparation for, among others, nationalist and Islamic
reformist movements. Notwithstanding the currently fashionable
demonization of "Orientalism," positive interactions were not absent.
Islamic curiosity about the West, although not matching the West's
about Islam, was also growing.[11] Islam's coexistence with the Christian
West should not have been impossible, given that the three great monotheistic faiths shared a vision of religious society in God's service.

But did they? The West was retreating from the ideal of a "community under God." Secularization and scientific-technological,
industrial, and military modernization undermined earlier cross-
civilizational correspondences, and tipped the political-military
equilibrium in favor of the West, soon immensely more powerful than the
Islamic world. Asymmetry caused the implosion of Islam's antiquated
structures, political loss, economic exploitation, and the decline of traditional cultural patterns. The question needs to be reformulated: not only
whether Islam constitutes a menace to the modern West, but also
whether Islam itself will survive the latter. Current east-west relations
reflect attempts to face the "Western danger," and correct the asymmetry.

One must also question to what extent "modern civilization" is still
synonymous with "the West." Modernity itself is progressively divest-
ing itself of its Western label. In Western Europe and North America,
white middle-class Christian predominance is giving way to multieth-

nic, multicultural civilization, composed of a variety of identity groups who mutually accept their differences as a minimum basis of coexistence. Protestant Anglo-Saxons, Latin Catholics, Blacks, Jews, and Muslims, too, participate in a common (if not yet completely level) economic and political field, where they meet primarily not as carriers of specific identity flags but as citizens. This de-culturized society in which all identities are equal is a rather abstract entity lacking proper physiognomy. Western civilization is reduced to a few common values and procedures, anonymous enough to be adopted by citizens of non-Western origins and by non-Western societies. In fact this is happening around the world. Moreover, in a pluralistic modern civilization, with its constitutionally separated private and public sphere, nothing prevents Muslims from forming their own church and fostering their own collective identity. Many Muslims opt indeed for this path. From modern civilization's viewpoint, there is no problem in coexisting with Islam as long as it plays by its consensual rules and behaves as any private religion. This includes trying to change the rules by peaceful and consensual means.

The problem is, of course, that Islam does not view itself as any religion, one among others, but as sole owner of the truth. An activist minority of Islamists sees itself as committed to establish, literally, God's government on earth, in the form of a militant community of believers who will eventually include all of humanity: society cannot legitimately remain religiously neutral; it can have no identity vacuum, but has the duty to surrender to Islam. Islamists thus reject a domesticated Islam under any non-Islamic, humanist, framework; and a significant minority is willing to use violence to realize its aims. *In contrast to other Muslims, hardcore Islamists constitute for modern civilization an inassimilable group.* Thus the real clash of civilizations that threatens to set the world on fire does not pit Islam against the Judeo-Christian West but, on one hand, a universalized modernity (which would accommodate a reformed Islam) against on the other, a radically antimodern version of political Islam. The latter uses the weapons of modernity against modernity itself, and is as universalized and culture-free as universalized modernity itself. The Islamists' Islam is no longer "just" a religion, but an all-encompassing ideological system that declares itself incompatible with the West. It would therefore be more correct to speak of a *clash of ideologies*. Culture wars between modernity and Protestant fundamentalism in the United States, or extremist Jewish settlers in Israel, or *Hinduttva* fanatics in India are all conceivable. However, radical Islamism is unique in combining mass violence with global pretensions.

Have all other attempts of the past half-century to regenerate the Islamic world—liberal, authoritarian, socialist, capitalist, pan-Arab, regional nationalistic, moderate Islamist—been proven a failure? Has the strategy of Islamist extremists to wage a war of "liberation" against the West on Western soil been the one success? The new Islamists wage their war not just to transform their Muslim societies, but to overhaul the whole international system. This system is still essentially Westphalian (i.e., based on sovereign states keeping a minimum of order among themselves through consensual institutions and regimes). Radical Islamists reject the underlying principles of this system: national independence, popular sovereignty, individual liberties, human rights. They do not want to replace it by a more pluralistic and multipolar system, but by a more monistic and unipolar one: a nonterritorial Islamic *umma* supreme over all remaining communities, and fighting until Islam's global supremacy is complete. Though not new, the program is being revitalized.

Osama bin Laden's strategy has unleashed a new hysteria in the West. After the Yellow Peril and the Red Menace, we have now a Green Danger, after the color of the Prophet's flag. It is too early to say whether al-Qaeda's strategy has brought the Islamist cause any gain; but it has already inflicted grave damage upon the Islamic world, the West, and the international community. "Islamist terror" (a term as vague as its opposite, "war against terror") is transforming international relations, with implications for Great Power diplomacy; North-South relations; U.N. functioning; international law; the interdependence between globalization, vulnerability, and collective security; the inverse relation between individual freedom and protection of society; and the ability of the state to cope with nonstate challengers. At a minimum, Islamism has been successful in hoisting itself to the top of the international agenda. More than any other conflict, the war between Islamism and the international community exemplifies how globalization produces at once ever more intense technical-economic interactions, and ever deeper cultural-identity fragmentation. The ongoing war is killing innocent civilians in every corner of the globe, without prior notice and without any justification that would make sense outside the circle of the "already converted." Although irregular and asymmetrical, this war is becoming so violent and far-flung that it threatens the bases of international coexistence itself—unless a more efficacious counterstrategy is developed. The key question thus becomes, What to do?

Conditions for Dialogue

The West's reaction to the frightening increase in violence coming from within the Islamic world has so far been clumsy: a mix of overreaction and underreaction. It has overreacted in terms of military intervention, with heavy "collateral damage," yet little diminution of terror. Underreaction takes the form of a plethora of well-meant interfaith seminars and encounters whose impact has been limited. Militarily protecting the modern urbanized world against terrorist attacks may be indispensable, but does not in itself improve relations between Islam and the West, and will hardly have positive effects unless tagged to policies designed to structurally change our unequal relationship with the Islamic world. *The most urgent task is to distinguish Muslims and Islamists.* With Islam and with the vast majority of Muslims, coexistence is possible and necessary, and should in principle enrich both sides. With violent Islamism, unfortunately, no dialogue appears possible.

Since 9/11, only the most naïve can deny that extreme Islamism constitutes a threat to coexistence. A future *modus vivendi* between Islam and the rest of the world will depend on a mutual agreement on the basis of this coexistence. Which one? The formula of "tolerance and dialogue for Islam, repression for Islamism," proposed a few years ago by the German-Syrian international relations scholar Bassam Tibi,[12] is a useful starting point but must today be qualified.

First, the difference between Islamists and other Muslims is not absolute. Turkey is a case in point: its democratic, pro-Western government has deep Islamist roots. This shows *there is no incompatibility of democracy with Islamism as such, but only with violent, antidemocratic Islamism.* One should be very careful not to generalize too carelessly. While they may be culturally Middle Eastern or South Asian, religiously observant Muslims may politically be democratic pluralists; just as "autochthonous" Europeans and Americans of Western cultural background may embrace violent Islamism. Fundamentalists are made, not born. Religious and political experiences may lead certain believers on an Islamist track. Yet between the already converted, and the half-modernized but still mostly traditional mass of Muslims, there lies a gray zone of believers who tend to accept the Islamist appeal but have made no irreversible commitment to it. The "call" may fall on willing ears for a variety of reasons, such as spiritual void. However, it is at least as probable that the simplifying Islam-is-the-solution slogan is what attracts a good number of candidate Islamists. Islamist anti-Western resistance may resonate with their frustration. Whereas the Islamist hard core is probably only susceptible to religious reasoning proper, the Islamistoid periphery may be swayed by political and other contingent circumstances. Islamist discourse may convince, not because of its theological antimodernism or political extremism, but despite these. Millions are looking for a way out of their collective impotence: a promise that earlier modernizing projects failed to keep. There must thus be whole populations whose transition to fundamentalism is not inevitable if the right policies are followed. Stemming the mass influx into Islamist movements cannot prevent future terrorist acts by small radical minorities, but would dramatically diminish their political significance.

Peaceful and mutually beneficial coexistence can only be grounded in mutual respect and tolerance—values that are already part of the repertoire of both civilizations, and therefore amenable to be reactivated, even in the current polarized context. Tolerance and celebration of difference are key ingredients of multiculturalism. However, tolerance implies passive coexistence and can easily evaporate whenever tensions rise. Active coexistence is based on knowing the Other, and on examining which of her identity components are compatible with our own. This is an active integration process that transforms the Other from tolerated stranger into partner. Interfaith dialogue may initiate such a rapprochement—on condition that it leaves its Islamophile ghetto and allows honest mutual criticism. In post-Christian society, such responsibility belongs not only to churches, but to all citizens.

Second, dialogue is not enough. Is it possible to combine (1) dialogue with "civilized," coexistence-prone, Islam– and (2) repression of "wild" Islamism? Where most Muslims are torn between two poles, such a dichotomous approach will not work (repression will only drive Islamists underground) unless framed in a wider policy of structural reform meant to change the balance of power between a powerful West and a powerless Islamic world. Absent visible signs of such a reform, dialogue will seem cosmetic to most Muslim leadership. At worst, it will degenerate into a farce: a few token Muslims unloading their complaints to a few Westerners eager to assuage their guilty conscience; one side accusing, the other apologizing: not a promising basis for encounter.

There is no a priori incompatibility. Precedents of and resources for communication between civilizations do exist. What brings ever more Muslims to embrace Islamist positions is Islamism's political proposal for dealing with a completely unbalanced world. In the Islamic world, its path is the only one left untested, and hence never disproved. Like fascism and communism, Islamism's answer may be wrong, but the question is right. Questions of power and resources inform Islamic-Western confrontation no less than culture. True, Middle Eastern culture tends to defeat itself by attributing all of its problems to malevolent outside forces.[13] However, outside influences only partly explain Islam's backwardness and involution. Other countries, such as the Asian Tigers, started at more or less at the same level, took responsibility for their own situation, and spectacularly overtook the Middle East. Nor need stagnation lead to a victim posture. India did not claim victim status despite years of lackluster economic growth. A region's or a civilization's development depends on a synergy of internal and external factors. Attitudes toward modernity and understanding of one's own history can be either resources or hindrances. Admittedly the Middle East carries its share of counterproductive cultural baggage. However, it also operates under a series of specific externally caused disadvantages. Even paranoiacs may have real enemies!

Debating who is the more culpable is futile. The Islamic world and the West have been trapped in a complex interaction for fourteen centuries. A chain of circumstances launched the West on the trajectory that landed it in the role of "guide–civilization" (i.e., that civilization that evolves psychosocial, organizational, and technological traits so successful that they transcend that culture's own limits and become universalized)—a role that had earlier been pioneered brilliantly by Islam. In this process, Islam, the earlier frontrunner, found itself victimized. Part of the victimization comes from outside, another part is self-inflicted and internally sustained. Denying either type of damaging influence is pointless: what matters is the effort to overcome its effects. This will demand the input of both progressive Muslims and interested outsiders to prevent a mutually fatal war of religions.

To be credible, communication with Islam demands serious international reform. Dialogue must also meet certain internal criteria. Authentic communication leaves room for criticism, not only Islam's of the West but also the West's of Islam. Discarding a priori any criticism of Islam as prejudiced engenders neither mutual respect nor rapprochement. Notwithstanding certain Islamophile and fashionably relativist attitudes saluting Islamism as cultural decolonization,[14] it is hard to see how dialogue is possible with an ideology that refuses pluralism and accepts violence as a legitimate means to realize its vision.

Defusing tensions will only be possible if dialogue avoids two opposed pitfalls. The first is entering dialogue with the agenda of converting Muslim interlocutors or of convincing them to change their Islam to make it more palatable to Westerners. Any rethinking of Islam's relationship to its sources can only be the result of an engagement among Muslims. Non-Muslim pressures in such a sensitive arena will be the kiss of death. The other pitfall is extreme cultural relativism (whether arguing from leftist Third Worldism, from a certain existentialist appreciation of violence, from postmodern fear of any value judgment, or from any other philosophy) that automatically justifies Muslim anger and violence. This is a useless posture, considered ridiculous within political Islam (the first ideology to reject any multiplicity of truths!). In the long run, the Left's refusal to judge at all is no less harmful than the overly judgmental and antipluralistic rejection of Islam by the Right. Understanding dissatisfaction is not the same as granting legitimacy to violence against civilians—regardless of whether the victims are Westerners or Muslims.

THE FUTURE OF ISLAM 12

Five Dilemmas

It is not the non-Muslim interlocutor's prerogative to tell Islam to change. If the future brings Islam nearer to modernity, it will be the fruit of reflection among Muslims themselves. It is, however, possible to list some critical themes—an inventory of dilemmas whose resolution will determine Islam's twenty-first-century course. Five of these stand out: Islam's relation to its sacred sources, to its internal divisions, to scientific reason, to democracy, and to the new impulses that will undoubtedly challenge it from "Western Islam." The resolution of these dilemmas will decide Islam's future relationship with the non-Muslim world.

The Critique of Sources

Will an Islamic reform dare historicize its sacred sources and free itself from the taboos of the Qur'an's exceptional status as divine message? An anti-historical reading of the Qur'an and *hadiths* has certainly harmed Islam's development. Islam has had courageous rationalists and proto-Enlightenment thinkers, such as Ibn Rushd (Averroes) and Ibn Khaldun. However, the "Aristotelian Left" has long been defeated—the *mu`tazilites'* political liquidation was complete by 850, in full Abbasid glory. Fragmentation into competing caliphates dates from the 900s: the "closure of the *ijtihad*" dates from before

1100[1]—well before the calamities of the twelfth through fourteenth centuries that are routinely blamed for Islam's decline. Reconstruction of liberal Islamic thought, then, although not impossible, will meet well entrenched opposition. Yet only such a critique of religious sources will permit rethinking those principles that most frustrate Islam's coexistence with modernity. Critical historical interpretation would ideally contextualize and relativize the most stringent principles engraved, apparently for all time, in its texts: hostility to the non-Muslim world, supremacy over non-Muslim minorities, subordination of women, and other questions. Islamists join hands with traditionalists in opposition to any epistemological opening demanded by reformists such as Arkoun. Which tendency will defeat the other?

Homogeneity or Heterogeneity?

Will a reform release Islam, theoretically the most universalistic of religions, from its built-in tribal and ethnic inheritance? Islam was conceived as a universal faith, yet since the time of the power struggle over Muhammad's succession among the branches of the Prophet's family, particularistic motives have infiltrated. Islam combatted but never defeated tribal loyalties. As a result, it never produced a homogeneous state, only a chain of more or less fragile polities that have depended more on personal loyalties and family bonds and less on government by abstract rules. Islam's expansion exported particularistic Arab tribal molds, and successive Muslim reigns allowed their survival and reproduction. Even the Ottoman Empire, its most durable exemplar, suffered worse internal fissures than its Western rivals; the difference in internal coherence eventually destroyed it. Islam's sociopolitical weakness permitted the West to become its heir who developed more solid political units and a more unified concept of state. Most Islamic countries continue to suffer from extreme internal divisions and fratricidal strife. Islamism aspires to do away with all particularisms (and as a matter of fact, with all culture) but in the name of an anti-modern revival. Will liberal Islam discover an alternative to the fundamentalist steamroller?

Modernity, Rationalism, and Science

Over a thousand years ago, Islam was at the forefront of scientific progress. Working on Greek classics lost to Christendom, it advanced in mathematics, astronomy, chemistry, optics, medicine, geography, and other sciences. New inventions made the Islamic empire powerful. Such progress, however, depended on an atmosphere of free thought; Sunnism's orthodox turn undermined this. Scientific inquiry, once welcome in Cairo, Baghdad, and Shiraz, long ago moved to Paris, London, and New York (and recently also to Tokyo, Bangalore, and Tel Aviv). It has not yet returned to Baghdad, Teheran, or Islamabad.

Science is at the heart of technological invention that allowed the West to conquer the rest of the world. Over the past millennium, the Islamic world has viewed science with suspicion. After all, it is based not on immutable revelation but on the institutionalization of doubt[2] and on accepting the uncertainty of outcome of any investigation. Islamic orthodoxy maintains a hostile attitude toward science and its corollaries, free thought and rationalism. There is scant difference here between the Sunni conservatism of Saudi Arabia and Pakistan, and Iran's revolutionary Shiism. In terms of education, the quantity and quality of scientific works produced, and discoveries and inventions, the Islamic world now lags behind not just the West but behind almost every other civilization.

For fundamentalists, this may be a fatal weakness. Islamism is, as we have seen, an outgrowth of modernity, an antimodern revolt emerging from the bosom of secularizing modernity. It is thus unthinkable without the object of its rejection. Islamists use in their struggle for power every achievement of reason-based modern science and technology. Yet theologically speaking, they oppose the rationalism that underlies explosives, airplanes, the Internet, and other Western inventions. Wherever they reach power, Islamists try to curb the exercise of reason. Even a relatively enlightened country like Pakistan has included religious knowledge—among other things, memorization of the Qur'an—as a criterion for exact science and engineering students, and appoints lecturers in science on the basis of their religiosity. In Afghanistan under the Taliban and in Saudi Arabia, the situation is worse. Such a framework weakens Muslims in relation to the West instead of empowering them. Bassam Tibi calls the Islamists' profound ambivalence about reason "halfmodern": they eat modernity's fruits while trampling its roots.[3] Ambivalence toward modern science permeates the Islamic environment well beyond the confines of fundamentalism. Simply transferring resources to the Islamic world will not produce empowerment: for this, Islam itself will have to undergo reform. A more rationalist and science-friendly Islam might presumably also be more compatible with the West. Opening to or closing off science, technology, and globalization: the choice will determine the quality of the Muslim future.

Is fundamentalists' rejection of modernity's values self-destructive? Their tactics—whether primitive-heroic (suicide bombs) or technologically sophisticated (jet planes)—are technically, but not technologically, innovative. In the meantime, the modern world is reacting to their threat by continuing to develop its own new technologies. In previous clashes of civilizations, the civilization better equipped to tap its people's economic, scientific, and military creativity has been the victor. Islamism has fervent followers, a critical resource that the West sorely lacks. But its mental closure may shut it off from the scientific innovations that are indispensable to defeating its enemy. The technological and scientific breakthroughs on which any future power shifts rest are unlikely to occur in an environment that stifles critical thought.

Democracy

Many Muslim societies face simultaneously grave developmental and cultural problems. Because there are few legitimate ways to express popular demands, and democratic traditions are either absent or suppressed, violence is often the only outlet. Worse, Islamism is also ideologically opposed to democracy. Does the failure of democratic development result from an innate antagonism between Islam and democracy (a Western import, after all)? Or can the tension be overcome? These questions are central to the recent debate on Islam.

In contrast to other religions, Islam is communal. (One can be a good Christian on a deserted island, but not a good Muslim.) Islam demands not only individual, but also collective, commitment. Its objective is not just the immediate community, but all of humanity. The question of individual rights occupies a smaller place in Islam than in Western juridical thought. Self-determination, the most crucial guarantee sanctioned by natural law, is explicitly denied in Islam: not the human being is sovereign, but God. Creatures belong to their Creator, Who has proprietary rights over them. God's sovereignty is incompatible with democracy, an illusory and illegitimate popular sovereignty. In many countries, Islamists are at the forefront of struggles against the authoritarian regimes of minority elites. They may thus appear, deceptively, to be a force for democratization. However, their place in the democratic rainbow coalition is merely instrumental. For Islamists, humans have only to prostrate themselves before God and accept His incommensurable and arbitrary power, a submission exemplified in the 1979 referendum that approved Iran's Islamic constitution—"one man, one vote, one time," in Bernard Lewis' sarcastic formula.[4] Once *shari`a* is imposed, politics is reduced to applying and interpreting an already (for all eternity) existing law—a task for religious specialists.

This is the theory. In practice, Sunni Islamist movements have not been eager to accept `*ulama* authority, but rather view themselves as the new interpreters of God's law. Even Shiite Islamists are strongly divided over the question of clerical rule. After the Islamic revolution, self-proclaimed charismatic leadership may give way to clerical-bureaucratic rule, as happened in Iran. However, not even there was a completely theocratic regime installed, but rather a theocracy-democracy hybrid, the outcome of a tug-of-war between conservative antidemocratic interpretations and the democratic will of the Muslim masses. Since `Abduh, reformist thinkers have highlighted the principle of *shura* (consultation): the community leader is duty-bound to consult representatives of the faithful before making his decision. This religious norm can be applied in a traditional way, as when the emir listens to his supreme `*ulama*; or more progressively, with the establishment of rules that may become virtually undistinguishable from parliamentary democracy.

Those who believe Muslims incapable of living under democracy have to explain how democracy took root in Turkey, Bosnia, Indonesia, and other Muslim lands. Modernist Muslims refuse any political privilege to "clergy" or other religious groups, and many of them would restrict the role of Islam to that of source of inspiration in a nation's public life. If this principle becomes intellectually hegemonic in the Islamic world, a significant step will have been taken toward Islam's integration into a global pluralistic community of civilizations. Although antidemocratic fundamentalist influence is currently stronger, the debate continues, and international coexistence may hinge on its outcome.[5]

The Challenge from Western Islam_____

Can Islamism defeat modern civilization? Not imminent, but not unthinkable. We have seen that while fundamentalists use rational means to attain their reactionary goals, they cannot really develop a new science and technology without arousing theological doubts. Their rejection of rationalism is therefore a deficiency of great consequence. An Osama bin Laden would certainly love to have at his disposal weapons of mass destruction, and in his hands they would constitute a real risk: he would not hesitate to use them to blackmail the West. But an Islamic superbomb of unknown, secretly researched technology is a farfetched nightmare. On the other hand, the accumulation of systemic problems in the West, in combination with coordinated attacks over multiple fronts and demoralization of modern society, may conceivably overburden the international community. In theory therefore, Islamism could perhaps win under one of the following scenarios: (1) a new nuclear-armed Islamic superpower with an Islamist program forces a dramatic reshuffling of the international power balance; (2) nonterritorial terroristic networks destabilize the global economy and/or international political regimes; or (3) Islamists successfully foster revolution *within* Western societies. Although all three scenarios seem to belong more to the realm of dystopian science fiction than to a rational calculus of probabilities, the third hypothesis is not devoid of consistency. This is why the role of Western Muslims could well be crucial for the future. We shall end our analysis with a brief speculation on the risks.

An Islamist Superpower?

Military challenges from the global south against the north will occur as long as justice and redistribution on a global scale remain pious wishes. But will such threats emerge from within the Islamic world? A Muslim superstate, although in secular and pan-Arab rather than religious garb, was Nasser's project in the 1950s and 1960s, and then Saddam Hussein's in the 1980s and 1990s. Both failed, and currently a renewed "neo-Bismarckian" endeavor is unlikely. Establishing a territorial base, unifying a sufficiently wide region and centralizing and arming it, and Islamizing its variegated populations would be extremely difficult. The Middle East is fragmented. Any hypothetical unification—assuming there exists a suitable candidate leader, a fundamentalist Nasser—would require a prolonged period in which to overcome the inevitable resistances. After this would follow another, presumably even longer period, to mobilize popular energies and prime the economy and military for a global hegemonic bid. All this would have to be done by using, say, oil income to overhaul the productive apparatus, but without provoking any preventive outside intervention—a highly improbable combination of conditions.

Nonterritorial Terrorist Networks?

Regardless of the possibility of Islamists coming to power in one Muslim country or another, a new generation of terrorists bred from the al-Qaeda stable might try to undermine the West through invisible transnational networks—either separately or in conjunction with other forces (e.g., antiglobalization *saboteurs*, criminal mafias, and drugs or arms dealers have been suggested). This scenario is slightly less implausible, because interruption of commercial and information exchanges may indeed set off an international economic crisis. It stands to reason, however, that this would provoke strong reactions from the developed world, particularly if terrorists were credibly suspected of possessing unconventional weaponry, and even more if they used them. Terrible though the occasion would be, it would probably trigger instant international solidarity against Islamist violence. For all its potential to push international relations into any number of undesirable directions, in a genuine "war against terror," victory of the Islamist militants would be improbable.

Islamist Revolution in a Western State? _____

There is, however, another peril. Western Europe and North America have imported a problem they may find ever more difficult to solve: impoverished Muslim immigrants with scant identification with the values of their adoptive fatherlands, eyed with growing mistrust by the native population. The xenophobic Right labels any Muslim population in the West as dangerous for societal cohesion. Inasmuch as Muslim minorities do become better integrated—and plenty of efforts in this direction are underway—one may disregard these alarmist voices. The question is, however, whether such efforts suffice to counterbalance forces opposed to integration. First-World socioeconomic difficulties may deepen the exclusion of vulnerable groups at Western society's margins—and here Muslim minorities are in the front line of risk. The informal apartheid of ethnically or religiously distinct "dangerous classes" may alienate and radicalize the masses of young Muslims even more. They would be grist for the mill of revolutionary Islamist movements, sparking off far more uncontrollable situations than have been seen thus far.

Another ominous factor would be the conversion to Islam of significant numbers of well-integrated Westerners. This phenomenon, still limited, is growing. This in itself is not more worrisome than modern citizens embracing Buddhism, any Christian church or sect, secular atheistic humanism, Krishna Consciousness (the "Hare Krishnas"), or the Unification Church (the "Moonies"). Human beings look for meaning and transcendence, and Islam's success in attracting newcomers points to its continuing and nonparochial relevance. However, a minority of converts to Islam may radicalize into violent Islamists. They would also be far more difficult to identify or disarm than second-generation Moroccans or Pakistanis. Would ex-Christians or ex-atheists who came to embrace Islamism put the project of modernity on hold?

All this highlights the significance of the crossroads that Western Islam is approaching. Three possible avenues are open. The first is modernism: making use of the West's freedom of expression to elaborate a reform of the Islamic religious and community experience compatible with further integration. The second is isolationism: maintaining a "resistance identity" with religion substituting for ethnicity. Last and most dangerous is the path of identification with international Islamist extremism, climaxing in attacks on the host society. It will take some time before winners and losers in this triangular ideological combat within Western Islam sort themselves out. But whichever of these alternatives comes out on top, Western Muslims will not escape their crucial role as harbinger of the future of the whole Islamic world.

CONCLUDING REMARKS

In the coming decades, the answers to the dilemmas sketched in these pages will define the new face of the Islamic world and, thus, the chances for coexistence between East and West. In the final instance, accommodation may well prove even more crucial for Islam's own survival than for Western modernity's. Although the options are many, they fall under three headings:

- **A victory of Islamism** would make religious practice more uniform by politicizing it, and would transform Islam into a coherent and doubtlessly anti-Western project. This is the road to confrontation, which currently seems to hold the best cards.
- **Secularization** would transform Islam into a private religion, conceivably with gradually diminishing impact on Muslims' social and political life. This is the secular West's preferred option for Islam. Although secularist options have apparently been resoundingly defeated in the crises of the twentieth century, the final verdict has not yet been given: globalization may yet lead to unexpected outcomes.
- **Islamic Reformation**—a remolding of Islam—may also produce a new, more pluralist and liberal, but not necessarily less intensely religious Islam. This would imply a rupture no less radical than that effected in the West by the Reformation or by the Enlightenment. For the time being a minority option, it engages a variety of significant Islamic thinkers.

All three options may develop simultaneously, in different places and in varied contexts. To prophesy which line will eventually prevail is impossible. However, the discussion within Islam is not taking place in artificial isolation, but in interaction with impulses originating in the wider non-Islamic world. The West (along with other civilizations) has every reason to help Islam in this difficult dialogue with itself and with us. This, unfortunately, has happened too little. As we have seen, reactions to the challenges have been inconsistent. In order to promote international security and intercultural coexistence, the policy that has most to recommend itself must consist of three interrelated components:

- For Islam: *dialogue*.
- For violent Islamism: *battle*.
- For the impoverished and enraged Muslim world: *justice, development, and democratization*.

Discussion about the future of Islam is essential for the Islamic world. It cannot but include Islam's relationship with the West—that competitor civilization that defeated the world of Muslims and has thrown it into ideological turmoil. For the majority of believing Muslims, no less than the salvation of their souls is at stake. For the rest of the world, what is at stake is the creation of better preconditions for coexistence with this "difficult" but enriching Other. The world would be a poorer place without its 1.3 billion Muslims. A real clash of civilizations would be a catastrophe for all of us.

NOTES

Introduction

1. "God" is used intentionally for "Allah," which is not a proper name but simply a contraction of *al-Ilahu*, (i.e., "the God"), pointing to the same Supreme Being Who manifested Himself in Judaism and Christianity.

Chapter 1: Islam in Time

1. Islam's lunar calendar "wanders" through the seasons with a lag of about ten days a year.
2. Cf. Chapter 9, note 10.
3. See Peters (1984), p. 174.
4. Hodgson (1974), vol. III, pp. 16–22, 26.
5. In the seventeenth century, an `Alawi sultanate was established in Morocco, where it continues in power today. See Laroui (1975), vol. II, pp. 48–57, 90–97.
6. Lewis (2002), pp. 64–81.
7. When the Greek Revolt broke out in 1821, Constantinople reacted by hanging the Greek Orthodox patriarch: Barber (1988), p. 138.
8. Lewis (1995).
9. 3:139 "So lose no heart nor fall into despair; for ye must gain mastery if ye are true in faith"; 30:47 "To help believers is incumbent upon Us"; 22:40: "Allah will certainly aid those who aid His cause, for verily Allah is full of strength, exalted in Might."
10. Ruthven (2000), p. 304.
11. Somewhere between 600,000 and 1.5 million Armenians perished in the Ottoman empire between 1915 and 1917, their disappearance wiping out a vibrant community of centuries' existence. Surviving Armenian communities and their sympathizers worldwide allege a deliberate

genocide, premeditated and implemented by the Enver Pasha triumvirate then ruling the empire. This position has been adopted by most scholars, and a number of states have outlawed denial of the "Armenian Holocaust." Successive Turkish governments, as well as many Turkish intellectuals and a smaller number of international scholars, have rejected this allegation, minimizing the number of victims or denying genocidal intent. Turkey has also persecuted intellectuals who tried to break open what remains a taboo in Turkish public life. The controversy, which goes beyond our discussion here, will be resolved only by dispassionate (and preferably multipartisan) analysis of the relevant archives.

12. Sivan (1985), p. 181.
13. Saadeh lived for a long time in Brazil, returning to Beirut in 1949; the Lebanese authorities deemed it prudent to have him shot at once: Ajami (1998), pp. 50–67.
14. Ruthven (2000), p. 308.
15. The causes of the Palestinian exodus continue to fuel polemics. See Morris (1987) and (2004).
16. See Sampson (1976).
17. Many Christian Arabs belong to the Greek Orthodox Church, whose elite was traditionally controlled by Greek clergy and often scornful of Arabs. In 1899, Arabic-speaking lower clergy and their flock took over the Antioch patriarchate. The Jerusalem patriarchate has kept its division between the high-Greek and lower-Arab clergy, which has led periodically to tensions.
18. Taheri (1988), pp. 166–167.
19. Bin Laden's two other accusations against the United States concerned the presence of American soldiers, "new crusaders" in Islam's holy territory, and the Palestine question. The accusations appear in his "World Islamic Front for Jihad Against Jews and Crusaders: Initial 'Fatwa' Statement," published in the Arabic Newspaper *al-Quds al-`Arabi* (London) on February 23, 1998, p. 3. Translation available at http://www.ict.org.il/articles/fatwah.htm

Chapter 2: Islam in Space: Islam's Expansion outside the Middle East

1. In Ayodhya, on the spot Hindus worshipped as the birthplace of their god Rama, he erected the Babri mosque named after him, which in 1992 became the target of Hindu revivalists whose campaign unleashed in 1992 the worst communal pogroms since India's independence in 1947: Vohra (1997), pp. 280–283.
2. Sikhism was the most significant attempt at syncretistically bridging Hinduism and Islam. Nanak (1469–1539) established in Punjab a religion combining *bhakti* (Hindu devotionalism) and Sufism; its adherents are known till today as *Sikhs* (disciples). However, ferocious persecution by the Mughals in the seventeenth century led to the transformation of this peaceful sect into a martial brotherhood. In the nineteenth century,

Sikhs dominated the Punjab. In the twentieth, their political demands were to further complicate community relations in the subcontinent: Smart (1998), 398–404.

3. Lapidus (1995), pp. 733–734.
4. See Rashid (2001), pp. 88–94.
5. The numbers of Indian Muslims are contested and may in fact be significantly higher.
6. Vohra (1997), pp. 223, 268–269.
7. Lapidus (1995), 757–766.
8. Lapidus (1995), pp. 823 ff; Smart (1999), p. 184.

Chapter 3: Islam among Others: The Muslim Diasporas

1. Lewis (2002), pp. 25–27. French *colons* in Algeria, Zionists in Palestine, Italians in Libya, and Greeks in Egypt and the Levant, among other groups. Except for the Jews, all eventually returned to their countries of origin after the Arab countries gained independence.
2. Or more—the exact numbers are a matter of controversy. The biggest communities are in France (at least 4–6 million), Britain (1.5 million), and Germany (2.5 million). The Netherlands have one million, and Spain and Italy each more than half a million Muslims: Haddad et al. (2000).
3. See Roy (2002).
4. Halliday (1999), pp. 160–194. Alain Gresh, "Islamophobie." In *Le Monde Diplomatique*, November 2001, p. 32.
5. See Eric Hobsbawm and Terence Ranger (eds.), *The Invention of Tradition*. Cambridge: Canto, 1996.
6. The numbers are subject to debate, some researchers claiming the real number is only 1–2 million.
7. See Tariq Ramadan, "Le temps de la réforme." In *Manière de Voir* 64 (*Le Monde Diplomatique*) June–August, 2002, p. 88.

Chapter 4: The Other in Islam: Minorities and Women

1. Goitein (1955); Cohen (1989); Bat Ye'or (2001).
2. See also verses 11:118, 16:93, and 42:8.
3. Roded (1999), pp. 3, 21; Ruthven (2000), p. 154.
4. Ruthven (2000), pp. 156–163.
5. Saadawi (1980), p. 146.
6. Saadawi (1980), p. 137; see Bouhdiba (1982), *passim*.
7. An example of overlapping religious and ethnic identities is clitoridectomy and other forms of genital mutilation practiced in North and Central Africa. (Female circumcision is not customary in the Middle East.) Although no Islamic justification exists for these traditions, they continue and are locally understood to be religiously sanctioned.

8. Lewis (2002), pp. 64–72. See Badran and Cooke (1990).
9. Taheri (1987), pp. 11–12.
10. See Zubaida (1997), Hoodfar (1997).
11. Saadawi (1980), p. 136.

Chapter 6: 1967–1981: The First Islamist Wave: Qutb's Egypt and the Sunni Jihad _____

1. Sivan (1985), pp. 66–68.
2. Maududi, *The Religion of Truth*. Lahore, 1967. pp. 3–4, quoted in Ruthven (2000), p. 328.
3. See Binder (1988), p. 195, who compares Qutb with Kierkegaard's proto-existentialism.
4. See Jürgen Habermas, *Der philosophische Diskurs der Moderne: Zwölf Vorlesungen*. Frankfurt/M, 1985.
5. Sivan (1985), pp. 94–107.
6. An English translation is available at http://www.youngmuslims.ca/online_library/books/milestones
7. Sadat was personally religious and had sympathized in his youth with the Muslim Brotherhood: Sadat (1981), pp. 34–35.
8. International Crisis Group Middle East and North Africa Briefing, April 20, 2004, *"Islamism in North Africa II: Egypt's Opportunity"*, p. 10. Accessible at http://www.crisisgroup.org/library/documents/middle _east_north.africa/egypt_north_africa/200404_islamism_in_north_africa _ii.doc.
9. Deadly terrorist attacks in Cairo and Sharm al-Shaikh (Sinai) in 2005 and Dhahab (Sinai) in February 2006 may serve as a counterpoint but do not invalidate the argument of an overall moderation of Egyptian Islamists.

Chapter 7: The 1980s: The Second Islamist Wave: Shiite Interlude _____

1. Indian Shiites, mostly Isma`ilites, constitute some 10 percent of all Indian Muslims and are concentrated in Gujarat and Maharashtra.
2. Kharijites have by now practically disappeared, except for some remote communities in Oman and the Algerian Sahara.
3. Ruthven (2000), p. 181 ff.
4. The survivors turned to a more pacific approach. The Agha Khan leads one of their branches.
5. Munson (1988), p. 57.
6. Bahá'is commenced as a sect in 1844 when Sayyid Ali Muhammad declared himself báb, or announcer, in contact with the Hidden Imam, and was executed for heresy. One of his followers, Mirza Hussein Ali (Bahá'u'lláh), received a revelation in 1852 that he was God's elect, in a line that included Jesus, Krishna, and Muhammad. Bahá'ism emphasizes correspondences among religion, science, gender equality, and peace—and have a markedly

more liberal tenor than normative Islam. Persecuted in Persia, it spread abroad and has between three and five million followers today.

7. Rodinson (1966), pp. 195 ff.
8. Munson (1988), pp. 118–124.
9. Taheri (1987) pp. 80–83, 239–240.
10. Olivier Roy, "Le post-islamisme?" In *Revue des mondes musulmans et de la Méditerrannée* no. 85/86 (1999), pp. 11–30.
11. Taheri (1987), pp. 72–76.

Chapter 8: 1991–2001: The Third Islamist Wave: The Seven Marks of Current Islamism_____

1. Roy (1992).
2. Kepel (2002).
3. Huntington (1993).
4. Wallerstein (1995), p. 22.
5. Walker, Tony, in *Financial Times*, January 10, 1991, quoted in Tibi (2002), p. 258, no. 30.
6. See Zakaria (2004).
7. Twenty-five million mostly Sunni Kurds speak an Indo-European language and constitute a nation of uncertain origin, spread over Turkey, Iraq, Iran, and Syria. Thirteen million live in Turkey, which long repressed Kurdish language and culture. From 1984 to 1999, a secessionist guerrilla of the Kurdish Workers' Party (PKK) provoked brutal repression. That war had cost 37,000 lives when the capture and condemnation to death of PKK leader Abdullah Öcalan led to a ceasefire. European Union pressure has since resulted in mitigation of cultural discrimination against Kurds, but in 2004 the PKK ended the truce, claiming Turkish reforms were merely cosmetic.
8. Sivan (1990).
9. Examples of Islamist pressure on free thought abound: Fazlur Rahman (1919–88) had to leave his native Pakistan and ended up teaching at the University of Chicago; Algerian philosopher Mohammed Arkoun now teaches at the Sorbonne in Paris. Other Arab intellectuals who found a more congenial workplace in the West include Syrian political scientist Bassam Tibi of Göttingen and Harvard, and Lebanese historian Fouad Ajami in New York. Many non-Muslim Arab intellectuals also found the climate in their countries uncongenial, including Palestinian Edward Said (1935–2003), who became professor of literature and theoretician of postcolonial studies at Columbia University (New York); poets Antoine Shammas and Nizar Qabbani; historian Amin Maalouf; and others. About the suffocating impact of a repressive political and intellectual climate on Middle Eastern intellectuals, see United Nations Development Programme/Arab Fund for Economic and Social Development, *Arab Human Development Report 2003* (3 vols.).
10. See Abu-Lughod (1989).

11. Eickelman and Piscatori (1996). Dale F. Eickelman, "The Coming Transformation of the Muslim World." Philadelphia, PA: Foreign Policy
Research Institute *WIRE*, vol. 7, no. 9, August, 1999. Accessible at http://
www.comw.org/pda/muslim799.html. See Roy (2002), pp. 165 ff.
12. Dudley Fishburn (Ed.). "Where's the World's Worst?" *The Economist—
The World in 2001*, p. 81.
13. Milosevic died in custody in 2006 before the conclusion of his trial for war
crimes.
14. Acronym for *Harakat al-Muqawwama al-Islamiyya*, Islamic Resistance
Movement.
15. Hamas's anti-Semitism can be gleaned from its Covenant (English translation accessible at http://www.palestinecenter.org/cpap/documents/charter.
html), which quotes the long-discredited anti-Semitic forgery of the Pro-
tocols of the Elders of Zion, as well as from its Holocaust denial, and similar themes.
16. Another terrorist outrage, claimed by a hitherto unknown Islamist outfit,
was perpetrated in the Hindu Holy City of Varanasi in March 2006,
claiming twenty lives.
17. Varshney (2002).
18. Meanwhile, in an unrelated, racial and economic (rather than religious)
war that has been assuming genocidal traits, Arab nomad *Janjaweed*
militia (tacitly supported by the Bashir regime in Khartoum) are ethnically cleansing African agriculturalists' areas in all-Muslim Darfur in
western Sudan. The latter have reacted by waging a war of secession.
Although an estimated 200,000–400,000 Darfur civilians had died by
2006, international enthusiasm for intervention has been lukewarm at
best. In May 2006, a peace accord brokered by the African Union was
signed by the Sudanese government and the largest branch of the rebel
Sudanese Liberation Army, calling for disarmament of the militia and
reincorporation of the rebels into Sudan's national army. However, violence has not halted.
19. Bergen (2002), p. 102.
20. Benzine (2004); Hafez (2000).
21. Muhammad Sa`id al-Ashmawi, *al-islam al-Siyasi* (Political Islam). Cairo:
Sina, 1987. p. 7. In Ayubi (1991), p. 203.
22. After Zeid had publicly doubted the Qur'an's literal truth, an Egyptian
tribunal condemned him for blasphemy and imposed obligatory divorce
from his Muslim wife. The couple was granted asylum in Holland. See
Ziad Hafez, "De nouveaux penseurs." In *Manière de Voir* 64 (*Le Monde
Diplomatique*) juillet–août 2002, pp. 89–93.

Chapter 9: What Do the Islamists Want? _____

1. Kamali (1999).
2. Roy (1996), p. 75.
3. *Hakimiyyat Allah* or "God-government," a neologism: Tibi (2002), pp. 96–102.
4. Roy (1996), pp. 65–66; see Juergensmeyer (2001).

5. Or "We love death. The US loves life. That is the difference between us two." Osama bin Laden, "Declaration of War against the Americans Occupying the Land of the Two Holy Places." Fatwa accessible at: http://www.pbs.org/newshour/terrorism/international/fatwa_1996.html.
6. Roy (1996), pp. 49, 84–86.
7. Tibi (2002), pp. 93, 103.
8. Tibi (2002), pp. 125–134. Pryce-Jones (1990) stresses the inherent internal cleavages of Arab societies, and their tendency to assess positions in pre-Islamic terms (kinship, honor, shame, etc.). However, his analysis has been faulted for being overly anti-Arab.
9. Lapidus (1995), p. 725.
10. Singular of `ulama`.
11. Sivan (1985), pp. 83–90.
12. The term is Tibi's: Tibi (2002).
13. Hiro (1988), p. 121.
14. See Burgat (2002).

Chapter 10: Causes of Islamism_____

1. Roy's taxonomy differs slightly, dividing between Islamism and neo-fundamentalism; the Afghan Taliban belong to his second category. Roy (1996), pp. 75–88.
2. Lewis (2002), pp. 156–159. See Hall, Edward. *The Hidden Dimension*. New York: Anchor: 1982: pp. 154–164.
3. Matthew 22:21.
4. Said (1987).
5. Roy (1996), p. 14.
6. Gellner (1992), pp. 13–16.

Chapter 11: Islam and the West: Clash of Civilizations or Transcultural Dialogue? _____

1. Lewis (2002).
2. Said (1987).
3. Edward Said's "There Are Many Islams" (September 16, 2001) was one of the first reactions of the Left to 9/11. Accessible at http://www.counterpunch.org/saidattacks.html; for a more complete catalogue, see Geoffrey Wheatcroft, "Two Years of Gibberish." In *Prospect Magazine* (September, 2003). Other defensive externalist reactions can be found in: Esposito (2002) and Ali (2002).
4. "[W]hosoever killeth a human being for other than manslaughter or corruption on the earth, it shall be as if he had killed all mankind, and whoso saveth the life of one, it shall be as if he had saved the life of all mankind": 5:32; "[E]njoy life while ye may, for you will come to know": 16:55; see also 2:177 and 2:256.
5. Among many other examples of such interfaith or intercivilizational dialogue, see the "European-Islamic Intercultural Dialogue" of the German

Institut für Auslandsbeziehungen, accessible at: http://www.ifa.de/islam-dialog/eindex.htm; the post-9/11 dialogue between American and Saudi intellectuals, accessible at http://www.americanvalues.org; and the Mumbai-based *Centre for Study of Society and Secularism*, accessible at www.csss-isla.com.
6. Matthew 10:34.
7. Lewis (2002), p. 98.
8. See Bowyer Bell (1978).
9. Huntington (1997), p. 254.
10. Naipaul (1977).
11. Rodinson (1978), pp. 60–64; Lewis (1982).
12. Tibi (2002).
13. Lewis (2002), pp. 155–159.
14. Burgat (2002).

Chapter 12: The Future of Islam: Five Dilemmas____

1. Hodgson (1974) II, p. 448.
2. Anthony Giddens, *The Consequences of Modernity.* Cambridge, 1990. In Ruthven (2000), p. 388.
3. Tibi (2002), pp. 46–71.
4. Lewis (2003), p. 112.
5. Esposito and Voll (1996).

GLOSSARY

(Arabic words unless otherwise indicated)

abangan: (Malay) in Java, only superficially Islamized follower of syncretistic faith

`Abbasids:* second caliphal dynasty (750–1258)

`abd:* slave (in many Muslim proper nouns, e.g., `Abdullah or `Abdallah, "slave of God")

abu: father of

agha: (Turkish) brother; lord; Ottoman military title

akbar: greater or greatest

`Alawites:* extreme Shiite sect in Syria venerating `Ali; also Moroccan dynasty (Alaouites, 1666–)

alevis: (Turkish) Shiites in Turkey

Allah: God (contraction of *al-Ilahu,* "the God")

Almohads: (*al-muwahhidun,* "the Unitarians") puritanical Muslim dynasty in Spain and Maghreb (1146–1275)

Almoravids: (*al-murabitun,* a military religious order) puritanical Muslim dynasty in Spain and Maghreb (1036–1148)

amir: (emir) prince or general; *amir al-muminin:* Commander of the Faithful, title of caliph

`asabiya:* tribal solidarity

`ashura:* in Shiism, commemoration of martyrdom of Hussein, the younger son of `Ali on the tenth day of the month of Muharram

ayatollah: sign of God; in Twelver Shiism, title of the highest *mujtahid*

a`yan: (Turkish) notables, local elite in late Ottoman Empire

Ayyubids: Sunni dynasty in Egypt and Syria (1171–1250)

badawi: (Bedouin) nomadic herders living in steppe or desert in Mashriq

Bahá'is: (also spelled *Baha'is*) followers of Bahaullah, prophet of syncretistic universalistic religion, founded as Persian Shiite sect in nineteenth century

bait: house

Ba`th: rebirth; the main pan-Arab party

bazar: market (often covered)

beur: North African youth in France

bey: (Turkish) lord; military title

bid`a: theological innovation

bint: daughter of

chador: in Iran, black feminine garment covering whole body

dar ul-Islam: the House of Islam, territory controlled by Muslims, in contrast
     to *dar ul-harb*, the House of War

darvish: (Persian) mendicant; member of a Sufi *tariqa*

da`wa: call; Islamic mission

deobandi: modernist Orthodox Islamic school in British India; in Pakistan,
     Sunni group favoring Islamism

dhimma: protection; security and freedom of religion granted to non-Muslim
     monotheists, the *dhimmi*

din: faith

Druze: religious community in Syria, Lebanon, and Israel that originated
     from an eleventh-century schism within Isma`ilism

falsafa: rationalist theology inspired by Greek philosophy

faqir: poor; itinerant Sufi

Fatah: opening, conquest; reverse acronym of *Harakat al-Tahrir al-Filastini*,
     Palestinian Liberation Movement (PLO); the largest, nonreligious,
     constituent of the PLO

Fatimids: Isma`ilite dynasty in Tunisia and Egypt (909–1171)

fatwa: juridical decision by specialist legist, the *mufti*

fida'i: (pl. *fida'iyyin*) martyr; Palestinian guerrilla

fiqh: understanding; *shari`a* jurisprudence or interpretive system; its practi-
     tioner is *faqih*; in post-revolutionary Iran, ultimate political power
     rests with the Supreme *Faqih*

fitna: fascination, temptation, or seduction; refers to female attraction as well
     as to civil war, namely, those of the era of the Rightly Guided Caliphs
     (656–89)

ghazi: warrior in *jihad*; in groups making frontier incursions (hence, razzia)

hadd: (pl. *hudud*) limit; Islamic punishment

hadith: news; tradition about Prophet Muhammad's sayings or acts

hajj: pilgrimage to Mecca; (s)he who completes it gains prestige as *hajji*

halal: allowed (said, e.g., of food)

haram: prohibited or set apart, religious sanctuary; harem, private quarters
     reserved for womanfolk

Hashemites: dynasty descending from Hashem clan, controlled Hijaz (until
     1924), reigning in Jordan (1922–) and Iraq (1920–58)

Hamas: zeal, fanaticism; acronym of *Harakat al-Muqawwama al-Islamiyya*,
     Islamic Resistance Movement, a Palestinian Islamist party

hanbalite: of the *fiqh* school of Ahmad ibn Hanbal (780-855)

hijab: screen or curtain; veil covering hair used by Orthodox muslimas *hijra:* (hegira) migration; Muhammad's flight from Mecca to Medina in 622, starting point of Islamic calendar

hizb: party

Hizbullah: Party of God, a Lebanese Shiite fundamentalist party

Ibadis: moderate Kharijites, today in Oman and Algerian Sahara

ibn / bin / banu: sons of

ijma`: consensus among the *umma's* representatives needed for legitimate decision

ijtihad: personal or innovative religious interpretation (in contrast to *taqlid*); the person qualified to make it is *mujtahid*

Ikhwan: (sing. *akh*) brethren, brotherhood; name of sedentarized Bedouin in Wahhabite communes, who in the 1920s constituted Ibn Sa`ud's irregular army in the conquest of the Arabian Peninsula

imam: (1) one who stands in front; leader of congregational prayer; (2) in Shiism, title of `Ali ibn Abi Talib and his descendants, supreme leader of the *umma* (equivalent to caliph in Sunnism)

intifada: rumbling, shaking; Palestinian uprising (1987–93 and 2000–)

infitah: opening; neoliberal reform of Egyptian economy under Sadat

Islam: submission (to God's will)

islamiyya: Islamism, Islamic fundamentalism

*isma`ili:* (Isma`ilites) Sevener Shiites, followers of Isma`il, son of Ja`afar al-Sadiq (d. 765)

jahiliyya: era of ignorance preceding the revelation of Islam

jama`a: society, association

jami`: central mosque of a Muslim community, where Friday sermon is held

jihad: struggle in God's path, referring both to self-control and to the Islamization of society and armed struggle against infidels; participant is *mujahid*

jizya: poll tax levied on *dhimmis*

ka`aba: quadrangular building in Mecca housing a black meteorite believed to be part of first temple

kalam: scholastic medieval theology that sought balance between reason and revelation

khalifa: caliph, successor the Prophet as spiritual and political leader of *umma*

khan: caravanserai, hostel for traveling merchants; (Turkish) title of sovereign, later honorary title

khariji: (pl. *khawarij*) (Kharijites) those who leave; puritanical schismatic group that in first *fitna* separated from `Ali ibn Abi Talib

khums: fifth of jihad spoils reserved for Prophet; in Iran, tax paid to Shiite clergy for community benefits

kiyayi: (Malay) rural `ulama in Java

kufr: unbelief, rejection of faith; (s)he who denies God is *kafir* or infidel

madina (Medina): city; Al-Madina is "the City," namely, where Prophet Muhammad established the first Islamic community in 622 (earlier called *Yathrib*)

madrasa: college for Islamic studies

Maghreb: west; the western part of the Islamic world—today Tunisia, Algeria, and Morocco

mahdi: rightly guided; Messiah-type figure of the future expected to restore righteous Islamic world; in Shiism, the Twelfth Imam

majlis: assembly, parliament

Mamluk: slave, person belonging to the ruler; Slave Sultan dynasty of Turkic or Circassian origin, in particular that ruling in Egypt, independently 1250–1516, and subsequently under Ottoman tutelage, 1516–1811

manara: minaret, tower of mosque

mansabdar: (Persian) fiefholder; military rank in Great Mughal India: provincial governor responsible for specified number of soldiers

Maronites: Christian community in Mount Lebanon, united since 1181 with Roman Catholic Church

Mashriq: east; the Oriental part of the Islamic world, broadly equivalent to the Levant, today the Fertile Crescent

mawali: (sing. *mawla*, servant, master) non-Arab converts to Islam who became clients of Arabs

millet: (Turkish, from Arabic *milla*, nation) autonomous religious community in Ottoman Empire

monophysites: (Greek) those who believe that Jesus Christ has one single nature (*monos physis*); predominant in Middle East but considered heretical by Byzantine Orthodox Catholic and Protestant Churches

muadhin: muezzin, Muslim announcing prayer hour or *adhan*

mufti: shari`a expert qualified to decree religious rule or *fatwa*

Mughals: (or *Great Mughals*) Indian Muslim dynasty of Mongol descent (1526–1856)

muhajarin: (sing. *muhajir*) migrants who (1) went with Muhammad to Mecca; or (2) other Muslim refugees, in particular Muslim migrants from India to Pakistan

mujahid: (pl. *mujahidin*) *jihad* warrior

mujtahid: in Shiism, high clergy qualified to enounce individual interpretation (*ijtihad*)

mulla: (Farsi: *mollah*) religious teacher or preacher in Shiism, equivalent of `ulama* in Sunnism

muslim: (m.)/*muslima* (f.) submitted; follower of Islam

mustadh`afun: (Farsi: *mustazafin*) the downtrodden, slum dwellers or oppressed in general

mu`tazila: separation; rationalistic theological school emphasizing free will and human responsibility

muwahhid: one who believes in God's unicity; Unitarian

Nahda: renaissance, the literary movement of Arab national rebirth

nakba: catastrophe; the Arab loss of Palestine in 1948

negara islam: (Malay) Islamic state

Ottomans: (Turkish: Osmanli, House of Osman) Turkish dynasty ruling Asia Minor, Middle East, and Balkans (1281–1922)

pancasila: (Malay) official Indonesian ideology of five principles, including belief in God

pasdar: (Farsi, pl. *pasdaran*) guard, the revolutionary guard in the Iranian Revolution

pasha: (Turkish) title of governor

priyayi: (Malay) in Java, member of Hinduized aristocracy

purdah: (Persian) separation or closure of women

qadi: magistrate applying *shari`a*

Qajar: Persian dynasty (1779–1925)

qasba: castle; magistrate's residence; small town

qawm: people, nation; *qawmiyya* is pan-Arab nationalism

qibla: prayer direction, toward Mecca, indicated in mosque by a niche or *mihrab*

quds or *muqaddas:* holy; al-Quds: Jerusalem, the Holy City

Quraish: Prophet Muhammad's tribe

Qur'an: (Koran) recitation; text of revelations received by Prophet Muhammad

Ramadan: month of fasting

rashid: rightly guided; refers to first four "orthodox" caliphs (632–661) recognized by Sunnis

Safavids: Persian dynasty (1502–1722)

salaf: ancestors; *al-salaf al-salih*, the worthy forebears (i.e., the pious Muslims of the first generation); tendency to emulate them is *salafiyya*

salat: prayer, worship of God, obligatory five times per day

santri: (Malay) in Java, Orthodox Muslims

sayyid: descendant of the Prophet in the lineage of `Ali and Hussein

Seljuks: Turkish dynasty ruling over Eastern Anatolia, Iran, and Syria (1055–1194); the Rum Seljuks controlled Anatolia (1077–1307)

shah: (Farsi) royal title; emperor of Persia

shahada: testimony; Muslim credo in God's unicity and prophesy of Muhammad, affirmation of which makes one a Muslim

shahid: witness; martyr who sacrifices his or her life for the cause of Islam

shaikh: (sheik) old one; tribal leader; person with religious authority; Sufi master

shari`a: originally "path toward a source," Islamic legal code

sharif: (pl. *ashraf*) venerable; in India, a person of Arab, Afghan, or Mughal ancestry; in Morocco, descendant of Prophet Muhammad

*shi`a:* faction; Shiism the party of `Ali ibn Abi Talib; follower is *shi`i* or Shiite; commonly used for Twelver Shiites who accept a lineage of Twelve Imams, from `Ali to Muhammad al-Mahdi

shirk: association (of other deities to God); polytheism; idolatry

shura: consultation; in Islamic political theory, noncommittal attempt at consensus by ruler; in modernism, equivalent of democracy

sipahi: (Turkish; in India: *sepoy*) Ottoman knight; Indian soldier in British army

sufi: follower of Sufism (*tasawwuf*); mystical tendency within Sunnism; possibly from *suf*, wool, garment worn by mystics

sultan: political authority, ruler (without religious connotation, in contrast to caliph)

sunna: beaten path; customs and manners sanctioned by tradition and/or Prophet's precedent (*sunnat al-nabi*); Sunnism; *ahl al-sunna*: the people of the Sunna; Orthodox Muslims or Sunnis

sura: Koran chapter

tabligh: missionizing in reformist Islam

takfir: judging someone to be an infidel; excommunication

talib: (pl. *taliban*) student (of religious seminary)

tanzimat: reorganization; reformist decrees promulgated in nineteenth century to modernize the Ottoman Empire

taqiya: caution; dissimulation or pretension of religious conformism

taqlid: imitation; acceptance of traditional source as basis of legal decision; traditionalism

tariqa: path of spiritual growth; hence, an organization caring for it—Sufi brotherhood

timar: (Turkish) in Ottoman Empire, nonhereditary land grant by ruler (Arabic: *iqta`*; Persian: *mansab*)

`*ulama:* (sing. `*alim*) sage or educated; in Sunnism, class of specialists in religious and juridical questions

Umayyads: first dynasty of caliphs (661–749)

umma: community of the faithful (also used in national sense), the universal Islamic ecumene

velayat-e faqih: (Farsi) the Custodianship of the Jurist; in contemporary Iran, Khomeini's political theory

Wafd: delegation; Egyptian bourgeois political party, 1918–52

Wahhabites: followers of Muhammad ibn `Abd al-Wahhab, ultra-puritanical preacher in the Arabian Peninsula (1703–92)

waqf (pl. *awqaf*): foundation based on donation of goods for religious or philanthropic purpose

watan: fatherland; *wataniyya* is local or regional patriotism

wazir (vizier)*:* highest civil servant appointed by sultan, minister

yeni čeri: (Turkish) new army; janissaries; Ottoman infantry corps formed of levies of converted Christian recruits

yishuv: (Hebrew) Jewish community in Palestine before the state of Israel

zakat: annual capital or income tax paid for social or welfare purposes

zamindar: (Persian) proprietor; in Mughal and British India, local administrator responsible for levying tax on harvest

BIBLIOGRAPHY

Abu-Amr, Ziyad. (1994). *Islamic Fundamentalism in the West Bank and Gaza: Muslim Brotherhood and Islamic Jihad.* Bloomington: Indiana University Press.

Abu-Lughod, Janet L. (1989). *Before European Hegemony: The World System A.D. 1250–1350.* New York: Oxford University Press.

Ahmed, Akbar S. (1997). *Jinnah, Pakistan and Islamic Identity: The Search for Saladin.* London: Routledge.

Ahmed, Leila. (1993). *Women and Gender in Islam: Historical Roots of a Modern Debate.* New Haven: Yale University Press.

Ajami, Fouad. (1998). *The Dream Palace of the Arabs: A Generation's Odyssey.* New York: Vintage.

Ali, Tariq. (2002). *Clash of Fundamentalisms: Crusades, Jihads, and Modernity.* London: Verso.

An-Na'im, Abdullahi Ahmed. (1996). *Toward an Islamic Reformation: Civil Liberties, Human Rights, and International Law.* Syracuse, NY: Syracuse University Press.

Arjomand, Said Amir. (1984). *The Shadow of God and the Hidden Imam.* Chicago: University of Chicago Press.

———. (1988). *The Turban for the Crown: The Islamic Revolution in Iran.* Oxford: Oxford University Press.

Arkoun, Mohammed. (1984). *Pour une Critique de la Raison Islamique.* Paris: Maisonneuve & Larose.

Armstrong, Karen. (1993). *Muhammad: A Biography of the Prophet.* San Francisco: HarperSanFrancisco.

———. (2000). *The Battle for God.* New York: Ballantine.

Ayubi, Nazih N. (1991). *Political Islam: Religion and Politics in the Arab World.* London and New York: Routledge.

Badran, Margot. (1994). *Feminists, Islam, and Nation: Gender and the Making of Modern Egypt.* Princeton: Princeton University Press.

Barber, Noel. (1988). *Lords of the Golden Horn: From Suleiman the Magnificent to Kamal Ataturk*. London: Arrow.

Bat Ye'or. (2001). *Islam and Dhimmitude: Where Civilizations Collide*. Fairleigh Dickinson University Press.

Beinin, Joel, and Joe Stork (eds.). (1997). *Political Islam: Essays from Middle East Report*. Berkeley and Los Angeles: University of California Press.

Benjamin, Daniel, and Steven Simon. (2002). *The Age of Sacred Terror*. New York: Random House.

Benzine, Rachid. (2004). *Les Nouveaux Penseurs de l'Islam*. Paris: Albin Michel.

Bergen, Peter. (2002). *Holy War, Inc.: Inside the Secret World of Osama bin Laden*. New York: Touchstone.

Binder, Leonard. (1988). *Islamic Liberalism: A Critique of Development Ideologies*. Chicago: University of Chicago Press.

Bouhdiba, Abdelwahab. (1982). *La Sexualité en Islam*. Paris: Quadrige/ Presses Universitaires de France.

Bowyer Bell, J. (1978). *Terror out of Zion: Irgun Zvai Leumi, Lehi, and the Palestinian Underground, 1929—1949*. New York: Avon.

Brown, Carl L. (2000). *Religion and State: The Muslim Approach to Politics*. Columbia University Press.

Brynen, Rex, Bahgat Korany, and Paul Noble (eds.). (1995–98). *Political Liberalization and Democratization in the Arab World*, 2 Vols. Boulder, CO: Lynne Rienner.

Burgat, François. (1994) (2002 nouvelle éd.). *L'Islamisme en face*. Paris: La Découverte.

Cahen, Claude (Hrsg.). (1968). *Der Islam I: Vom Ursprung bis zu den Anfangen des Osmanenreiches*. Frankfurt am Main: Fischer Taschenbuch Verlag.

Cohen, Mark R., and A. L. Udovitch (eds.). (1989). *Jews among Arabs: Contacts and Boundaries*. Princeton: Darwin Press.

Cole, Juan R. I., and Nikki R. Keddie. (1986). *Shi'ism and Social Protest*. New Haven: Yale University Press.

Crone, Patricia. (1980). *Slaves on Horses: The Evolution of the Islamic Polity*. Cambridge: Cambridge University Press.

Curtis, Edward E., IV. (2002). *Islam in Black America: Identity, Liberation, and Difference in African-American Islamic Thought*. Albany: State University of New York Press.

Dekmejian, R. Hrair. (1995). *Islam in Revolution: Fundamentalism in the Arab World*. Syracuse: Syracuse University Press.

Eickelman, Dale F., and James Piscatori. (1996). *Muslim Politics*. Princeton: Princeton University Press.

Esposito, John L. (1999). *The Islamic Threat: Myth or Reality?* New York: Oxford University Press.

———. (ed.). (2000). *The Oxford History of Islam*. Oxford: Oxford University Press.

———. and John O. Voll. (1996). *Islam and Democracy*. New York and Oxford: Oxford University Press.

————. (2002). *Unholy War: Terror in the Name of Islam*. New York: Oxford University Press.

Feldman, Noah. (2003). *After Jihad: America and the Struggle for Islamic Democracy*. New York: Farrar, Strauss, Giroux.

Fisk, Robert. (2001). *Pity the Nation: Lebanon at War*. Oxford and New York: Oxford University Press.

Fuller, Graham. (2003). *The Future of Political Islam*. New York: Palgrave Macmillan.

Geertz, Clifford. (1971). *Islam Observed: Religious Development in Morocco and Indonesia*. Chicago: University of Chicago Press.

Gellner, Ernest. (1981). *Muslim Society*. Cambridge: Cambridge University Press.

————. (1992). *Postmodernism, Reason and Religion*. London: Routledge.

Giddens, Anthony. (1990). *The Consequences of Modernity*. Stanford, CA: Stanford University Press.

Gerges, Fawaz A. (ed.). (1999). *America and Political Islam: Clash of Cultures or Clash of Interests?* Cambridge: Cambridge University Press.

Gilsenan, Michael. (1982). *Recognising Islam: An Anthropologist's Introduction*. London: Croom Helm.

Goitein, S.D. (1955). *Jews and Arabs: Their Contacts Through the Ages*. New York: Schocken.

Grünebaum, Gustave Edmund von. (Hrsg.). (1980) (1971, 1st). *Der Islam II: Die Islamischen Reiche nach dem Fall Konstantinopel*. Frankfurt am Main: Fischer Taschenbuch Verlag.

Haddad, Yvonne Yazbeck. (2000). "The Globalization of Islam." In *The Oxford History of Islam*. Ed. John Esposito. Oxford: Oxford University Press. 601–641.

————. (ed.). (2002). *Muslims in the West: From Sojourners to Citizens*. New York: Oxford University Press.

Hafez, Kai, et al. (eds.). (2000). *The Islamic World and the West: An Introduction to Political Cultures and International Relations*. Leiden: E.J. Brill.

Halliday, Fred. (1996). *Islam and the Myth of Confrontation: Religion and Politics in the Middle East*. London and New York: I.B. Tauris.

Hefner, Robert W. (2000). *Civil Islam: Muslims and Democratization in Indonesia*. Princeton: Princeton University Press.

Hiro, Dilip. (1988). *Islamic Fundamentalism*. London: Paladin.

————. (2002). *War Without End: The Rise of Islamist Terrorism and the Global Response*. New York: Routledge.

Hodgson, Marshall. (1974). *The Venture of Islam,* 3 Vols. Chicago and London: University of Chicago Press.

Holt, P.M., et al. (eds.). (1970). *Cambridge History of Islam*, 2 Vols. Cambridge: Cambridge University Press.

Hoodbhoy, Pervez. (1991). *Islam and Science: Religious Orthodoxy and the Battle for Rationality*. London: Zed.

Hoodfar, Homa. (1997). "Devices and Desires: Population Policy and Gender Roles in the Islamic Republic." In *Political Islam: Essays from Middle*

East Report. Ed. Joel Beinin and Joe Stork. Berkeley and Los Angeles: University of California Press. 220–233.

Hooglund, Eric (ed.). (2002). *Twenty Years of Islamic Revolution: Political and Social Transition in Iran since 1979*. Syracuse, NY: Syracuse University Press.

Hourani, Albert H. (1991). *A History of the Arab Peoples*. London: Faber and Faber.

———. (1993). *Arabic Thought in the Liberal Age: 1798–1939*. Cambridge: Cambridge University Press.

Hunter, Shireen T. (ed.). (1988). *The Politics of Islamic Revivalism: Diversity and Unity*. Bloomington and Indianapolis: Indiana University Press.

———. (1998). *The Future of Islam and the West: Clash of Civilizations or Peaceful Coexistence?* Westport, CT: Praeger.

———. (ed.). (2002). *Islam, Europe's Second Religion: The New Social, Cultural and Political Landscape*. Westport, CT: Praeger.

Huntington, Samuel. (1993). "The Clash of Civilizations?" *Foreign Affairs* 72, 3.

———. (1997) (1996, 1st). *The Clash of Civilizations and the Remaking of World Order*. New York: Touchstone.

Ibn Warraq. (1995). *Why I Am Not a Muslim*. Amherst, NY: Prometheus.

Inalcik, Halil, et al. (1994). *An Economic and Social History of the Ottoman Empire, 1300–1914*, 2 Vols. Cambridge: Cambridge University Press.

Israeli, Raphael. (2002). *Islam in China: Religion, Ethnicity, Culture, and Politics*. Lanham: Lexington Books.

Jaber, Hala. (1997). *Hezbollah: Born with a Vengeance*. New York: Columbia University Press.

Jansen, Johannes J. G. (1996). *The Neglected Duty: The Creed of Sadat's Assassins and Islamic Resurgence in the Middle East*. New York: Macmillan.

Juergensmeyer, Mark. (2001). *Terror in the Mind of God: The Global Rise of Religious Violence*. Berkeley: University of California Press.

Kamali, Mohammad Hashim. (1999). "Law and Society: The Interplay of Revelation and Reason in the Shariah." In *The Oxford History of Islam*. Ed. John Esposito. Oxford: Oxford University Press. 107–153.

Karsh, Efraim, and Inari Karsh. (1999). *Empires of the Sand: The Struggle for Mastery in the Middle East, 1789–1923*. Cambridge, MA: Harvard University Press.

Keddie, Nikki R. (ed.). (1972). *Scholars, Saints and Sufis: Muslim Religious Institutions in the Middle East since 1500*. Berkeley: University of California Press.

Kepel, Gilles. (1993). *Le prophète et Pharaon: Aux sources des mouvements islamistes*. Paris: Seuil.

———. (1993). *Muslim Extremism in Egypt: The Prophet and Pharaoh*. Berkeley: University of California Press.

———. (1994). *A l'ouest d'Allah*. Paris: Seuil.

———. (2002). *Jihad: Expansion et déclin de l'islamisme*. Paris: Gallimard.

———. (2003). *Jihad: The Trail of Political Islam*. Cambridge, MA: Harvard University Press.

Kelsay, John, and James Turner Johnson (eds.). (1991). *Just War and Jihad: Historical and Theoretical Perspectives on War and Peace in Western and Islamic Traditions.* Westport, CT: Greenwood.

Kinross, Lord. (1988). *Ottoman Centuries.* New York: William Morrow.

Kramer, Martin S. (ed.). (1987). *Shi'ism, Resistance, and Revolution.* Boulder, CO: Westview Press.

Kurzman, Charles (ed.). (1998). *Liberal Islam: A Sourcebook.* Oxford: Oxford University Press.

Lapidus, Ira. (1995). *A History of Islamic Societies.* Cambridge: Cambridge University Press.

Laroui, Abdallah. (1967). *L'idéologie arabe contemporaine: Essai critique.* Paris: François Maspéro.

———. (1975). *L'histoire du Maghreb: Un essai de synthèse.* 2 vols. Paris: Maspéro.

———. (1977). *The Crisis of the Arab Intellectual.* Berkeley: University of California Press.

Lawrence, Bruce B. (1998). *Shattering the Myth: Islam beyond Violence.* Princeton: Princeton University Press.

Levtzion, Nehemia, and Randall L. Pouwels (eds.). (2000). *The History of Islam in Africa.* Athens: Ohio University, Center for International Studies.

Lewis, Bernard. (1985). *The Muslim Discovery of Europe.* New York: W.W. Norton.

———. (1990). *Race and Slavery in the Middle East: An Historical Inquiry.* Oxford: Oxford University Press.

———. (1995). *The Middle East: 2000 Years of History from the Rise of Christianity to the Present Day.* London: Phoenix.

———. (2002). *What Went Wrong: Western Impact and Middle Eastern Response: The Clash between Islam and Modernity in the Middle East.* New York: Perennial.

———. (2003). *The Crisis of Islam: Holy War and Unholy Terror.* New York: The Modern Library.

Maalouf, Amin. (1989). *Les croisades vues par les arabes.* Paris: J'ai Lu.

Malik, Iftikhar Haider. (1999). *Islam, Nationalism, and the West: Issues of Identity in Pakistan.* New York: Palgrave Macmillan.

Mamdani, Mahmood. (2004). *Good Muslim, Bad Muslim: America, the Cold War, and the Roots of Terror.* New York: Pantheon.

Manji, Irshad. (2005). *The Trouble with Islam Today.* New York: St. Martin's Griffin.

Mardin Serif. (2002). *Religion, Society and Modernity in Turkey.* Syracuse: Syracuse University Press.

Marty, Martin E., and R. Scott Appleby (eds.). (1991). "The Fundamentalism Project." In Vol. I, *Fundamentalisms Observed.* Chicago: University of Chicago Press.

Mernissi, Fatima. (1987). *Beyond the Veil: Male-Female Dynamics in Modern Muslim Society.* Bloomington: Indiana University Press.

Mishal, Shaul, and Avraham Sela. (2000). *The Palestinian Hamas: Vision, Violence, and Coexistence.* New York: Columbia University Press.

Momen, Moojan. (1985). *An Introduction to Shi'i Islam: The History and Doctrines of Twelver Shi'ism*. New Haven: Yale University Press.

Morris, Benny. (1987). *The Birth of the Palestinian Refugee Problem, 1947–1949*. Cambridge and New York: Cambridge University Press.

———. (2004) *The Birth of the Palestinian Refugee Problem Revisited*.

Mortimer, Edward. (1982). *Faith and Power: The Politics of Islam*. London: Faber and Faber.

Munson, Henry, Jr. (1989). *Islam and Revolution in the Middle East*. New Haven and London: Yale University Press.

Naipaul, V. S. (1977). *India: A Wounded Civilization*. Harmondsworth: Penguin.

———. (1999). *Beyond Belief: Islamic Excursions Among the Converted Peoples*. New York: Vintage.

Nasr, Seyyed Hossein. (2002). *Islam: Religion, History, and Civilization*. San Francisco: HarperSanFrancisco.

Peters, Rudolph. (1996). *Jihad in Classical and Modern Islam: A Reader*. Princeton: Markus Wiener.

Pickthall, Mohammed Marmaduke. (1953). *The Meaning of the Glorious Koran*. An explanatory translation by M. Pickthall. New York: Mentor.

Pipes, Daniel. (2002). *Militant Islam Reaches America*. New York and London: W.W. Norton.

Pryce-Jones, David. (1990). *The Closed Circle: An Interpretation of the Arabs*. London: Paladin Grafton.

Rahman, Fazlur. (1979). *Islam*. Chicago: University of Chicago Press.

Ramadan, Tariq. (2003). *Western Muslims and the Future of Islam*. New York: Oxford University Press.

Rashid, Ahmed. (2001). *Taliban: Militant Islam, Oil and Fundamentalism in Central Asia*. New Haven and London: Yale University Press.

———. (2002) *Jihad: The Rise of Militant Islam in Central Asia*. New Haven: Yale University Press.

Robinson, Francis (ed.). (1999). *The Cambridge Illustrated History of the Islamic World*. Cambridge: Cambridge University Press.

Roded, Ruth (ed.). (1999). *Women in Islam and the Middle East: A Reader*. London and New York: I.B. Tauris.

Rodinson, Maxime. (1966). *Islam et capitalisme*. Paris: Seuil.

———. (1978). *Islam and Capitalism*. Austin: University of Texas Press.

———. (1978). *La fascination de l'Islam: Étapes du regard occidental sur le monde musulman*. Nijmegen: Association néerlandaise pour l'étude du Moyen-Orient et de l'islam. 2002.

———. (1989). *Europe and the Mystique of Islam*. London: I.B. Tauris.

———. (1961). *Mahomet*. Paris: Club François du Livre.

———. (1971). *Mohammed*. London: Penguin Books.

Roy, Olivier. (1992). *L'échec de l'Islam politique*. Paris: Seuil.

——— (1996). *The Failure of Political Islam*. Cambridge, MA: Harvard University Press.

———. (2002). *L'islam mondialisé*. Paris: Seuil.

Ruthven, Malise. (2000) (new ed.). *Islam in the World*. London: Penguin.

————. (2002). *A Fury for God: The Islamist Attack on America*. London: Granta Books.

Saad-Ghorayeb, Amal. (2002). *Hizbu'llah: Politics and Religion*. London: Pluto Press.

El Saadawi, Nawal. (1980). *The Hidden Face of Eve*. London: Zed.

El-Sadat, Anwar. (1981). *In Search of Identity: An Autobiography*. New York: Fontana Collins.

Said, Edward W. (1987). *Orientalism*. London: Penguin.

————. (1997) (revised ed.). *Covering Islam: How the Media and the Experts Determine How We See the Rest of the World*. New York: Vintage.

Salame, Ghassan (ed.). (1994). *Democracy Without Democrats?: The Renewal of Politics in the Muslim World*. London: I.B. Tauris.

Sampson, Anthon. (1976). *The Seven Sisters: The Great Oil Companies and the World They Made*. London: Hodder and Stoughton.

Sardar, Ziauddin. (1989). *Explorations in Islamic Science*. London: Mansell.

Saunders, J. J. (1990). *A History of Medieval Islam*. New York: Routledge.

Schimmel, Annemarie. (1975). *Mystical Dimensions of Islam*. Chapel Hill: University of North Carolina Press.

Sharabi, Hisham. (1988). *Neopatriarchy: A Theory of Distorted Change in Arab Society*. Oxford: Oxford University Press.

Shari'ati, Ali. (1979). *On the Sociology of Islam: Lectures by Ali Shari'ati*. Berkeley: Mizan Press. (Hamid Algar, trans.).

Shaw, Stanford Jay. (1977). *History of Ottoman Empire and Modern Turkey*. 2 vols. Cambridge: Cambridge University Press.

Sivan, Emmanuel. (1985). *Radical Islam: Medieval Theology and Modern Politics*. New Haven: Yale University Press.

————. (1990). "The Islamic Resurgence: Civil Society Strikes Back." In *Journal of Contemporary History* 25: 353–364.

Smart, Ninian. (1998). *The World's Religions*. Cambridge: Cambridge University Press.

————. (1999). *Atlas of the World's Religions*. London: Calmann & King.

Stern, Jessica. (2003). *Terror in the Name of God: Why Religious Militants Kill*. New York: Ecco.

Taheri, Amir. (1985). *The Spirit of Allah: Khomeini and the Islamic Revolution*. London: Hutchinson.

————. (1987). *Holy Terror: The Inside Story of Islamic Terrorism*. London: Sphere Books.

————. (1988). *The Cauldron: The Middle East Behind the Headlines*. London: Hutchinson.

Tibi, Bassam. (1990). *Islam and the Cultural Accommodation of Social Change*. Boulder: Westview.

————. (2001). *Kreuzzug und Djihad: Der Islam un die christliche Welt*. München: William Goldmann.

————. (2002). *Die fundamentalistische Herausforderung*. München: C. H. Beck.

————. (1998). *The Challenge of Fundamentalism: Political Islam and the New World Disorder*. Berkeley: University of California Press.

Tripp, Charles. (2002). *A History of Iraq*. Cambridge: Cambridge University Press.

Varshney, Ashutosh. (2002). *Ethnic Conflicts and Civil Life: Hindus and Muslims in India*. New Haven: Yale University Press.

Vohra, Ranbir. (1997). *The Making of India: A Historical Survey*. Armonk, NY and London: M.E. Sharpe.

Wallerstein, Immanuel. (1995). *After Liberalism*. New York: The New Press.

Watt, William Montgomery. (1961). *Muhammad: Prophet and Statesman*. London: Oxford University Press.

Wirsing, Robert G. (1994). *India, Pakistan, and the Kashmir Dispute: On Regional Conflict and Its Resolution*. New York: St. Martin's Press.

Zakaria, Fareed. (2004). *The Future of Freedom: Illiberal Democracy at Home and Abroad*. New York and London: W.W. Norton.

Zubaida, Sami. (1993). *Islam, the People and the State: Essays on Political Ideas and Movements in the Middle East*. London: I.B. Tauris.

———. (1997). "Is Iran an Islamic State?" In *Political Islam: Essays from Middle East Report*. Eds. Joel Beinin and Joe Stork. Berkeley and Los Angeles: University of California Press. 113–118.

INDEX

ABOUT THE AUTHOR

PETER R. DEMANT is a Professor of History at Universidade de São Paulo, Brazil, where he lectures in international relations and contemporary Asian history. From 1991 to 1999 he lived in Jerusalem, where he was senior research associate at the Harry S Truman Research Institute for the Advancement of Peace at Hebrew University of Jerusalem. He is a specialist in Middle Eastern and Islamic affairs.